UP FRONT
FINANCING

Wiley Series on Small Business Management
Rick Stephan Hayes, Editor

Simplified Accounting for Non-Accountants
 by Rick Stephan Hayes and C. Richard Baker

How to Finance Your Small Business with Government Money:
SBA Loans
 by Rick Stephan Hayes and John Cotton Howell

Accounting for Small Manufacturers
 by C. Richard Baker and Rick Stephan Hayes

Simplified Accounting for Engineering and Technical Consultants
 by Rick Stephan Hayes and C. Richard Baker

Simplified Accounting for the Computer Industry
 by Rick Stephan Hayes and C. Richard Baker

The Complete Legal Guide for Your Small Business
 by Paul Adams

Running Your Own Show: Mastering Basics of Small Business
 by Richard T. Curtin

Up Front Financing
 by A. David Silver

UP FRONT FINANCING

The Entrepreneur's Guide

A. David Silver

A Ronald Press Publication
JOHN WILEY & SONS
New York   Chichester   Brisbane   Toronto   Singapore

This publication is designed to provide accurate and
authoritative information in regard to the subject
matter covered. It is sold with the understanding that
the publisher is not engaged in rendering legal, accounting,
or other professional service. If legal advice or other
expert assistance is required, the services of a competent
professional person should be sought. *From a Declaration
of Principles jointly adopted by a Committee of the
American Bar Association and a Committee of Publishers.*

Library of Congress Cataloging in Publication Data:

Silver, A. David (Aaron David), 1941-
    Up front financing.

    (Wiley series on small business management)
    "A Ronald Press publication."
    Includes index.
        1. Small business—Finance—Handbooks, manuals, etc. 2. Venture
capital—Handbooks, manuals, etc.
I. Title.   II. Series.

HG4027.7.S53   658.1'592   81-21985
ISBN 0-471-86386-6   AACR2

Printed in the United States of America

10 9 8 7 6 5 4 3 2 1

This book is dedicated to the memory of Blaine D'Arcey, whose career as a venture capitalist in the Rocky Mountain region over two decades serves as an inspiration to all of us fortunate enough to have known him!

PREFACE

We are extremely fortunate to live in a time and place in history where there exist mechanisms to finance and support people who seek to solve serious social, medical, or industrial problems through the free enterprise system. Moreover, the mechanisms for providing launch capital and management support for scientists, inventors, and innovators are becoming more defined. Chester Carlson, the inventor of xerography, struggled for 12 lonely years in the 1940s and 1950s until the Haloid Company decided to back his project. There was no organized venture capital industry 30 years ago. Today, however, there are billions of dollars of venture capital in 20 or so different forms available to launch products such as photocopiers. Entrepreneurs are able to choose between alternative forms of launch capital and alternative sources within each form.

The process of raising venture capital is becoming more systematic as venture capitalists become more experienced and as successful entrepreneurs join venture capital funds to provide assistance for selecting appropriate investments and monitoring their managements. The increased amount of venture capital and the heightened publicity that surrounds it create a demand–pull effect on entrepreneurs. As more entrepreneurs leave their jobs to start companies, more pressure is put on the financial markets for greater amounts of venture capital. These forces are positive because over a decade or so, employment will increase, difficult problems will be solved entrepreneurially, and wealth will be created and reinvested into the next decade of innovations.

A. DAVID SILVER

New York, New York
February 1982

$\equiv$ ACKNOWLEDGMENTS $\equiv$

I have had the opportunity to work with and for a number of highly skilled investors, lenders, investment bankers, and entrepreneurs since first entering the venture capital field in 1968. It has been my good fortune to have participated in a wide variety of financings with many different lenders and investors throughout the country.

The "deal business" requires lots of travel, and airplanes have become for me excellent places to write. Entrepreneurs have asked me for some time to write a book that would describe the different methods of financing new and emerging companies, as well as leveraged buy-outs, to make the fund raising process less awesome. With greater numbers of people becoming entrepreneurs, the book seemed like an excellent idea.

The entrepreneur–venture capital process, I have come to learn, is a lot like the writer–publisher process. The two sides get together, in one case to build a business and in the other to build a book.

I had the concept and the plan, which are good entrepreneurial beginnings for a book. Luck and timing came about when Marilyn Dibbs of John Wiley & Sons, publishers, had the same idea at the same time and suggested that her firm would like to publish my book. We quickly got together on terms, a happy moment for any entrepreneur.

The hard work was done by Elizabeth A. Meyers and Barbara Behr, both of whom prepared the manuscript; Nancy Burleson, who painstakingly hammered it into shape; and Michael J. Hamilton of John Wiley & Sons, who agreed to make the investment and provided excellent editorial input from start to finish.

A.D.S.

CONTENTS

	Introduction	1
1.	Leveraged Buy-Out	7
2.	Private Venture Capital Funds	23
3.	Corporate Venture Capital Subsidiaries	33
4.	SBICs and MESBICs	39
5.	Business Development Corporations	55
6.	Tax Shelter	61
7.	Research and Development Grants	77
8.	Public Offerings	81
9.	Public Shells	87
10.	Government Guaranteed Loans	91
11.	Accounts Receivable, Inventory, and Equipment Loans	95
12.	Customer Financing	103
13.	Joint Ventures and Licensing	115
14.	Preparing the Business Plan	121
15.	Questions and Answers	147
Appendix 1.	Sample Option and Proxy Used to Gain Control in Leveraged Buy-Outs	221
Appendix 2.	Sample Business Plans	225
Index		241

UP FRONT
FINANCING

═══ INTRODUCTION ═══

There are more than 20 different methods of financing the small business. All of them should be considered by the capital-short entrepreneur and several of them utilized to raise the most capital in the shortest time span at the lowest cost.

The U.S. financial market is like a variegated family vegetable garden. If the tomatoes are in short supply one year, the corn will be plentiful and vice versa. Even in the most severe drought that weakens the entire garden, there is still enough food to feed the family. When the new issue market dried up in the mid-1970s, the Government developed three new loan guarantee programs that offset the lack of demand for new common stock offerings. When private venture capital was in short supply in the late 1970s, a variety of new limited partnership financing methods were created to absorb some of the demand. Most other developed nations have one-crop gardens: government financing for small business. Thus, when the government is in a capital pinch, small business is unfortunately starved out. Not so in the United States where the Federal Government all but ignores financing for small business, directly providing only a fraction of its capital requirement each year.

The 20 or so methods of financing a small business do not apply equally to all companies. For example, companies in a research and development stage can attract tax shelter dollars more easily than venture capital; companies at a start-up stage can attract venture capital more easily than debt financing; and companies in an expansion phase can attract debt financing more easily than venture capital.

At any point in time the small business is in at least one of the following stages:

1

1. Research and development
2. Start-up
3. Expansion
4. Work-out
5. Buy-out

If the management team is clever, it can be in several stages at the same time, thus opening up a greater number of sources of capital. For example, it is not unusual for an expansion stage company to raise venture capital for expansion, obtain a line of credit for working capital, and arrange a tax shelter financing to develop a new product. Similarly it is not unusual for a start-up company to blend together venture capital and debt financing to accomplish a leveraged buy-out.

Each of the methods of financing is approached in the same manner: by a combination of written and verbal presentations made to sophisticated investors and lenders. For the small businessman who does not have many contacts in the financial market, or who cannot prepare an adequate business plan or discuss his goals and objectives easily with others, there are investment bankers willing to help for a fee.

The business plan must be a very accurate and precise, yet highly readable, memorandum. Its key sections are the operating statement projections, the product description, and the background of the management team. If these three sections are interesting to the investor or lender—and frequently he has time enough to skim only these sections—he will welcome a visit by the entrepreneur. It is at this visit, where the entrepreneur tells his story, that the capital will change hands. It takes about 15 minutes for a lender or investor to determine if an entrepreneur is intelligent, three or four phone calls to determine if he is honest, and a 30 minute study of the business plan to determine if the business is interesting. But honesty, intelligence, and a good business plan must be communicated well; thus, the most successful entrepreneurs are generally excellent speakers.

In raising capital for his small business, the entrepreneur should constantly remind himself of the first man to eat a lobster and the difficulty he surely had in trying to convince others that it was tasty. It is extremely difficult to get an investor's or lender's attention to consider a new "deal," as investment opportunities are called. But once gotten, it can be converted to an investment by an enthusiastic and systematic verbal presentation. "Raising money is talking," someone once said, and that short sentence explains why some undeserving companies attract financing while more viable ones do not.

THE FIVE QUESTIONS

Although an investor may have certain industry criteria that he favors, such as oil and gas or high technology, these criteria are set aside frequently to make room for exciting exceptions. The exceptional deal has provided the right answers to the five questions that an investor asks each time he reads a new business plan:

1. How much can I make?
2. How much can I lose?
3. How do I get my money out?
4. Who says this deal is any good?
5. Who else is in the deal?

In asking these questions, the investor is attempting to accept or reject the business plan quickly to maximize his time. It is in his interest, as much as that of the entrepreneur, to avoid 30 days of investigation that results in a turn-down. Thus the investor is inclined to turn down a deal quickly if the answers to these five questions are not what he was looking for.

For example, if the operating statement projections are too flat, the deal could be turned down because the rate of return is inadequate. Or if the projection ramp is too steep, the turn-down may be the result of unrealistic projections. The answer to the question "How much can I lose?" has to do with the use of proceeds of the financing. The entrepreneur may need product development money at a time when the investor has an excess of development stage risk in his portfolio. To the third question, "How do I get my money out?" the investor wonders if this company can be taken public, or sold to a larger company—the conventional means of capitalizing on an investment—or if it will be a cash cow. When the investor asks the next question about management track record he would like the answer to be that the entrepreneurs were involved in the founding of Hewlett-Packard or Weight Watchers International and that they have blessed this investor with the opportunity to finance their second company. This does not happen on a daily basis, and in fact investors are faced with lesser of evil choices most of the time because most entrepreneurs have track records ranging from none to poor. What the investor likes to see, however, is that the entrepreneur exhibits the judgment to hire skilled managers, primarily in the areas of marketing, manufacturing, finance, and engineering. The purpose of the fifth question is for the investor to find others who have endorsed the company by agreeing to provide products, credit, contracts, or purchases.

If all of this sounds wooden and mechanical, then pray tell how one Fred Smith, age 29, raised $96 million from Prudential Insurance, General Dynamics, and 26 venture capital funds to launch Federal Express Corporation in the pit of the 1973 recession, on the basis of a term paper he had written in college and without any substantive previous business experience. Or, why did it take Chester Carlson, the patent lawyer, 12 years to raise capital to finance the development of the first Xerox machine? Perhaps it had something to do with the fact that there was no business plan, merely a demonstration by a tall, cragged man in a wrinkled raincoat involving a small piece of stainless steel, a rabbit's foot, some dark powder, and a piece of paper. Some small companies have trouble paying for postage, while others have to send back offers to invest because they are oversubscribed. Apple Computer Corporation raised more venture capital in 1978–1980 than the rest of the personal computer industry in total, although it is not reputed to manufacture the best hardware or offer the most useful software. Its founders were two unseasoned engineers under age 26, but the manager they hired to run Apple, Michael Markulla, was considered one of the marketing stars at Intel Corporation, and he attracted venture capital from Arthur Rock and others. Peter Farley, the molecular biologist who founded Cetus Corporation, raised over $36 million from industrial corporations and venture capitalists in the mid-1970s, and then $125 million from the public in early 1981, without a product or more than a few million dollars in contracts. Dr. Leonard Schoen, the founder of Arcoa Corporation, operator of the U-Haul System of one-way truck and trailer rentals, has raised all of Arcoa's capital privately through tax shelter oriented limited partnerships that own the trucks and trailers and lease them to the company. The seed capital for *Psychology Today* came very rapidly from recipients of a direct mail test who subscribed to the magazine at an overwhelming rate, thus providing the cheapest of all forms of capital: customers' money. Yet in the shadow of these success stories lies the wreckage of thousands of economically viable, socially useful businesses that have been unable to attract financing.

By reason and example the seeming mystery of raising capital to launch, expand, turn around, or acquire a small emerging business is made clear. The various methods are outlined, discussed, and compared. The answers to the five questions asked by venture capital investors are explained in terms of where they fit into the business plan.

At least one, and frequently several, forms of capital are available for every new or emerging business. Although three companies may have similar characteristics, one company is launched with government-guaranteed bank loans, another via an R&D tax shelter, and the third is begun with customer advances. The many different sources of capital discussed in the following chapters will remind you of a vegetable garden. To accomplish the task of raising launch capital you need a sound business plan, intelligence, and tenacity.

1

LEVERAGED BUY-OUT

Whenever and wherever entrepreneurs gather to boast and tell stories, those held in most awe by all the others are those whose stories begin, "I was flat broke, so I decided to buy a company." Why not? when there are many companies whose owners want out and many entrepreneurs who need a base to build a business on. What makes this financing method, known as the "leveraged buy-out," so interesting is that it requires very clever balancing on the entrepreneur's part, much like a five-person acrobatic team crossing a high wire on one another's shoulders.

A leveraged buy-out is the purchase of a company using its assets to secure loans that are used to pay the seller. If the assets are inadequate to attract the full amount of the sales price, the seller must be persuaded to take notes or the buyer must attract equity capital. The more equity capital required, the smaller percentage ownership the entrepreneur is able to keep. If the company's asking price is too high or the cost of debt financing too dear, then more equity capital is required to the point of diluting the entrepreneur's interest, and at some point he will have to walk from the deal.

The best candidates for leveraged buy-outs are divisional spin-offs from large industrial corporations. These giants periodically go through a housecleaning exercise in which they discard small divisions or subsidiaries that were appendages of larger companies that were acquired or that were acquired many years ago when the corporation's goals and objectives were perceived differently. These small divisions are frequently not attractive to other corporations because of their size, thus making them candidates for entrepreneurial purchase. Private or family owned companies are less attractive leveraged buy-out candidates because the record keeping is usually sloppier, and there is no assurance that the family is truly a willing seller. Sometimes they will put their company on the market merely to establish a value for estate planning purposes. In a divisional spin-off, the board has authorized the president to sell, and he is instructed to get the best price with the most cash. Further, the division is usually audited every year, and the key general ledger items are normally maintained on computer.

Exhibit 1 presents the financial statements of a wholesale distributor of electronic components offered for sale by a large corporation at a price of net worth plus $1,000,000.

EXHIBIT 1.   Leveraged Buy-Out Candidate—Electronic Parts Distributor

BALANCE SHEET
FYE 1981

Assets		Liabilities and Net Worth	
Cash	$ 67,800	Accounts payable	$ 425,000
Accounts receivable	2,203,600	Accrued expenses	504,000
Inventories	2,881,200		
Total current assets	5,152,600	Total liabilities	929,000
Equipment and leasehold improvements—net	582,900	Net worth	4,778,900
Other assets—net	(27,600)		
		Total liabilities	
Total assets	$5,707,900	and net worth	$5,707,900

OPERATING STATEMENT
FYE 1981

Sales	$15,999,000
Cost of goods sold	10,159,000
Gross profit	5,840,000
Selling general and administrative expenses	4,159,000
Net operating income	1,681,000
Corporate interest charge	263,000
Corporate rent	279,000
Corporate management fee	141,000
Net profit before taxes	$ 998,000

From this financial information, an entrepreneur can raise approximately $4,000,000 in debt, collateralized by the assets of the company, and the balance of $1,800,000 to $2,000,000 in the form of venture capital or a combination of venture capital and notes held by the seller. With very little of his own money at risk, an entrepreneur could own between one-fourth and one-third of the company described in Exhibit 1.

The accounts receivable and inventory of a wholesale distributor are very attractive collateral to a secured lender. The customers that make up the accounts receivable are generally retail organizations or manufacturers who pay their bills within 90 days and who can be located and usually collected from if their bill is unpaid in 90 days. The inventory is in a finished goods stage, usually labeled, easily counted, and readily disposed of at auction or to a competitor if the lender has to liquidate the company to repay his loan.

Turning next to the operating statement, we see that the division earns about $1,000,000 per annum, which at today's high interest rates could support comfortably about $3,000,000 of borrowing (i.e., $22\% \times \$3,000,000 = \$660,000$, which can be paid by the company's earnings and have a margin of safety). But, how much money does the division make when we deduct corporate charges and the expensive overhead allocation that divisions of large corporations are saddled with? This is the more important number and it is known as "adjusted net income." The adjusted net income of the division, $1,681,000, represents the earnings of the division on a stand-alone basis, free of corporate charges for capital and services. This relatively high level of income could support the entire purchase price of $5,800,000 at an interest rate of 22% per annum (p.a.) (i.e., $\$5,800,000 \times 0.22 = \$1,276,000$ in annual interest which is less than $1,681,000 in adjusted net income).

We are in the comfortable position of having a strong cash flow to support borrowing. Now we return to the balance sheet to see how much we can borrow. The most tangible asset is accounts receivable. If the seller guarantees the collectibility of 100% of the accounts receivable, then a secured lender will loan $2,200,000 with the receivables as collateral. The maximum loan ratio on finished goods inventory is probably not more than 60%, which in this case would generate just under $1,800,000. The two current assets are able to provide an aggregate loan of $4,000,000. There is probably some collateral value in the shelves, desks and office furniture, and equipment as well as in the customer list, particularly if rented to others. This additional collateral could yield another $200,000 of loan value. Thus, the entrepreneur has found $4,200,000 in capital to buy the division, and so far he owns 100% of it.

Now the balancing act begins. The entrepreneur will normally shoot for perfect leverage and ask the seller to take a note for the balance of the purchase price, or in this case, $1,600,000. Clearly the division's income will support interest on additional debt of that amount, and leave several hundred thousand dollars to spare, but will it support a fast repayment? Large corporations are not inclined to loan money to entrepreneurs to help them buy their divisions, and to pile on so much debt that they will get the division back upon foreclosure. In this case, a loan from the corporation could not be repaid inside of five years, assuming no material improvement in the company or material reduction in interest rates. The seller might be willing to take back a $500,000 note for one year secured by an important asset, such as the division's name or catalogue mailing list (if the secured lender will release it), and then only if he saw a substantial equity investor in the company.

To lure an equity investor into the deal, the entrepreneur will have to persuade the best members of the division's management team to stay—a persuasion normally made easier by offering raises and made bloody simple by offering stock—and additionally by developing a business plan that portrays why this division will grow faster and earn more money when managed by the entrepreneur and the equity-encouraged division managers. For investing substantially all of the risk money in the deal, the equity investor will certainly seek control, and it becomes an intense negotiation, usually with several different venture capital funds, to see which one will ask for the smallest equity participation and the easiest stock repurchase or equity bonus plan to the entrepreneurs and managers.

In the meantime, the seller has not been sitting idly by. He has given the entrepreneur a fixed time to come up with $5,800,000, after which time he will take one of the other offers that always seem to be there. The secured lender cannot leave his commitment outstanding for more than a short time, as well, because of other demands for funds. Further, the division management who have been called on to do a tap dance for the investors are beginning to realize that they don't need the entrepreneur to pull off the buy-out. There are several other forces at work creating delays that the entrepreneur must counterbalance, such as lawyers, accountants, appraisers, committees, and their other time commitments, all of which make the entrepreneurs' ability to prioritize events and balance the various players critical to consummating a leveraged buy-out.

The division just described is an attractive company with outstanding cash flow. The purchase price is less than four times cash flow, which is cheap for this level of quality. The entrepreneur and his managers would probably be able to own one-third of the company if they fully leveraged the buy-out, after which their percentage ownership could increase through performance or options. A mature entrepreneur with 10 to 15 years of toil remaining in his business career might reasonably expect to make a couple of million dollars on this deal. An empire builder might need to own more of his buy-out. To own more of a buy-out, the entrepreneur has to find a less attractive company to buy. Here he will not be faced with severe time constraints, the threat of competitive bids will be a smaller factor, and he will end up owning more of the company. There are degrees of unattractiveness ranging from the small, no-growth manufacturing company to the bankrupt situation that needs a work-out plan acceptable to creditors and the court. In the first instance the company may never be able to grow sufficiently to retire the debt used to purchase it; in the second instance the factors that led to the bankruptcy may creep back into the picture after the acquisition.

An example of the financial statements of a less attractive company—a typical small, urban manufacturer of metal stampings—appears in Exhibit 2.

Assume that a family owns this small metal stamping business and that it is seeking $450,000 in cash. The adjusted net income includes net profits before taxes of $114,000, plus the seller's salary of $80,000 and various perquisites aggregating $25,000, for total adjusted net income of $219,000. If the full $450,000 is borrowed at an interest rate of 22%, annual interest charges would be $100,000, or ample coverage, even after adding back the entrepreneur's salary of $60,000 per annum.

Commercial finance companies are eager to assist in financing the transfer of ownership by way of the leveraged buy-out method. In this instance they would be prepared to advance 80% of the value of good (less than 90 days old) accounts receivable and 50% of the value of finished goods and raw material inventory. In this example those loan ratios would generate about $280,000. Where does the balance of the purchase price, or $270,000, come from?

Frequently in older manufacturing companies, the machinery and equipment, tools, dies, jigs, molds, blueprints, and drawings have been depreciated to extremely low levels. In this example the assets are carried on the books for $85,000, whereas their replacement value is probably 10 times as much and their market value perhaps four times

EXHIBIT 2. Financial Statements of a Typical Small Manufacturer

BALANCE SHEET
FYE 1981

Assets		Liabilities and Net Worth	
Cash	$ 12,000	Accounts Payable	$112,000
Accounts receivable	218,000	Accrued expenses	62,000
Inventory	306,000	Taxes payable, other	24,000
Total Current Assets	536,000	Total liabilities	198,000
Equipment—net	85,000	Net worth	450,000
Other assets	27,000		
Total Assets	$648,000	Total liabilities and net worth	$648,000

OPERATING STATEMENT
FYE 1981

Sales	$1,200,000
Cost of good sold	840,000
Gross profit	360,000
S, G&A expenses	256,000
Net profit before tax	$114,000

larger. In the old days, walls were built two feet thick, floors of solid concrete went down three and four feet, the metal stamping and cutting machinery was oiled and cleaned every day for the last 30 years, and the replacement value of these assets is frequently 40 to 50 times their book value.

Secured lenders make loans on equipment using neither replacement nor book value. Rather, they rely on something known as liquidation value, or quick-sale value. This is the estimate by a skilled appraiser of how much cash the lender could raise if he had to sell the machinery and equipment at auction within 60 days. In most instances the entrepreneur will be required to pay for the appraisal, but it is advisable to ask the secured lender to recommend several appraisers whom they trust. Prior to paying the appraiser to visit the plant and inspect the equipment, the entrepreneur should submit detailed information on the equipment and have the appraiser estimate the liquidation value. This is known as a "desk appraisal," and it is free. If the desk appraisal is too low to proceed, then the deal can be broken off before any expenses are incurred.

Secured lenders are generally willing to loan as much as 75% of the liquidation value of machinery and equipment. Thus, in the metal stamping company example, the needed $270,000 would be available if the liquidation value of the machinery and equipment is appraised for at least $360,000. In the event that it is appraised for less, the entrepreneur has at least four alternatives to raise the difference: (1) convince the sellers to hold a note for the difference, possibly securing it with second liens on all assets; (2) obtain a 90% guarantee on the equipment loan from the Small Business Administration (of which more later) to increase the lender's advance; (3) raise venture capital by offering a portion of the company's common stock to others; and (4) sell the equipment to a limited partnership of wealthy individuals for a price sufficient to close the gap, thus providing them with tax shelter, and lease the equipment back over 7–10 years, with low rental payments in the early years. Usually one of these methods will work if they are doggedly pursued. These negotiations and financial arrangements must be done quickly because sellers can get nervous and back out of a deal, as can lenders.

More time is available to the entrepreneur who purchases a company that has filed for protection under Chapter XI of the Bankruptcy Act, otherwise known as voluntary bankruptcy. This is so because the bankruptcy court freezes the company's obligations at the time of the bankruptcy filing (these are called the "pre-petition debts") and allows the company a period of time—usually around six months—to develop a plan to pay the pre-petition debts and get back on its feet. If no plan is offered, the company is liquidated for the benefit of creditors. In Chapter X, or involuntary bankruptcy, the six months shrinks to about two, because the creditors have gotten angry at the company and have put it into bankruptcy, feeling that in liquidation they will fare better than in reorganization.

One of the more interesting and exciting entrepreneurial challenges is to purchase a company in Chapter XI utilizing nothing more than verbal communication skills. Frequently in these situations the company is more viable than its owners believe. Many Chapter XI's result from the inheritance of a business by the incompetent children of a dynamic father. The father ran it with instincts, timing, contacts, friends among the suppliers and customers, and other important factors not available to the sons. Moreover, in his day the prime rate of interest was not more than 6%. He would not have been as successful with prime at 20%.

Thus the sons or their appointed managers see that sales are higher (inflation), but profits are lower. They are borrowing more than ever; the suppliers are demanding payment in 30 days, whereas Dad could hold them off for 90; and the customers are paying in 60 days, whereas they used to pay in 30. One or two creditors ask to see the company's financial statements, notice that the goods they supply are pledged to the bank, that net worth is shrinking or at least not growing, and they put the company on C.O.D. or credit limits until there is a balance sheet improvement. The sons no longer have a friend at the bank. Dad's banker friend died, and the sons now deal with a 22-year-old fresh-faced person who must channel all loan requests to Central Credit or some other committee of credit officers. To the bank, which has to make money, the company's balance sheet looks sick also. Not only does Central Credit turn down the request for more money, but it also asks the sons to begin reducing the loan and have it "cleaned up" within six months. The sons panic and go downtown to the law firm that they have used for contracts, leases, rents, and commercial collections to discuss the problem. In the flicker of a gnat's eyelash, the lawyers file for protection under Chapter XI to buy six months time. Everyone believes the situation is much worse than it is, completely ignoring the asset values that the father created, but focusing on the tightness of credit. This company becomes a fattened calf for the hungry, wolfish entrepreneur.

Dozens of these companies exist. You can receive numerous submittals by placing an ad that says you are a buyer of companies in Chapter XI in the *Wall Street Journal* or newspapers read by lawyers and bankers. After combing through the various submittals, the obvious one to go after has the following characteristics:

1. Numerous suppliers (pre-petition creditors) owed relatively small amounts of money; that is, less than $2,500.

2. Relatively few major suppliers owed large sums of money; that is, over $25,000.

3. A large customer list, made up of corporate purchasers, not governments or individuals.

4. Relatively more finished goods and raw material inventory than work in process.

5. Substantially fully depreciated property, plant, and equipment with no or minor amounts of loans outstanding against it.

6. Nature of the business is preferably a wholesale distributor or a manufacturer of an industrial component sold to several industries such as construction, aerospace, transportation, or restaurants, hotels, and housing.

7. The company should be sufficiently profitable to pay you a salary that compensates you for alternatives foregone, after reducing the family's salaries and perquisites.

A first step is to meet with the worried owners and their advisors and ask every question you can think of about the nature of the company's operations. Do not tip your hand by being pointed in your questioning. For example, do not say: "Do you have many suppliers owed small amounts?" Rather, ask to see the list of pre-petition creditors submitted to the court. Or if the company is on the precipice of Chapter XI, ask to see the complete list of trade debt. Find out who in the company talks to the credit managers of the suppliers. Frequently it is a clerk whose quavering voice has done the company more harm, without the owners' knowledge, than any other single fact. A firmer, more positive voice can relax the creditors for several months, even if payments to them become slower while cash is bundled into larger packages to deal with more pressing problems such as the Internal Revenue Service (IRS), telephone company, and utilities, as well as larger creditors.

It is best to gather all of the material after the initial meeting and take it to your hotel room for a long, careful analysis. Inform the owners that you will make up your mind in the morning. Practically every detail is important in analyzing a potential work-out situation, because the difference between a comatose and a salvagable company is marginal. The key is cash flow. "Cash before pride," the work-out experts will tell you, as they hack away at bloated personnel rosters, excess inventory, unused equipment. What assets can be liquidated or used creatively as collateral and what expenses can be slashed to generate cash? Assuming there is enough cash to keep the company afloat, given an acceptable pay-out plan to creditors and lenders, is it worth it? Or asked another way, assuming that you risk personal assets and work an 18-hour day for 12 months to turn around a sick company, is the ownership of that company worth the effort?

Further, are there any variables beyond your control that, if unleased, would surprise you and jeopardize the turnaround? For example, measure the effect of a 20% interest rate increase on the cost of capital during the work-out. Is there a better-faster-cheaper competitive product ready to come onto the market? Has some once-considered harmless litigation been swept under the rug? If there is a union, could it strike midway through the recovery?

Once you have considered as many negative occurrences as you can, and if you believe that sufficient cash can be generated on the company's assets, given a reasonable pay-out schedule to trade creditors and lenders, then it is time to return to the conference room and make the offer to the beleaguered owners. You must set the tone of this meeting as "serious-dramatic." An opening sentence might be, "Gentlemen, you have 60 days to survive at most." Or, "The condition of your company is critical, and I do not know if I or anyone else can save it."

The objective from their point of view is to come out of the trouble with some ownership and their pride—the wrong objective with which to enter negotiations with an entrepreneur. Your objective is to obtain as much ownership as possible for the least amount of personal risk. The most practical offer you can make is an option to obtain voting control of the common stock subject to your increasing the company's working capital or net worth at stated intervals: 30, 90, and 180 days, for example. As the benchmarks are met, additional shares are issued to you until you reach 80%, or 67%, or whatever number you can get through negotiation. It is also important to have the proxy to vote 51% of the common stock while effecting the work-out, so that you may sell material assets, make stretch-out deals with creditors, and move quickly without requiring a board action. A sample option and proxy agreement appears in Appendix 1.

Let us walk through a work-out situation to see how an entrepreneur might use the company's assets plus creditor responsiveness to stretch-outs to obtain majority ownership.

By practically every measure of efficiency the company portrayed in the financial statements of Exhibit 3 is headed for bankruptcy. On the surface, of course, it has a deficit working capital and an inadequate equity base to support its current level of sales. But a more detailed investigation shows average accounts payable days of 96 days; accounts receivable of 74 days; and 4.7 inventory turns per annum. The company employs 200 people who receive $145,000 every two weeks, yet there is only $35,000 cash on hand. Every asset is pledged to secure a loan. Who would want this company? Any management decision seemingly would amount to no more than rearranging the deck chairs on the Titanic.

An entrepreneur would want this company because in those financial statements there is cash that can be brought to the surface. And the reward for saving this company is control of a $20 million manufacturing company—an event that would take 10 years to accomplish from a standing start.

First of all, there are personnel inefficiencies, but not many. The product has a low labor content, as indicated by the high sales per employee ratio of $100,000. Nonetheless, the company can be put through a shake-up with 10% fired and others doubling up while the company works itself out. That is a savings of $29,000 per month plus $6,000 per month in obligations to the Federal Insurance Contributions Act (FICA).

The bank has underloaned on accounts receivable and inventory, and it should be replaced with a commercial finance company that is more comfortable with asset-based loans. The current assets can support a revolving credit of $5,000,000, assuming that only 15% of the receivables are over 90 days old and that two-thirds of the inventory is in raw material and finished goods. A commercial finance company would respond favorably to an overall business plan rather than on the strength of the assets alone. This would generate $900,000 in cash after paying off the bank.

Appraisals of the plant and equipment should indicate some improvement in their value as collateral. Let us assume that the chattel and real estate mortgage can be refinanced to yield $500,000 more.

EXHIBIT 3. Financial Statements of a Company Candidate for Leveraged Buy-Out

BALANCE SHEET

Most Recent Date

Assets		Liabilities and Stockholders' Equity	
Current assets:		Current liabilities:	
Cash	$ 35,000	Accounts payable	$ 4,860,000
Accounts receivable	4,080,000	Accrued expenses[a]	665,000
Inventories	4,260,000	Notes payable[b]	3,975,000
Total current assets	8,375,000	Total current liabilities	9,500,000
Equipment—net	1,130,000	Mortgages payable[c]	450,000
Plant, real estate	875,000		
Other assets	115,000	Total liabilities	9,950,000
		Stockholders' equity:	
		Common stock	75,000
		Retained earnings	470,000
		Total stockholders' equity	545,000
Total assets	$10,495,000	Total capitalization	$10,495,000

OPERATING STATEMENT

	Most Recent 12 Months	Most Recent Month
Sales	$20,000,000	$1,650,000
Cost of goods sold	15,000,000	1,250,000
Gross profit	5,000,000	400,000
Selling expenses	1,585,000	107,000
General and admin. expenses	1,360,000	110,000
Net operating income	2,055,000	183,000
Interest expenses	1,325,000	145,000
Depreciation	240,000	20,000
Net profit before taxes	490,000	18,000
Provision for taxes	245,000	8,000
Net profit after taxes	$ 245,000	$ 10,000

[a]Includes payroll for approximately 200 employees (145,000 every two weeks) and unpaid, overdue withholding taxes of $375,000, plus overdue payments to representatives.

[b]Note payable to local bank secured by accounts receivable and inventories, plus owners' personal signatures.

[c]Note payable to local bank secured by chattel on equipment and mortgage on real estate.

Finally, the accounts payable can yield the necessary working capital to meet the first 30 day test of the option period. At least $1,500,000 of accounts payable can be shifted to long-term debt and paid out over two years including a 90-day grace period. Remember, the old assistant controller had the suppliers' credit departments in a state of near panic by the time the entrepreneur arrived. The entrepreneur may have to guarantee some or all of these term notes.

The increase in interest expenses of $300,000 per year is offset largely by the personnel reductions. Further, the products that the company sells probably have not had a price rise in a few years—now is an excellent time.

The cash raised should be used to pay overdue withholding taxes, overdue representative commissions, to reward key people who assist in the turnaround, to introduce production efficiencies, and to accomplish other entrepreneurial goals.

Raising money by way of the purchase of an existing company, using its assets to borrow on, and stretching out its debts to gain time and ownership is not a new method. However, it has become increasingly popular and, indeed, systematized by managers of leveraged buy-out investment companies. These people are skilled at identifying companies whose stocks trade publicly at prices less than book value and whose assets are substantially written down, hence further deflating their value. They offer the control block a price above market value, which is typically at or near book value but less than appraised or liquidation value, obtain the block, and tender for the balance of the shares. Buy-outs of relatively large publicly held companies are occurring with greater frequency as leveraged buy-outs become part of the lexicon of entrepreneurs.

On a smaller scale, for example, in buy-outs of companies with sales up to $20,000,000, the first acquisition in many cases is the springboard to building a major company. Teledyne, Gulf + Western, and LTV, three of *Fortune's* top 50 companies, were each begun with a small leveraged buy-out. Charles Bluhdorn, the founder of Gulf + Western, after buying a small, troubled auto parts distributor, picked up New Jersey Zinc, E. W. Bliss, a Dominican Republic sugar refiner and approximately one-fifth of that country's real estate, Paramount Pictures, and several other companies. Frequently an entrepreneur will go after a distributor initially because the receivables are from corporations, the inventory is all finished goods, and there is a considerable amount of real estate and plant suitable for refinancing. The automobile and truck parts industries make particularly good waters to fish because the suppliers to these fields will be unusually helpful to an entrepreneur. One shock absorber manufacturer might offer 90-day terms if its line is stocked and a competitor's line is removed.

For the entrepreneur who merely wants to have his own business, set his own hours, and pay himself whatever he feels like, there are numerous leveraged buy-out candidates under $20,000,000 in sales. Attracting a supply of them to review and select from is not particularly difficult, although it does require time, systematization, and a war-chest of $15,000–$25,000 to permit a six-month effort that involves travel, investigation time, telephone, and postage. The best sources of sellers are merger and acquisition brokers, many of whom are listed in the Yellow Pages of the telephone book. The First National Bank of Maryland publishes a monthly list of companies for sale. The *Wall Street Journal* also lists companies for sale under the Business Opportunities column in the Classified Advertisements section.

There are several ways to get hurt doing leveraged buy-outs. The first is by falling in love with the company. This affliction could lead to overpaying, overborrowing, or overguaranteeing loans in order to sit at the president's desk. The second most common disease is an insufficient audit, which leads to buying a company that is too sick to turn around. The company's financial statements must be carefully audited as well as its personnel, its contracts, its supplier relationships, its customer relationships, and then, last but not least, its industry and its competition. Just because a company is inexpensive or financable does not mean it should be bought. The third most common error in doing buy-outs is to rely on anyone but yourself to accomplish anything. Hire a sharp securities lawyer for the closing and not a friend or relative. Hire a sharp accountant to help you understand the financial statements and not a trainee. In analyzing the company use first-class, top flight experienced people and avoid the advice of management insiders, sellers, sellers' lawyer and above all, avoid free advice.

2

PRIVATE VENTURE
CAPITAL FUNDS

The decade of the 1980s is the Age of Entrepreneurship. There is no better evidence of this than the formation of private venture capital funds. In 1970 there were no more than 10 such funds in the United States. In 1981 there were approximately 180, with 30 more raising capital to begin operations. In 1970 the 10 funds—primarily affiliates of wealthy families such as the Rothschilds, Rockefellers, Whitneys, and Phippses plus one or two pioneers including the legendary Arthur Rock—had roughly $400 million in available capital. In 1981 the available capital exceeded $5 billion. In 1970 there were perhaps 10 professional venture capitalists in the country, that is, people experienced in all phases of company launching. By 1981 the number of professional venture capitalists had grown more than 15 times.

What is the catalyst behind this formation of capital? On the one hand, investment managers are getting better at selecting entrepreneurs. They have earned their stripes as employees of small business investment companies or corporate venture capital subsidiaries where compensation included salary plus bonus tied to the performance of the portfolio. But they were denied "a piece of the action." After many years of making entrepreneurs rich, the desire to have an equity interest in the companies they select becomes an overwhelming desire. They calculate the rate of return that they have turned in for their employer and write an offering circular that in effect says, "We have earned Allstate or Citicorp an average return of 30% per annum for the last 10 years, and we can do the same for you Mr. Investor." In the period

1978–1981 close to three billion dollars was raised in this manner, primarily from pension funds and insurance companies.

A second stimulus to the accelerated formation of private venture capital funds was the simultaneous liberalizing of several unrelated Federal laws. In 1979 the Labor Department reversed a temporary ruling that prohibited pension funds from entrusting some of the funds under their management to independent third parties. At about the same time the capital gains tax was lowered by Congress, which helped to make equity investments more attractive. Quite independent of those actions, but at approximately the same time, the Securities and Exchange Commission permitted the sale of securities without a registration statement more quickly and with less hassle than had previously been the case.

On the surface these macroeconomic events may appear to have very little effect on the entrepreneur sweating out a meeting with his Uncle Harry to borrow $10,000 to test an engineering idea. But Uncle Harry reads the paper, and somewhere he will notice that venture capital is "in" or "out" and like the novine creatures that we all seem to be when making investment decisions, Uncle Harry will want to be with the "in" crowd.

Private venture capital funds are generally partnerships of 10-year lives, owned 80% by the providers of the capital and 20% by the investment managers. However, the 20% is generally calculated net of capital losses. For example, if the fund begins with $50 million and in the second year one of its investments goes public at a $10 million gain and another is written off for a $1 million loss, the investment managers do not receive a dividend of 20% of $10 million less 20% of the $1 million loss; rather, the $1 million loss is deducted from their $2 million share of the gain. In other words, when they raised the $50 million, the investment managers told their investors, "We'll share the gains 80/20, but the losses will come out of our shares." The investment managers are rewarded only on "realized" capital gains; thus, they want all of their investments to go public or be acquired within three to five years if possible. The focus on achieving capital gains in a short period of time naturally creates a focus on companies that will grow quickly when given fuel.

Managers of private venture capital funds make a concerted effort to minimize their losses, primarily because losses hurt them in their pocketbooks. Many of the investment opportunities they screen look exceptionally good to them. Frequently they turn down deals after a lengthy analysis when all signs have pointed to a closing. The long "no" or lengthy turn-down is very costly to an entrepreneur because he has discarded other financing options while concentrating on the seemingly interested venture capital fund. It generally takes 45–60 days after a business plan has been submitted to a venture capital fund to obtain a commitment for financing. If the commitment has not been given by then, there is a good chance that it never will. One would think these things should move along more quickly, but venture capitalists act slowly and carefully. Also, they have small staffs and large portfolios to manage, new deals to read, board meetings to attend, and administrative duties. Most venture capitalists travel extensively and are physically unable to respond as quickly as one would like. Thus, an entrepreneur is well-advised to allow 90–120 days to obtain a financing, including 45–60 days once a venture capital fund has shown interest.

It is prudent to send the business plan to 20–30 private venture capital funds. Frequently an investment banker can be helpful or, alternatively, one of the directories that categorizes the funds by their areas of interest. Among the nearly 200 private venture capital funds, the investment criteria differ in several key respects. The entrepreneur should ask several questions of the venture capitalists at the time of the initial call to determine if the business plan meets the investor's criteria.

Private venture capital funds categorize investment opportunities into four life cycle stages, as well as industry areas and geographical locations. The four stages are as follows:

1. Start-up
2. First stage
3. Mezzanine
4. Buy-out

A start-up situation is a company without revenues. Most private venture capital funds have a strong preference for start-ups. This is true for several reasons: First, they can obtain more ownership in a start-up situation and frequently control. Second, they know a great deal about the risks involved in start-ups and how to manage those risks. Third, if the entrepreneur or inventor needs buffering or support, such as in administration or finance, the venture capital fund can fill the slot temporarily or find someone to fill it.

Start-ups are frequently broken down into three subcategories: (1) dining room table; (2) laboratory; and (3) garage. The dining room table start-up is not really a company. There is an idea or concept for a new product or service, an entrepreneurial team, and a timetable of events (or PERT chart) with dollar values assigned to those events. In a dining room table situation, the costs of the launch are known as well as the events that need to take place. At this very early stage, usually no money has been invested. Many entrepreneurs incorrectly set out to find venture capital at this stage—the incurable inventor with the patentable idea is the most typical—without the timetable, cost breakdown, management team, or product application identified. They are rarely satisfied with proper financing.

It is frequently better for the entrepreneurs to raise family or friendly capital to move a dining room table deal to a more advanced stage of development, because if all the capital that needs to be raised, according to the PERT* chart, is raised from private venture capital funds, the entrepreneurs will in all likelihood give up control from the outset. Because many emerging companies require several rounds of financing, the entrepreneurs' ownership would very likely be whittled down to less than 20%. Family money "wants to help." Family members and friends are usually willing to give their proxy to the entrepreneurs to vote their shares. They frequently are able to provide a few more dollars after the first round, if necessary; they are generally willing to sell some of their shares to provide a sweetener to venture capitalists in future rounds of financing; and, they usually understand that they will be diluted significantly in future rounds of financing.

If the PERT chart indicates that the launch will require $1,200,000 over a period of 15 months until monthly cash receipts begin to exceed monthly cash expenditures, it might be possible to have the expenses of the first six months funded by family and friends. If the PERT chart calls for $85,000 in equipment, $20,000 in parts, and the salaries of three people for six months, say $45,000, or $150,000 overall, it is reasonable for many entrepreneurs to raise that sum. To improve the return to investors, the new company can form a subchapter S corporation and allow the investors to take most of the loss as personal income tax deductions. Thus, to an investor in the 50% income tax bracket, the net dollars invested would be $75,000. Further, one or more of the investors might wish to own the equipment and lease it to the company to use the investment tax credit ($8,500 in this example) plus accelerated depreciation to save income tax payments and to lower his net cash investment. An attorney familiar with securities laws should be consulted in regard

*PERT chart preparation is explained in Chapter 14, "Preparing the Business Plan."

to the sale of stock to family and friends to ensure proper legal house-keeping from inception.

The laboratory stage of the start-up period generally occurs when a product is in development but is not sufficiently completed to be tested. Few of the risks of the very earliest stage have been abated. That is, the major questions—Can it be produced? Can it be sold? and Can it be sold at a profit—still exist. What distinguishes the laboratory stage from the dining room table stage is that *a risk has been taken.* The entrepreneurs have begun to spend time and money to develop a product that they believe has commercial value. They may have left their jobs, which shows, more than any other action, faith in the product. More likely than not at this stage, they have kept their jobs and are moonlighting with the new product. Venture capitalists like to see an entrepreneur risk his time and his job because they risk their time and job with every investment they make.

Many entrepreneurs seek funding at the laboratory stage of emergence, although it is preferable to complete product development before raising professional venture capital. The ownership level that is necessary to attract venture capital at this stage is generally too great to leave enough incentive for the entrepreneurs. It is advisable to attempt to grow to a more advanced stage before obtaining professional venture capital. A tax shelter oriented financing is recommended.

Who might invest at this stage? A local industrialist or wealthy doctor or other professional who has an affinity for the entrepreneur's project or area of interest. The investment should be structured in a manner that saves income taxes or otherwise reduces the investor's risk to make the decision-making process move along rapidly. Frequently private individuals have difficulty in saying "no" rapidly and string along the entrepreneurs rather than "hurt their feelings." For the entrepreneur who legitimately cannot approach family or friends, because of an impoverished background or other circumstances, it is useful to visit the local Industrial Development Authority office and ask for the names of local private investors who might be inclined to invest to increase employment or otherwise benefit the community. Of course, certain communities reach out for the entrepreneur and pull together the financing for him, but this occurs principally in the Deep South and in certain industrial areas that have been losing employment.

The garage stage is that start-up period at which most early stage companies receive professional venture capital. The term "garage" probably originated in the early 1960s when companies such as

Hewlett-Packard were beginning; the entrepreneurs had built a proto-type of a new device or machine, and they would invite investors and customers to come over to the garage for a demonstration. Actually, Hewlett-Packard, which has sales of more than $4 billion and is still considered entrepreneurial and exciting by its employees, began in a garage, although other high technology companies frequently rent small offices. In the garage stage the entrepreneurs have built a proto-type, tested its performance, estimated the costs of tooling and unit costs of production in volume runs, and may have run a few tests on customers' premises. In a nonmanufacturing garage start-up the con-cept would have been tested by way of pro-forma customer interviews or, as with a magazine start-up, a "dummy" used to conduct a limited dry circulation test.

Garage start-ups may be a little more or a little less advanced than the prototype stage and may require as little as $20,000 or as much as $500,000 to complete the research and development cycle, but they are the most popular investment candidates for more than half of the pri-vate venture capital funds. The entrepreneurial team has generally taken the career risk, they have personal or family money at risk, they have worked together for awhile and uncovered and worked out many of the kinds of problems that arise in highly risky, intense, tightly controlled environments. The product risk is also mitigated somewhat by actual proof that the product can be produced and that it works as advertised. What remains is the marketing risk. Can the product be sold at a profit? If the people and production risks are minimized, many pri-vate venture capital firms will tackle the marketing risk head-on. This is particularly the case where the market for the product is very large and rapidly growing. (More on this in Chapter 14, "Preparing the Business Plan.")

Several of the older private venture capital funds are sufficiently ex-perienced with start-up stage investments that they will orchestrate the launch. They will contact a topflight biologist or chemist and ask him to prepare a plan to develop some solutions to problems that he has been tackling in a university environment. They will provide the venture capital, the management, and the networking with major cor-porate customers, banks, and suppliers until the company develops some cash flow and its entrepreneurs begin to evolve into managers. Genentech Corporation, the genetic engineering company whose stock jumped on the first day of public issuance to a value in excess of the market value of the Chase Manhattan Bank, was launched out of the venture capital fund of Kleiner, Perkins and Company of San Francisco in 1978. Tandem Computer Corporation was begun in much the same way when James Treybig, its founding entrepreneur, was pulled out of Hewlett-Packard by Kleiner, Perkins and asked to design a product and prepare a business plan to get it to market. But those are the rare launches that are industry-specific: vertical market extensions of microprocessors, genetic engineering, and robotics, the three areas that produce Pavlovian reactions among venture capitalists.

First-stage investments are equally popular with private venture capital funds. In this stage the company has generally been operating for one year after the product development period, and it has made a number of sales—primarily test and demonstration sales. For example, 30 or 40 customers have each ordered one or two products to test and flesh out. The products have been debugged in a user environment and frequently modified. The entrepreneurs have learned something about customer service and, moreover, have been in the marketplace and gotten their hat handed to them a few times when the product was delivered late or was missing a part. In one or two instances, a customer is willing to place a large order if the company can demonstrate a more solid financial footing. The customer wants to know that if it wants products in 24 months, or service or parts some months in the future, there will be a manufacturer to provide maintenance and service. If the company cannot obtain capital, it probably will lose the order.

Prior to making an investment in a first-stage company, a professional venture capitalist always makes an in-depth investigation of how the product is received and, indeed, used in the marketplace. As many as a dozen customers might be called and asked to speak candidly about the product as well as the service, training, parts replacement, price, and the possibility of expanded used. Customer types are broadly spoken of by venture capitalists as distributors, end-users, and original equipment manufacturers ("OEMs"). Distributors or dealers purchase the product for resale, occasionally adding value such as software but primarily retailing the product in their geographic market for a commission. End-users buy the product to use it for a specific in-house function. OEMs purchase the product to integrate it with one of their manufacture and resell the two as a system. OEM orders can become very large, steady, and profitable. To a venture capitalist, it is a positive feature when a first-stage company stresses OEM sales because it minimizes marketing expenses, produces longer production runs, and ramps sales faster. Of course, excessive reliance on one or two major OEM accounts is excessively risky because should they vanish for whatever reason, the emerging company would begin bleeding red ink in bucketfuls. A mixture of OEM, end-user, and distributor sales is the happy medium, although sales through marketing representatives to distributors or dealers is frequently a less expensive means of generating sales in the early years than is fielding a sales force.

Professional venture capitalists are also interested in suppliers and supplier relationships. They expect the first-stage company to have tested the components of most of the available sources of supply and have solid reasons for why each supplier was selected. They expect that the first-stage company will have a procedure for testing incoming components to control their quality. Further, they expect that there are alternative sources of supply for each component. This is called being "second sourced," an important requirement, especially for critical components, because a supplier could fail, be struck, or encounter production delays.

The value-added aspect of first-stage companies is critical to the private venture capital fund. The fund's life cycle is usually about 10 years; thus the investment managers seek companies whose products materially improve the users' efficiency or profitability. If the products are proprietary that is, protected by patents, formulas, trade secrets or know-how, all the better. What is crucial is lead time. If the value added to the end-user is 30% or better in terms of speed, efficiency, or price (or a combination of the three) the product may have a two- or three-year lead time over larger competitors. Wealth creation through the entrepreneurial process is the maintenance of a monopoly position for as long as possible. Companies such as Polaroid, Xerox, Monogram Industries, Digital Equipment, Intel, Federal Express, and others made such dramatic impacts on the lives of their customers that they created new industries. Their products and sometimes their corporate names became generic means of classifying the functions they performed, as in "Let's Xerox it" and "I'll Federal Express it to you."

The valuations of first-stage companies are markedly greater than start-ups, other things being equal. Whereas $500,000 might purchase 40–50% of a start-up, it rarely gets more than 25% of a first-stage company. That is a sweeping statement, and there are a multitude of exceptions. Nonetheless, many of the risks encountered at the start-up stage have been reduced or eliminated at the first stage. The valuation procedure is discussed in Chapter 14.

The mezzanine, or second-stage, financing occurs generally two or three years after start-up. The company is operating at a sales level around $5 million and requires another boost to $20 million. The boost is usually to expand nationally from a regional base, to broaden the product line, or to systematize the marketing effort and hire and train a captive sales and installation force. Frequently, mezzanine financings can be provided with debt or by way of a public offering, but prudent entrepreneurs realize that venture capital at this stage is relatively inexpensive. A $1 million injection might cost as little as 5–10% ownership if the growth curve has been fairly vertical, earnings trending up, and sound management practices in place.

Private venture capital funds like to put 10-20% of their capital at the mezzanine level to balance the general riskiness of their portfolio. Often they invest at this stage to avoid having their previous investment severely diluted. To gain more equity at the mezzanine level, private venture capital funds occasionally purchase some of management's stock. They also investigate the prospects of a public offering prior to investing with the thought of going public fairly soon after their capital goes in.

Some private venture capital funds have corporate partners to whom they have promised co-investing opportunities. Thus if a fund puts in $1 million at a first-stage level, it may offer the mezzanine level to one of its corporate partners. The corporation may have other reasons for investing, of which more in Chapter 3, "Corporate Venture Capital Subsidiaries."

Finally, the fourth stage at which certain private venture capital funds are active is the leveraged buy-out, discussed in detail in Chapter 1. This is a radically different kind of investment from the high technology start-up and requires radically different kinds of expertise. There are few leveraged buy-outs financed, for example, by San Francisco-area venture funds because of the plethora of high technology start-ups in that marketplace. On the other hand, New York and Chicago have several active leveraged buy-out funds. The role they play in leveraged buy-outs is to fill the gap between the purchase price and the money that can be borrowed on the assets and from the sellers.

As is discussed in greater detail in Chapter 14, the private venture capital funds are interested in achieving a rate of return, on start-up and first-stage investments, between 45 and 60% per annum compounded. This translates into 10 times their investment in five years of four times in three years on the high side, to seven times in 10 years and three times in three years on the low side. The range between high and low depends upon the investment managers' assessment of the degree of risk. Exhibit 4 translates compound annual rates of return into re-

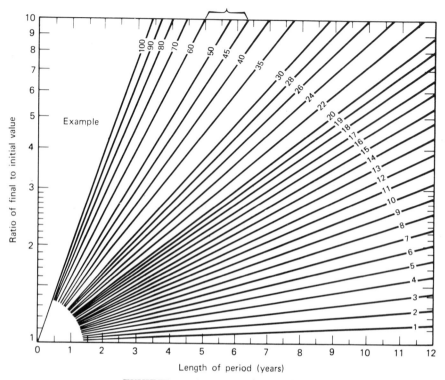

EXHIBIT 4.   Compound growth rates

turn on investment ("ROI") and can be used as a shortcut method of
determining compounded annual growth rates with sufficient accu-
racy for most purposes. The brackets indicate the target region for venture capital at the start-up and first-stage level. A start-up is expected to
pay out in five years and a first-stage deal in three, although in reality
events frequently do not occur as planned. Mezzanine financings and
leveraged buy-outs are expected to pay out in less than two years, and
because they are less risky, they would fall along the 30% line, or two
times in two years. This exhibit comes into play in Chapter 14, where
the financial statement projections set forth by the entrepreneur match
up to these rates of return lines.

3

CORPORATE VENTURE CAPITAL SUBSIDIARIES

The formation of venture capital activities within corporations is a difficult proposition at best for the simple reason that the investment managers, if good, will not stay; if bad, will be fired; and if average, will leave after five years for more salary. In any event, the portfolio will be unattended, and the corporation will have to divest itself of the bad investments, stay with the average investments until they can be sold off, and try to get the good ones public. Good venture capitalists will not work for a straight salary for more than five to seven years on average, and that is usually the only form of compensation that corporations can offer. If their track record is good, the venture capitalists frequently will set up their own funds. Thus corporate venture capital subsidiaries are characterized by several different features including frequent changes in personnel and abrupt changes in policy as well as more than the normal amount of red tape to close and an in-house legal opinion on virtually every imaginable issue before, during, and after closing. If the entrepreneur is willing to put up with these negatives, the positives are quite interesting and sometimes overriding, namely:

1. A tendency to overfund the company.
2. A longer horizon—10 years rather than five in the case of start-ups.
3. Additional fundings at first and second stages, frequently without seeking additional equity.
4. Joint-venture, license, and technology transfer opportunities.

5. Internal assistance in accounting, advertising, budgeting.
6. Assistance in high level contacts in banks, with suppliers, and with potential corporate customers.

The formation of corporate venture capital subsidiaries comes in waves, and the waves are currently coming in strong. The first wave occurred in the mid-1960s when Richard Gerstenberger was Chief Executive Officer of Dow Chemical Company, one of the earliest corporations to form an active venture capital subsidiary. Each time he agreed to serve on the board of another corporation, as he did at Eaton Corporation, he would convince the board of the merits of venture capital investing, and a new source of venture capital would spring up. However, because of the difficulty of rewarding corporate venture capitalists with pieces of the action, the waves soon wash out, and the activity becomes silent. Corporations that are no longer in venture capital are as numerous as those just getting into it. The ex-venture capitalists include Dow Chemical, Eaton, Union Carbide, Diamond Shamrock, Boise Cascade, GTE, Johnson & Johnson, Gulf Oil, Motorola, Time, Inc., and Allied Corporation.

The reasons that corporations form venture capital subsidiaries are valid from the corporations' point of view, but frequently lead to unhappy relationships with their portfolio companies. Corporations do not form venture capital subsidiaries to achieve capital gain income—the primary reason that private venture capital funds are formed. Wealth creation for the stockholders of Exxon was not the reason for the formation of their highly successful venture capital subsidiary, Exxon Enterprises. No matter how successful Exxon Enterprise's investments might have been—even if it had invested in Digital Equipment Corporation, the proverbial biggest venture capital play of all time, $70,000 into $500,000,000 in less than seven years—the impact on Exxon's earnings per share would have been miniscule. Wealth creation is not the objective. But because it is the objective of most entrepreneurs, disagreements occasionally arise that place entrepreneurs and corporate investors at opposite ends of the table.

The reasons that corporations play this noncorporate game are worth summarizing as follows:

1. To incubate future acquisitions that can become new divisions.
2. To gain windows into new technologies and new markets that they can step into in the future.

3.   To obtain licenses to manufacture or sell new products.
4.   To provide work for plants that have unused capacity.
5.   To teach entrepreneurial thinking to middle managers.
6.   To find a home for excess cash flow.

There are several other reasons as well, but the overriding ones are to incubate small companies that may be worth acquiring to form a new division and to develop a window into new markets. Exxon carried out these objectives beautifully, as indeed Exxon does many things first class. In the mid 1960s it formed Exxon Enterprises and made venture capital investments in three areas: (1) information processing; (2) educational products; and (3) medical products. After a few years, it decided to concentrate on information processing as the new market that offered the greatest opportunity to become sufficiently large to become a division of Exxon. New investments in teaching machines and medical instruments were ceased, and investments in computer and communications device manufacturers were intensified. By the late 1970s Exxon observed that several of its investments in the information processing field had become industry leaders, primarily Zilog (microprocessors), Qyp (facsimile transmission), and Vydac (word processing). It had other investments as well that had grown less rapidly, but had excellent potential, primarily in telecommunications equipment. True to the objectives it laid out a decade before, Exxon acquired these companies, merged them under the Exxon Enterprises umbrella, and had formed a new division well on its way to $300,000,000 in annual revenues. The near-term benefits to Exxon stockholders? Miniscule. The long-term benefits to Exxon stockholders? Major. When oil no longer fuels the world, Exxon can sell electronic mail systems.

The success of Exxon Enterprises has not failed to gain the attention of other large oil and chemical companies. Most of them formed venture capital activities in the late 1970s, although apparently without the clear set of goals outlined by Exxon. It would appear, based on what can be observed publicly, that the other oil companies are interested in biotechnology, alternative and regenerative energy sources, and information processing. The non-oil companies that are riding the venture capital wave seem to be interested in a variety of new markets, ranging from medical instrumentation to computer games.

The corporate venture capital subsidiaries are appropriate sources of venture capital primarily for large projects: $3,000,000 to $25,000,000 start-ups. If the start-up does not begin to show positive cash flow for five years, it will be rejected by private venture capital funds (their horizons are much shorter), but appreciated by corporations. If the project requires plants in various sectors of the country or world, the corporate venture capital subsidiaries can provide plant space in lieu of capital. The same applies to manufacturing or marketing licenses. For example, if an entrepreneurial team owns U.S. and certain foreign patents on a process of converting bark into an enriched animal feed and needs $5,000,000 to launch a U.S. manufacturer, but wishes to maintain 51% ownership internally, it might offer to an oil company in exchange for the $5,000,000, 49% stock ownership plus rights to implement the patent in Europe for example. To an investor who could not use the European rights 65% ownership might be required to make the same investment.

Some of the biotechnology companies formed in the late 1970s cleverly offered rights to possible future developments in exchange for corporate venture capital. Cetus Corporation, Berkeley, California, raised $36,000,000 of start-up capital, yet its founders maintained control because its corporate investors were traded rights to the fruits of Cetus' research in genetic engineering in lieu of equity. Thus Standard Oil of Indiana, National Distillers, and DeKalb Agresearch entered the corporate venture capital business to gain through Cetus' laboratory that which they apparently were lacking in their own.

The early laboratory successes of Cetus, Biogen, Genentech, and other biotechnology companies created a period of wild speculation whereby virtually every major pharmaceutical company in the world began offering from $5,000,000 to $50,000,000 to molecular biology Nobel laureates (and potential laureates) in university laboratories throughout the world, if they would devote their time and energy to genetic engineering and manufacture. Should Genentech, with less than $5,000,000 in revenues, and most of that in short-term contracts, have a greater market value than Control Data, Chase Manhattan Bank, or Intel? Such is the enthusiasm for entrepreneurial energies pointed at such major problems as cancer, diabetes, and malnutrition.

With some of the newly formed agriculture genetics companies working furiously on nitrogen fixation of soils, a process that will eliminate the need for fertilizer and herbicides, large corporations such as Monsanto and American Cyanamid, for defensive reasons, have invested huge sums in plant genetics companies.

The strongest arguments in favor of obtaining venture capital from a large corporation are that they have a tendency to overinvest, they have far greater patience, and they generally take a minority equity position along with contractual rights to the eventual product. They would like to have the contractual right, going in, to acquire control of the company in the future, but entrepreneurs are reluctant to yield this sweetener. Why build a company merely to sell it at a previously determined value on a previously determined date? It eliminates the value of the "chase," the entrepreneurial *raison d'etre*. Corporate venture capital operations that insist on a wedding and value of the dowry at the time of the first blind date quickly see their flow of deals dwindle to a handful.

Companies in the most favorable position to seek corporate venture capital, therefore, have the following characteristics:

1. Early start-ups (dining room table or laboratory).

2. Large capital requirements (in excess of $5,000,000, preferably $20,000,000 and up).

3. Requirements for multiple plants or multiple sites.

4. Very large market size potential; that is, the investor can visualize revenues in excess of half a billion dollars within 10–20 years.

5. Availability of multiple product fall-out resulting from the research for various licenses and various secondary market developments.

Synthetic fuels, new forms of protein, alternative energy sources, new metals, undersea mining, new forms of transportation, satellite broadcasting, new chemical compounds, and genetic engineering are examples of the kinds of areas that interest corporations in venture capital. It is important to remember that whereas private venture capital funds seek to turn their money every three to five years, corporate venture capital subsidiaries can sit with an investment for a much longer period of time.

VENTURE CAPTIAL ACTIVITIES OF FOREIGN GOVERNMENTS

The foregoing discussion applies to the government venture capitalists as well, with one exception: it is usually a requirement that the new company grant an exclusive manufacturing and marketing license to the foreign government, or agree to manufacture the product in their country. As with large corporations, foreign governments are interested in obtaining a variety of valuable properties other than wealth. For example, there is not one country in the world that would not give its eye teeth for Santa Clara County, California, known the world over as "Silicon Valley" because it is the birthplace of the microprocessor. The Germans, French, English, and Swedes have acquired companies in Silicon Valley, and the Japanese have replicated it with government financing. Israel has come the closest to creating a miniature Silicon Valley near Tel Aviv.

Like large corporations, the foreign governments with venture capital activities are slow to move. Whereas a private venture capital fund can do a deal in 30 days, start to finish, the foreign venture capitalists require 6 months and sometimes longer. This is because the decision-making power is vested across the ocean with some thrice-removed committee.

Beware of corporate development officers disguised as venture capitalists! Many are the corporations who attempt to kill new companies whose products may become competitive. If a corporation has its future riding on zippers or snaps, it would love nothing more than to see Velcro taken off the market. How best to do that? Invest in the Velcro company and then obstruct its growth and development.

Before taking a check from a venture capitalist—private or corporate—ask to speak with several of its portfolio companies. Make sure there are no man bites dog stories.

4

SBICs AND MESBICs

As any business person knows, the United States Government does less for small businesses than does any other technologically advanced country in the world. The German and Japanese Governments are virtual partners with business, enabling the rapid entry into new world wide markets of start-up companies through low cost loans to finance new product development and production. The United States Government is not a partner of the entrepreneur; although it occasionally operates businesses (mail delivery is a good example) in competition with entrepreneurs. It has very few programs to assist entrepreneurs and, on balance, when one considers the rules, regulations, and red tape involved in dealing with the Government, one can only comment that we have a long way to go in this country in the area of small business assistance.

The vehicle through which the Federal Government aids small business has been, since 1946, the Small Business Administration (SBA) of the Department of Commerce. The SBA affects small business primarily through two programs, Government guaranteed loans (this program is discussed in Chapter 10) and through the Small Business Investment Company (SBIC) program. To place in perspective just how small these two programs are, relative to private capital formation, let us count the number of jobs they create. A careful study was done in 1978 by the American Electronic Association to demonstrate that when an entrepreneurial company raises money it creates jobs and when a mature company raises money, it deletes jobs. The study showed that it takes $70,000 to create one new job in the electronics industry. The study further showed that approximately $30,000 of the $70,000 was traditionally provided by venture capital, and the balance was provided by borrowing and reinvested profits. Other similar kinds of studies done by various states have come up with the same figure for manufacturing companies in general. So $30,000 seems to be a reliable number for the capital cost of a new job.

The combination of SBA loan guarantees and SBIC loans for emerging businesses aggregates approximately $3.5 billion per annum, of which approximately $2.5 billion is in the form of SBA loan guarantees. When we divide $30,000 into $1.0 billion, which is the capital component, we arrive at 33,333 new jobs created each year in industry through the Government assisted SBIC program. In a country with 8–12 million people unemployed, that is a drop in the bucket. Moreover, the SBA programs as a whole account for only 50,000 new jobs annually, and that is in a good year. Fortunately, a new manufacturing job usually begets a new service job (teacher, gas station attendant, hairdresser, etc.) in the town where the plant is built. Thus, one could say that the SBIC program is responsible for generating between 50,000 and 70,000 new jobs per annum in the aggregate. To put that in perspective, 70,000 is about twice the unemployment level of Youngstown, Ohio in a recession year—not much government muscle behind small business in this country, relative to the overdraft facilities that the Government of Japan has given to electronics, automotive, and steel manufacturers. On a positive note, there is room for expansion and growth of government assistance in the United States, whereas the string has played out in Germany and Japan.

The SBIC program has had two lives since General Georges Doriot, the father of venture capital, formed American Research and Development Company in Boston just after World War II. General Doriot, a Harvard Business School professor, believed that businesses could be launched systematically through a blend of entrepreneurship, invention, and capital. He and others persuaded Congress to provide a "development bank" at whose window company launchers could borrow four dollars for each one dollar of equity capital and in turn loan that to entrepreneurs. Initially, one could form an SBIC if he could demonstrate $150,000 in capital. Even to this day, ownership of an SBIC license is open to any nonfelon, with or without banking or investment experience. In its first life cycle, 1946–1971, SBIC formation was slow and gradual until the new issue stock market in the mid-1960s bid the prices of SBICs sky high. Investors perceived that owning stock in a publicly held SBIC was a means of owning some of the growth companies in their portfolios. General Doriot's American Research, after all, had launched Digital Equipment Corporation, with the legendary $70,000 that was on its way to becoming $500 million in value. It could happen in other SBIC portfolios as well.

This clamoring for SBIC stocks naturally hastened the formation of SBICs in the mid-1960s. By demonstrating $150,000 in securities or other forms of capital (not necessarily cash) one could obtain $600,000 in borrowing ability at the SBA at low rates and 12–15 year terms. The $600,000 could be invested in new growth companies, and the growth companies could then be taken public, and the SBIC could get its money back. Sounds good on paper. That is what about 500 new licensees believed, and a period of excessive company launching began. Incompetent venture capitalists loaned money to incompetent entrepreneurs, and practically everyone involved created jobs for the bankruptcy lawyers. Only a handful of licensees from that era still remain in business after the stock market collapse of 1970–1971 and the recession of 1974.

In the midst of that first life of the SBIC program, the Department of Commerce created a new division to assist minorities seeking to enter the entrepreneurial process. The division was known as the Office of Minority Business Enterprises, or OMBE, and having participated in some of the early planning sessions in 1966–1967, I am aware of its purpose and goals. OMBE was created to assist blacks in owning businesses in inner cities. As white flight led to black blight in burned-out downtowns like Detroit and Chicago, OMBE looked for mechanisms by which blacks could own automobile dealerships, retail stores, and fast food franchises to enhance commerce in fast eroding downtown business districts. OMBE came up with a stepchild of the SBIC program—then in full flower—called the Minority Enterprise Small Business Investment Company or MESBIC. The MESBICs would loan venture capital to minorities. If you wanted to form a MESBIC you showed a net worth of $150,000 to the SBA, and it would loan initially and then invest $600,000 (a ratio of 4 : 1) in your preferred stock, with a 3% dividend rate after five years and a 20-year redemption period. Many large corporations formed MESBICS—Ford Motor, General Foods, Equitable Life—and, indeed, blacks and other ethnic groups for the first time had a special way of becoming entrepreneurs. Approximately 200 MESBIC licenses were granted, and the program was launched at top speed. Alas, the 1974 recession eliminated many mi-

nority entrepreneurs whose retail establishments were thinly capitalized and about half of the MESBICS, like many SBICs, collapsed and
died.

To breathe new life into the MESBICs, the definition of a "minority"
was broadened in 1976 by the SBA, thus enabling MESBICs to broaden
their portfolios to include a variety of businesses, not merely inner city
retailers and small manufacturers. The 1976 redefinition included men
and women deprived of economic advantages for any number of reasons. Thus Caucasian males over 50 years of age, persons deprived of
economic opportunity for reasons of ill health, American Indians,
women of all races and ages, persons of Hispanic origin and Vietnam-
era veterans could obtain venture capital from a MESBIC. The formation of MESBICs took on a new head of steam, as clever investors saw
the 4 : 1 leverage as a new Government trough at which to feed. Indeed,
several movie production companies formed MESBICs, right after the
movie tax shelter loophole was closed in 1976. The Hollywood MESBICs
would loan money to produce black and martial art films employing
hundreds of minorities, and then the parent company, having risked
but one-fourth of the capital, would distribute them. Several larger
MESBICs have operated almost like SBICs funding emerging businesses with the caveat that they are majority owned by "disadvantaged" people. Disadvantaged borrowers should bear in mind that
these MESBICs are interested in first-stage and mezzanine-stage
companies that manufacture a fairly basic product. When a MESBIC
seeks to stretch the definition of the term "disadvantaged," permission
must be obtained from the SBA, but that has not been difficult. For
some reason, not clear to the SBA or other observers, there have been
very few women and physically disadvantaged people stepping up to
the MESBIC window. However, Hasidic Jews, classified as disadvantaged because they represent a minority group within the Jewish reli-
gion, have been obtaining MESBIC loans.

"A MESBIC is a workout," says a MESBIC president I know. "The Department of Commerce hammerlocked large corporations in the late
1960s to throw a few dollars at the then most prevalent social problem:
civil rights. The ticket price was low, and they would stick an inexperi-
enced MBA in there to run it. The deals began to sour by the 1974 recession, and most MESBIC portfolios began to run with red ink."

According to Peter F. McNeish, Acting Associate Administrator for
Investment, Small Business Administration, "200 MESBIC licenses have
been granted since the program began in 1968. Approximately 72

MESBICs have failed, but the 128 survivors are for the most part better capitalized and better managed than ever before. They have an aggregate capitalization of $110 million and $134 million in SBA leverage as of June 30, 1981."

Walter Durham, President of MESBIC Financial Corporation of Dallas, owns the oldest MESBIC license. His fund has 24 companies in the portfolio and a net worth of close to $2 million. Durham was there at the beginning trying to put his initial $150,000 capitalization into black and Hispanic companies that had a reasonable shot at meaningful growth. But it was not enough money to permit diversification or investment in larger deals. It was too small to help portfolio companies with additional capital.

Like many of the entrepreneurs he finances, Durham set about raising some venture capital in 1972 and called on every large corporation in Dallas and some outside Dallas, like IBM and Xerox, with large facilities in the state. He pulled together $1.5 million of additional capital. The SBA at that time revised its policy and began buying 3% preferred stock from MESBICs rather than their debentures, so MESBIC Financial Corporation theoretically had nearly $5 million to work with.

MESBICs have to go out and find the really good deals. "We heard of Star Adair Insulation Company in Odessa, owned by a Mexican-American named Ignacio Cisneros," says Durham. "His company provides insulation services to refineries, power plants, and petrochemical plants to reduce their energy costs. Star Adair had grown from $6 million to $10 million in revenues in one year and was looking at $15 million in the coming year."

Ignacio Cisneros, the 49-year-old founder and president continues, "We had grown to 400 employees with business from Prudhoe Bay to Florida and jobs in 25 states throughout the country. We were supporting our growth with short-term debt at prime + 2%. At the time Walt Durham came to me, I was choking on growth and needed long-term capital and financial expertise."

Durham put together in May 1981 a syndicate of three MESBICs including Minority Equity Capital Company, New York and Amoco Venture Capital Company, Chicago, who invested with Durham $1,600,000 in Star Adair's common stock and its seven-year debentures with detachable common stock purchase warrants and entitling the MESBICs to 25% ownership. The Star Adair financing is typical of a large MESBIC financing in a fairly mature, rapidly growing company. The formation of a syndicate to provide the $1.6 million is a common practice among venture capitalists, because it offers a means to share the front-end investigative work and the back-end monitoring job.

MESBICs tend to finance a lot of deals that are indigenous to their areas: leveraged buy-outs in Eastern industrial centers; black-owned manufacturing and service businesses in the industrial Midwest; and Mexican-owned oil-related businesses in the Southwest. A typical Southwestern deal, for example, is Ben Baca's well site service business in Cuba, New Mexico, funded by Associated Southwest Investors of Albuquerque. Baca noticed the beginning of deep well drilling for oil and gas in the San Juan basin and a shortage of service contractors. The oil companies would hire one person who happened to own a backhoe and rely on him for a variety of services. Baca formed a company, Well Location Contractors, in 1980 to provide equipment and roughnecks to all job sites in the area. In late May Associated made Baca a $75,000 seven-year loan, partially secured by the drilling equipment with warrants attached to buy 25% of the company's common stock at the founder's price. This is typical of a relatively low risk regionalized MESBIC investment.

The second life of the SBIC program began in 1978 at the dawn of the Age of Entrepreneurship. Survivors of the first-stage SBICs had begun an exodus from the SBIC industry to form private venture capital funds. Their places were taken by entrepreneurs who had made a few dollars in the late 1960s and early 1970s and who sought to become financiers. The private venture capital funds also formed SBICs. Private venture capital funds would raise, say $30 million from institutional investors and reinvest $5 million in a new SBIC. This would give them $50 million to invest. To the institutional investor who puts up $30 million for 80% of the capital gains of the fund, he is ahead of the game from day one; $50,000,000 × 0.80 = $40,000,000. If the fund merely breaks even, the investor gets back $4.00 for every $3.00 invested. The combination of entrepreneurs forming SBICs and venture funds forming SBICs led to a resurgence of activity in the SBIC program. From a low of perhaps 50 active (that is able to make new loans) SBICs in 1975, there are close to 450 today, and more than 100 applications for licenses at SBA.

The background of the SBIC and MESBIC programs is useless information to the struggling entrepreneur trying to cover the payroll checks he wrote last week, but it provides an overview that is extremely important to the entrepreneur who is negotiating with an SBIC for a $500,000 first-stage investment. SBICs (MESBICs are included in the reference to SBICs unless otherwise stated) act differently from private venture capital funds. The differences are dramatic in the commitment letter or term sheet that a private venture capital firm gives an entrepreneur and the one given by the SBIC. Whereas the private venture capital fund is usually a 10 year partnership that does not pay interest on its partners' investments, the SBIC must cover operating costs plus the cost of interest on SBA loans and the cost of noninterest paying loans in the portfolio. If an SBIC offers to loan an entrepreneur $500,000 at an interest rate of 15% of which $100,000 is convertible into one-third the company's common stock, the SBIC will in all likelihood be turned down by the entrepreneur who receives a counterproposal from a venture capital fund offering to buy one-third of the company's common stock for $500,000. As a general rule, SBICs need current income and private venture capital funds (and corporate venture captial subsidiaries) do not.

Only small businesses can obtain funding from SBICs. The definition of a small business changes from time to time to meet the needs of an inflationary economy. The definition of a small business in terms of SBIC funding, as defined by the Code of Federal Regulations (CFR) 121.3-11, is as follows:

1. Business not dominant in its industry.
2. Independently owned and operated.
3. Net worth is less than $6 million.
4. Average net profits after taxes for the prior two fiscal years is less than $2 million.

If these tests are not met, the SBIC has the option of attempting to qualify the borrower under CFR 121.3-10, the SBA guidelines, which are industry specific. That is, the size limitations are raised for distribution industries that sell at retail prices and lowered for manufacturing industries that sell at wholesale prices.

The borrower must meet at least one of these regulations. If a borrower is borderline—that is, its sales are too large, but number of employees and net worth are within the guidelines—the SBIC can ask SBA for a waiver. The bottom line in government sponsored programs, bear in mind, is job creation. Thus a borderline applicant's request for waiver will be better received if lots of new jobs are at stake.

SBICs make long-term loans with equity features. They do not invest in common stock.* SBICs are most comfortable in making loans to first-stage and mezzanine-stage companies. These companies have a greater chance of repaying the loans than do start-ups. Naturally, start-ups are visible in virtually every SBIC portfolio, but only after the SBIC's first few years of operations when there is positive cash flow and a low risk, well-diversified, initial portfolio.

An SBIC is not permitted to loan more than 20% of its capital to any one company without obtaining permission from the SBA to "go overline," that is, go over the 20% line, usually in order to save its first loan. Therefore if an SBIC is capitalized at $500,000, even though it has $2,000,000 in funds available to it, no more than $100,000 can be loaned to any single company. Because most emerging companies require more than $100,000, SBICs generally group together into syndicates to make loans. For the entrepreneur who has attracted the interest of one SBIC in his deal, the money-raising job may only be one-fifth accomplished. Putting together a syndicate of SBICs can be a tedious proposition, but frequently the lead SBIC will make introductions to others.

Just as the SBIC officers spend time interviewing the entrepreneur, the entrepreneur should also investigate the SBIC. The key points in this inquiry are the following:

1. How large is the SBIC's capitalization?
2. How many companies are there in the SBIC's portfolio?
3. What is the decision-making process?
4. Has the SBIC ever acted as the lead lender in putting together a syndicate?
5. Does the SBIC require current income over and above interest on the debentures?

The answer to the first question will give an indication of the size of the possible commitment. The answer to the second question will give an indication of how active the SBIC has been. If it has a $2 million capitalization and a portfolio of 90 companies, with only three loan officers, it is busier than a man trying to drain an alligator swamp. The entrepreneur should be prepared for many delays in trying to get his deal accomplished. If, on the other hand, the capitalization is $2 million with a

---

*Occasionally SBICs participate with private venture capital funds in syndicates where all of the participants buy common stock.

portfolio of 18 companies serviced by three people, the deal should be processed quickly. However, the venture capital industry is under-staffed and delays of two to three weeks in reading a business plan are normal.

The entrepreneur should ask for permission to contact several port-folio company presidents to determine how they viewed their working relationship with the SBIC. It is advisable to ask in particular to contact a portfolio company where the entrepreneur had to be replaced by a manager to see if the transition was handled smoothly with a minimum of ruffled feathers.

I find the question about the decision-making process fascinating. Each SBIC differs in the manner in which they commit to a deal. The worst case for an entrepreneur is where the SBIC's board of directors meets monthly to pass on submittals by the loan officers. This is an unsatisfactory system because the entrepreneur can be 45 days or more (assuming it takes 15 days to prepare a recommendation memo-randum) from a decision. Then if the board requires a modification, there will be further dealys. If after all of that, a syndicate must be put together to fund the entire amount, another 60 days could get tacked on to the financing.

The entrepreneur should determine the steps in the investigation process (known as "due diligence") for two reasons: (1) timing of events and (2) preparation on the entrepreneur's part to expedite the process. The usual timing of events is as follows:

1. Visit to the company's office to see the product, the production process, meet members of management, and observe the record-keeping process.

2. At this visit, normally, other information is requested such as the most recent month's results, the next month's budget, cop-ies of major contracts or purchase orders, breakdowns of cus-tomers by product, geographically, industry, their uses of the product, and by percentage of sales, plus other data omitted from the business plan.

3. The entrepreneur is then invited back to the SBIC's offices to meet other members of the staff or loan committee, where many of the original questions are asked over again. In this situ-ation the loan officer who made the plant/office visit is spon-soring the loan and seeking internal support.

4. The next step is the submittal of the terms and conditions of the loan; or it could be a turn down.

The terms and conditions of an SBIC loan are very different from an investment by a private venture capital fund. The SBIC borrows 80% of its capital, and it is on the hook both to cover the costs of that capital and to repay it. As a result, an SBIC *rents* its capital to an emerging company for approximately five years, and then seeks to have it returned when the company is larger and is able to afford a repayment schedule. Under the terms of the Act by which Congress created the SBIC program, SBICs are not permitted to have their loans fully repaid inside five years, and they are not permitted to own more than 49% of the common stock of a company.

Two fairly standard loan arrangements are the convertible debenture and the combination of a straight debenture (no conversion privilege) plus common stock. In the former case, if we use $500,000 as the total amount of the loan, $100,000, or 20%, might be convertible into a portion of the company's common stock, and $400,000 might be repayable in equal annual installments for four years beginning with the fifth year. The debenture can bear interest at an annual rate up to 5% above Federal money market rates. In the high interest rate period that has prevailed since 1979, SBIC loan rates have been as high as 18% per annum.

An alternative SBIC loan arrangement, using the foregoing example, is an outright purchase of common stock for $100,000 plus a $400,000 debenture that repays in four equal annual installments beginning in the fifth year. Although these two structures appear similar, in the first case the SBIC has the right to have the convertible portion of the loan repaid if it does not view the company's prospects as exciting, whereas, in the second case, the SBIC is a stockholder from the beginning, for better or for worse. Although it is not transparent, the latter relationship is preferable because the SBIC thinks like a stockholder rather than a lender from the outset. Among other things, it might be more reluctant to pull the rip cord on the default provisions of the debenture if in so doing it wiped out its own equity.

A debenture is an unsecured obligation to pay. A note is similar, but can be, and frequently is, secured or collateralized. SBICs generally subordinate debentures and notes to senior indebtedness such as bank debt and trade debt. They want the company to be able to obtain conventional bank financing, which for small companies frequently means pledging their accounts receivable and inventories. This is not to suggest that SBICs are opposed to securing their position. On the contrary, they might ask for liens on equipment and plant subject to prior liens. In restaurant and other retail chain financings, they frequently ask for an assignment of leaseholds. They practically always take a position in the capitalization senior to the management. For example, SBICs prohibit payments of dividends unless payments on the debenture are current and other tests are met. In the event of liquidation, the debenture ranks senior to the common stock.

For SBICs that earn quite a bit of income taxable at ordinary rates, the preferred stock is frequently used rather than the debenture. Since dividend income is paid after taxes, SBICs usually charge their borrowers a dividend rate one-half of what they would have charged as an interest rate. Thus a preferred dividend rate might be 7.5–9% per annum.

SBICs are not loathe to charge director's fees and to seek reimbursement for attendance at board meetings. Some SBICs charge participation fees such as 5% of net income, and some charge consulting fees if they choose to send in a consultant. Although these niggling little fees can add up over the course of a year, they are frequently worth paying in order to raise a big chunk of subordinated money.

The term sheet that an SBIC presents a borrower—and many of the terms are common to private venture capital funds—contain three important sections: (1) the positive covenants; (2) the negative covenants; and (3) the co-sale agreement.

POSITIVE COVENANTS

Positive covenants, or the "Thou Shalls" are intended to force the company to do certain things regularly, the failure of which places the company in default and makes the debenture immediately due and payable in full. Although there is generally a "cure" period of 90 days after default is called, default is a serious affair because it could automatically trigger default of senior indebtedness. Entrepreneurs should attempt to avoid "cross default" covenants so that all debt is not called at once. A cross default covenant provides that if the company is in default on one loan, perhaps its bank loan, then it is also in default on its SBIC debenture. The standard list of positive covenants includes a myriad of items, some specific to each situation, but generally including the following:

1. Submittal to the SBIC of actual monthly results (cash flow statement and balance sheet) within 10 days after the end of each month.

2. Submittal of audited fiscal year end financial statements within 60 days after the end of the fiscal year.

3. Submittal of the succeeding year's monthly budget within 30 days prior to the end of the fiscal year.

4. Maintenance of a positive net worth or combination net worth plus subordinated debt of a certain predetermined amount.

5. Maintenance of a positive working capital balance of a certain predetermined amount.

6. Maintenance of adequate fire, casualty, theft, and key man life insurance.

7. Payment of all taxes when due.

8. Maintenance of all patents, trademarks, and rights to do business in various states.

9. Prompt reporting of litigation whenever it occurs.

10. Hiring of certain key people within 90 days following the closing, as agreed to prior to the closing.

Whereas SBICs cannot *control* a borrower, unless the SBA determines that it is warranted in order to protect their principal, private venture capital funds can take control at any time. The latter are more apt to introduce a variation of the positive covenants that gives them the right to elect a majority of the board of directors in the event that the net worth test (number 4 above) is not met. Literally, they can fire the management and replace them with their choices. SBICs tend to operate through the default provisions set up in the debenture or note agreement signed by both parties at the closing. If the company is in default, but cannot pay off the debenture, the SBIC can seek a variety of remedies to have its loan repaid. SBICs are quite experienced at this and exert tremendous amounts of influence at the board level and with the borrower's bank, if necessary, if they believe their principal could slip down the drain. It takes many winners in the portfolio to make up for losers; also, losers eat up a lot of time that could be spent reviewing new deals. Thus SBICs tend to move swiftly when certain red flags appear—hence the working capital and net worth tests—to save their principal. For example, the following scenario is possible:

1. Eight straight months of losses (seen in the monthly statements).

2. Trade debt builds up, thus pulling the working capital below the test level (seen in the monthly statements).

3. Default is called.

4. Ninety days pass without a remedy of the working capital test.

5. Suit is filed demanding repayment.

6. Judgment is obtained.

7. The assets, including bank accounts, are attached.

8. Management agrees to certain changes (removal of officers allowing a new chief executive officer to come in, or other changes) to free up the assets.

9. The SBIC rewrites the debenture to a secured or guaranteed note.

This scenario has been played out many times, but variations have occurred just as frequently. For instance, the managers could open a bank account unknown to the lenders when they enter default, allow cash to build up as receivables are collected and improve their negotiating posture thereby. This is not a small business tactic by any means. In October 1981, at a time when International Harvester was in default on over $2 billion of bank loans, it sold a division for $550 million and hid the cash from its banks. This action is not recommended unless the company's management believes that its side of the story should be heard.

NEGATIVE COVENANTS

The negative covenants or the "Thou Shall Nots" are a list of items that the borrower may not do without the approval of the SBIC. The list can be quite broad, and it generally includes specific items relating to the company and a statement such as the following: Without the approval of the debentureholder (or usually two-thirds of them if there are three or more), the company may not:

1. Issue shares of its common stock.

2. Issue securities senior to the debentures.

3. Pay a dividend on the common stock.

4. Create a subsidiary.

5. Sell off a major asset ("major" is usually defined).

6. Purchase a major asset ("major" is usually defined).

7. Increase salaries of or pay bonuses to its officers by more than a stated percentage.

8. Borrow money on an unsecured basis in an amount greater than the amount of the debenture.

9. Borrow money on a secured basis in excess of a predetermined amount.

10. Enter into any monthly lease or rental obligations in excess of a predetermined amount.

In the event the company fails to comply with a negative covenant it becomes in default under the terms of the Purchase Agreement, and the above-described scenario begins to unfold.

CO-SALE AGREEMENTS

The third area stressed by all venture capitalists, but originally created by SBICs as a means of exercising greater control without owning 51% of the common stock, is the area of restricting sales of stock by the entrepreneurs. These terms and conditions are called co-sale agreements. They provide that the entrepreneurs cannot sell their stock to a third party without offering it first to the SBIC. If they could, the SBICs might find themselves in the position of backing a new group, not to their liking, overnight. The co-sale agreement also provides that should the entrepreneurs receive a bona fide offer for their shares of common stock ("bona fide" requires definition, and could mean the offeror must have a net worth of $50 million or more or must be a listed company), the SBICs must be given the chance to better that offer and 90 days to do it, and the SBICs must be permitted to sell when and if the entrepreneurs sell. The SBICs are bound by the same rules as the entrepreneurs in the co-sale agreement.

There is a saying in the SBIC industry that good terms do not make for good investments. No matter how creative the structure of the loan, a deal will not become a 100 to 1 winner as a result. But good terms do cut losses, and that is all they are meant to do.

Although entrepreneurs should negotiate hard and astutely to try to get the most odious of the covenants removed or softened, it is frequently a losing battle. SBICs know many ways to lose money because dozens of events have occurred in their portfolios to cause them to write off loans. Therefore they insert these potective covenants based on experience with other borrowers. The leverage is very much in their favor when negotiating the terms and conditions.

After they have put money in the company, the leverage flips over to the borrower. The borrower can seek to renegotiate terms based on various changing conditions. For example, it can immediately raise more money for new product development by way of a research and development (R&D) tax shelter financing. It can seek government guaranteed loans. It can file for a public offering and offer to have some of the SBIC's stock sold. Entrepreneurs generally like risks more than do SBICs, and, as sure as the night follows the day, entrepreneurs will do certain things with the company after the financing that are permissible under the covenants yet cause the SBICs to become nervous. Sometimes they succeed and sometimes they fail.

One of the negotiating mistakes most frequently made by entrepreneurs is that they attempt to leverage venture capitalists. That is, they attempt to squeeze the highest valuation and the most favorable terms out of the most sophisticated investors who live by a myriad of rules and self-imposed rate of return requirements. Negotiations frequently abort as a result of the entrepreneur holding out for a few percentage points of ownership, when in fact the valuation of the company is normally fairly small at this stage of financing relative to its future worth. If, on the other hand, the entrepreneur capitulates on valuation, as long as it is reasonable, leverage will come later in the form of senior debt financing and a public offering. Alas, entrepreneurs are frequently hard headed about the worth of their companies and they negotiate bitterly with venture capitalists until both sides take hard and fast positions at opposite ends of the pole. Financial markets change quickly and a bird in the hand, the old men of Wall Street are fond of saying, is worth 86 in the bush.

5

BUSINESS DEVELOPMENT CORPORATIONS

Perhaps the most flexible lenders in the country are the Business Development Corporations, or BDCs, which are chartered by 27 states to make loans to small businesses where the end result is *job creation.* BDCs are a well-kept secret. Very few entrepreneurs know of their existence, hence they are substantially underutilized. Curiously, more than half the states do not have BDCs, and many of the non-BDC states are capital importers with few venture capital funds. The states that have BDCs are as follows:

Arkansas	New Hampshire
California	New York
Florida	North Carolina
Georgia	North Dakota
Iowa	Oklahoma
Kansas	Pennsylvania (Pittsburgh)
Kentucky	Pennsylvania (Philadelphia)
Maine	Rhode Island
Maryland	South Carolina
Massachusetts	Virginia
Mississippi	Washington (Seattle)
Missouri	Washington (Spokane)
Montana	West Virginia
Nebraska	Wyoming

BDCs are owned by a group of private investors who take the trouble to obtain a license from the state or owned by financial institutions and large corporations in the state. Funding is generally provided by individual financial institutions and corporations in the state whose interests are served by the increased availability of jobs.

The California BDC, launched in 1978 by a group of successful entrepreneurs, obtained its funding by way of a public offering. The New York BDC, more than 20 years old, is owned and operated by most of the large commercial banks, who designate officials to serve on a rotating loan committee that meets once a month to pass on loan requests generated by the permanent staff.

The inherent flexibility of BDCs arises from the following factors:

1. They can make conventional loans, like a commercial bank, secured or unsecured.

2. They can enter into purchase/leasebacks, whereby they might buy or build a plant for a small company and lease it to the company.

3. They are generally lenders under the SBA 501 program, which means that they can make loans 90% guaranteed by the SBA.

4. Many BDCs own and operate SBICs, thus enabling them to provide venture capital along with debt.

5. BDCs are a sifter of information about local investors. They can pull together a syndicate of private investors to co-invest with their SBIC, finance a building, or fill an equity gap.

The smaller the state, the more creative the BDC must be because there are normally few banks, no SBICs, and an absence of systematic small business financing methods. Take Wyoming, where the BDC is one of the most important financial institutions in the state. It has been known to provide practically 100% financing for start-ups, if the business plan meets with its criteria. One incident involved two young entrepreneurs who wanted to open a supermarket in a small town that had none. They had $40,000 between them, but the project called for more than $1,000,000. The BDC bought the land and financed the construction of a building, which it leased to the entrepreneurs for 20 years. They would own it after that. With a 90% SBA loan guarantee the BDC financed the equipment and fixtures of the store as well as initial inventory. The entrepreneurs risked their $40,000 on start-up expenses and working capital. The downside for the BDC was the value of the land, which was expected to appreciate, and a vacant general purpose building, should the supermarket fail to make it.

Although not BDCs, the states of Alaska and Massachusetts have venture capital pools created to assist entrepreneurs in their states. The Alaska Renewable Resources Fund, created by the state in the late 1970s and funded with a portion of that state's royalties from Prudhoe Bay oil royalties, makes venture capital investments to stimulate entrepreneurship in job creating industries indigenous to Alaska. Fishing related businesses have been a popular recipient of Alaska's funds.

The Massachusetts Technology Development Corporation (MTDC) is funded by the large financial institutions headquartered in the state. It makes subordinated loans up to $250,000 per company to technology-based companies that can raise $500,000 of venture capital. MTDC takes back an option or warrant to purchase a small percentage of the borrower's common stock, and agrees to resell it to the borrower at a mutually agreeable price.

NETWORKING

This is a good place to disucss one of the most important, but least utilized, methods of raising money for small companies: networking. In a previous decade, the term would have been "getting people involved who can assist you and in so doing benefit themselves." Networking means using people in the state or region who can assist the entrepreneur through contacts and action in accomplishing the financing.

Let us examine for a moment the steps taken by major corporations in accomplishing billion dollar financings. First an investment banker is engaged to analyze the financing, produce several alternative structures, and recommend the least cost path to accomplish the goal. A team is set up inside the corporation to generate PERT charts, cash flow statements, cost analyses, profit and loss statement projections, and eventually a business plan for the project. The management of the project may come out of that team, or an executive search firm is engaged to find management. An accounting firm is hired to bless the numbers generated by the project team. The corporation sends its squad into the state or region to negotiate tax deals, land purchases, rights of way, energy sources, water availability, and personnel resources. The state or region that offers the best package of people, energy, natural resources, and tax benefits gets the project. The winning state puts the laurel wreath around the elected official, who gets to pose for pictures with the platinum shovel as the project is begun. That usually results in votes.

In this scenario 20 to 30 people become involved in making sure the project succeeds, and each one stands to benefit in some way, from the junior accountant who anguishes over the financial statement projections to the highest government official who takes credit for 5,000 new jobs in the state. They have been pulled together by one major goal, and they work to make it happen because their individual interests are served.

The same kind of networking can be done entrepreneurially and on a smaller scale. The kickoff point is the BDC, or if one does not exist in the entrepreneur's state, with the Industrial Development Agency (IDA) of that state. All of the states have IDA offices whose function it is to create employment in the state. IDAs place ads in business journals, tooting their states' horns about great highway networks, rail facilities, deep water ports, cheap energy, hardworking people, and so forth. Their goal is to get clean industry to put plants in their states and hire huge numbers of low skilled people. The larger the projected employment of a company, the more enthusiastic they become. Each job in a factory begets a service job for that person's family. A study by the Connecticut IDA showed that 100 new factory jobs create 100 new teachers, beauticians, gas station attendants, television repairmen, and so forth. Whereas a start-up situation can create 20 jobs in the first year, 40 the second, and 60 in the third; that leads to 120 jobs overall and about $100,000 in annual state income taxes. Thus the argument for waiving real estate taxes for a few years.

Some states will provide training for new employees up to some small dollar amount. Connecticut has a kitty of $150,000 for woking capital plus a grant program of up to $350,000 per company for research and development in a scientific field. TIE Communications, Inc., a Stanford, Connecticut manufacturer of telephones that competes with Western Electric took advantage of the Connecticut R&D grant five years ago, and it was an important injection of capital at that time. Many of the southern states will waive real estate taxes for a dozen years, and Puerto Rico, for a time, offered a 17-year holiday on corporate income taxes. That program has been modified, resulting in a loss of industry to Ireland, which assesses no corporate income tax.

The entrepreneur should visit the BDC and the IDA in his state and discuss his plans, stressing the benefits to the state or locale. Visits with local architects and the president of the local junior college should be scheduled to discuss the number of graduates with the skills needed by the entrepreneur. The town fathers should be visited, including the bank president, insurance salesmen, and newspaper publisher. A local accountant should be used to bless the numbers. The local equipment dealer can provide the cost of a wall-to-wall factory layout. A local investment banker can structure the optimal financial packages.

This will cost the entrepreneur less than $5,000 and about five days of hard work. At each visit, of course, he ticks off the names of the other enthusiastic people he has met and who have agreed to be helpful. He states that the project will cost about $2,500,000 and that he has not raised it yet, but plans are unfolding. There is always the "by the way, who would you recommend for . . . ." And one contact leads to another five people who could be helpful. Finally, about 30 people in the community begin to talk about the deal and think of the boat they can buy if it goes through from their legal or accounting fee, equipment sale, construction job, land and brokerage, and so forth. The network eventually leads to several energetic lenders or investors—informal BDCs, if you will—who put the $2,500,000 financing together by one of several methods.

Typically, a new plant and the land it sits on might cost $900,000, the equipment $450,000, another $1,000,000 for working capital and the balance of $150,000 for fees. The BDC or an informal one pulled together by the IDA might finance the land and building and lease it back to the company. The BDC or a local lender can finance 80% of the equipment on a secured basis. The $1,000,000 in working capital can be arranged with a $500,000 SBA guaranteed loan and $500,000 of venture capital.

Thus, the $2,500,000 project ends up with a $640,000 venture capital requirement. The SBIC affiliate of the BDC might swing for $140,000 of the $640,000 and the remaining $500,000 can be divided between the people in the network, the entrepreneur, and a nearby SBIC or venture capital fund. Perhaps a couple of the pension funds of local employers could invest $50,000 apiece, and the person selling the land could turn back $50,000 of his profit. One of the bank's directors who has been vocal in his demands for new jobs in the community could put in $50,000 of his money. The local law firm that has the task of making this octopus transaction come together might invest $15,000 and the equipment dealer could go for $7,500.

If enough people in the community stand to benefit from the launch, the company will get launched. Networking works just as well, by the way, on a leveraged buy-out of a plant that might shut down if an entrepreneur is not found who will purchase it and save the jobs. As you recall, leveraged buy-outs almost always have equity gaps that must be filled. Frequently the IDA can point the entrepreneur to active purchasers of industrial real estate in the state who can fill the equity gap by doing a purchase/leaseback of the plant and making the terms very attractive to the entrepreneur in order to own the plant.

6

TAX SHELTER

For the entrepreneur who resists the notion of selling equity in his company for the purpose of developing a product, testing a marketing plan, erecting a plant, or selling licenses to a product, or for the entrepreneur who wants to complement an equity financing with an equal amount of capital, tax shelter financings are an excellent vehicle. The essence of a tax shelter financing is that wealthy, private investors can use the losses generated by the start-up project to reduce their income taxes, and at such time in the future that the project is commercially successful, the private investors will receive income equal to a small percentage of sales. The arrangement lasts usually for 10 or 15 years, at which time it dissolves. The investors receive tax savings in the early years and income in the later years, but no equity in the company. The company receives launch capital, preserves its equity, and gives up a royalty tied to sales or income.

Before jumping into a tax shelter financing, the entrepreneur must weigh the trade-offs: equity versus a royalty. For example, assume the case of a two-year old company that has designed and developed a product that it produces and sells to an industry segment for $120,000 and on which it earns a 50% gross profit margin. Assume further that it has sold about 20 of these products and foresees in two to three years another 100 sales before the product begins to reach the top of its life cycle, after which it will tail off as a result of market saturation and competition. Further, assume that the entrepreneurs who run the company gave up 33% of the ownership for their initial launch capital.

The royalty versus equity decision arises when the entrepreneurs face the issue of financing the development of a smaller version of the product that will sell for a lower price and reach a broader market segment. For example, assume that the company sells computer-based mailing list management systems and that its first product addressed large fund-raising and direct mail organizations such as political parties and magazine publishers. There is a much larger market segment among smaller direct mail companies that need a mailing list management system, such as churches and publishers, but they cannot afford $120,000 to improve the efficiency of list management. Indeed, their lists are smaller and hence the need for smaller computer memory size, number of terminals, speed of printer, and so forth. They would be willing to pay $40,000, perhaps, but they would require other features such as programs to handle their accounts payable, bookkeeping, and the like.

The entrepreneurs determine that there are approximately 500,000 small and medium sized list handling organizations in North America, and they might penetrate 5% of the market in 5 to 10 years, a $1 billion target. Because a list management system is not proprietary, the entrepreneurs determine that they will have to act quickly to develop the product and then market the product broadly and at a great cost, far in excess of what the cash flow from the initial product will permit.

The development budget indicates about 2,000 people-hours, or five software engineers working 200 hours each and five hardware engineers doing the same. These people will have to be hired and carried for at least one year until the product is turned over to the marketing team. At a salary level of $45,000 per person, plus another 20% for Social Security, health insurance, and Workmens' Compensation (usually referred to as FICA and benefits), the people budget is $540,000. The entrepreneurs estimate another 20% for additional laboratory space, or $90,000, and $300,000 for market research, field testing, advertising and brochure preparation, and transportation of people and product to customer test sites. Finally, the entrepreneurs allow an additional $200,000 for slippage due to delays and mistakes and another $100,000 for legal fees, investment banking assistance, and additional administrative salaries to oversee and account for the project. The downscale product development and market testing budget, thus, is a hefty $1,230,000.

The company's actual financial statements for its second year of operations and its budget for the third year appear as follows:

	Actual Second Year of Operations	Budget Third Year of Operations
Units sold	14	25
Revenues	$ 1,680,000	$ 3,000,000
Cost of goods sold	840,000	1,500,000
Gross profit	840,000	1,500,000
Selling expenses (15%)	252,000	450,000
General and administrative expenses	360,000	600,000
Net operating income	228,000	450,000
Interest expense	64,000	80,000
Net profit before taxes	$ 164,000	$ 370,000
Provision for taxes	50,000	150,000
Net profit after taxes	$ 114,000	$ 220,000

The company raised $400,000 to develop the first product, and spent all of it; so that its net worth is equal only to the second year earnings, or $114,000. The interest expense of $64,000 results from borrowing $250,000 under an SBA term loan at prime plus 3%, plus interest on credit cards used for travel and bank charges.

The balance sheet of this hypothetical company is not very strong. An aggregate of $114,000 in net worth plus $250,000 in term loans supports an equivalent amount of inventory and equipment. Accounts payable roughly equal accounts receivable. There is not very much cash, about $17,000, certainly not enough to hire engineers, design a new product, or implement creative marketing strategies. It is time to raise venture capital.

As we mentioned at the top, the company cannot support more debt and no lender would be willing to take an unsecured position in a fragile situation such as this. Therefore, the choice of financing vehicles comes down to two, equity capital or tax shelter, and we're back to the trade-off: ownership or royalty. I have a bias in situations such as this, which does not mean that I am right and opposing views are wrong: do not part with equity to finance research and development of a new product. Wherever there exists a financing method other than equity to finance an asset, use it and hold on to your equity. The same logic, as

shown in Chapter 11, "Asset-Based Borrowing," applies to plant, equipment, accounts receivable, and inventory. Equity should be held in reserve as long as possible and exchanged for capital at such time as either there are no other alternatives or the highest value can be
obtained. Tax shelter investors are more leveragable than equity investors. This preference for tax shelter money to develop new products is
merely a bias, but in the case of research and development, a systematic method of using government dollars exists and should be carefully
explored.

The essence of tax shelter financing is that the government permits
deductions from income taxes of business-related expenditures in the
year incurred. If an individual anticipates owing $20,000 in Federal in-
come taxes next April 15, he can spend that amount of money on research and development or certain other business-related purposes
and save or reduce the tax payment. The government picks up approximately 50% of the investor's payment in a tax sheltered investment and
frequently more. In certain instances, as we shall see, the government
reduces the tax rate on income that flows back to the investor if his investment was for research and development.

There are *traditional* and *aggressive* tax shelter investment opportunities. The former involve fixed assets such as office and apartment
buildings, oil and gas drilling, and equipment. The latter involve research and development, market research, franchising, advertising,
and new ideas developed by a breed of geniuses known as tax lawyers.
It is the aggressive tax shelter that is of the most interest to the entrepreneur. The term "aggressive" suggests new and relatively untried,
more subject to audit and riskier than the traditional tax shelter. An entrepreneur should *never* set up an aggressive tax shelter financing
without the assistance of a sophisticated tax lawyer and investment
banker. The offering is likely to receive very few takers and if so, may
unravel in the future owing to multiple investor audits unless it is structured perfectly.

Returning to the case of the computer systems integrator, the
$1,230,000 of capital required would cost the entrepreneurs approxi-
mately one-third of the company's equity capital versus approximately
a 6% royalty based on its future sales of the new product. Which
financing would you do if you were the entrepreneur? To make a rational decision, we have to do a cost of capital analysis in which we
measure the cost today of an expenditure that occurs in the future. In
the case of the cost of equity, we ask what is the value of one-third of my

company when I go public three years hence? In the case of the tax shelter financing, we ask what is the cost today of giving up 10% of product sales for the next 10 years?

We need to make some assumptions, primarily a three-year operating statement projection for the company and a 10-year sales projection for the new product.

A simple three-year operating statement projection for the company is based on extrapolating sales of the first product as it peaks in its life cycle and begins to taper off and estimating the ramping up of sales of the new product. We will assume that gross profit margins remain the same, that selling expenses are 15% of sales, and that general and administrative expenses increase at the rate of $150,000 per annum. Interest on the SBA loan begins to taper down as that loan is paid off.

THREE-YEAR OPERATING STATEMENT PROJECTION[a]

	Year 1	Year 2	Year 3
Revenues			
Product 1—Units	25	40	35
Product 2—Units	—	6	24
Product 1—$000	$ 3,000	$ 4,800	$ 4,200
Product 2—$000	—	240	960
Total revenues	3,000	5,040	5,160
Cost of goods sold	1,500	2,520	2,580
Gross profit margin	1,500	2,520	2,580
Selling expenses	450	756	774
Gen. and admin. exps.	600	750	900
R&D expenses	800	400	—
Net operating income (loss)	(350)	614	906
Interest expenses	80	64	50
Net profit before taxes	(430)	550	856
Provision for taxes	—	40	400
Net profit after taxes	$ (430)	$ 510	$ 456

[a]Dollars are expressed in thouands.

Assuming that the company arranges a public offering for its common stock after completion of year three, and that the underwriter is willing to raise $2,000,000 for 25% of the company's common stock, an

$8,000,000 valuation or a 17.5 times price/earnings ratio, then the entrepreneurs have created personal wealth of approximately $2,664,000 computed as follows:

Ownership after the initial $400,000 financing	= 0.667
Ownership after the $1,230,000 R&D financing	= 0.667 × 0.667 = 0.445
Ownership after the $2,000,000 public offering	= 0.445 × 0.75 = 0.333
$8,000,000 × 0.333	= $2,664,000

The entrepreneurs have created a paper wealth of $2.6 million, and must abide by certain rules before selling any of their stock. The SEC's rules on selling insider stock are discussed in Chapter 15. The first-round investors have been diluted to a 16.7% ownership position after two subsequent financings. They have achieved a return of 6.7 times their original investment in five years ($2,664,000/$400,000) or an approximately 46.5% compound return on investment. The second-round investors have been diluted only one time from 33.3% ownership to 25% ownership. Their $1,200,000 investment is now worth $2,000,000, a disappointing compound return of approximately 19% per annum over three years.

To analyze the return to the company's stockholders from the tax shelter approach involves plotting a curve for sales of the second product, deducting the cost of the royalty, and then estimating the value of the company after the public offering sometime in the future. There are several ways to estimate the ramping up of a new product's sales curve which are discussed in Chapter 14, "Preparing the Business Plan." However, let's assume that sales grow at the rate of 50% per annum for three years, then by 25% for three years, then by 10% for three years, as follows:

Year 1	Development	
Year 2	A few test/demo sales	
Year 3	24 units	$ 960,000
Year 4	36 units	1,440,000
Year 5	54 units	2,160,000
Year 6	68 units	2,720,000

Year 7	85 units	3,400,000
Year 8	106 units	4,240,000
Year 9	116 units	4,640,000
Year 10	127 units	5,080,000

If this 10-year sales projection is realistic, and if the investors are entitled to the same return on investment as the venture capitalists who
bought the company's stock in the alternative scheme, or about 20%
per annum compounded, then a royalty of approximately 10% of sales
is appropriate. Remember, to many investors the cost of the investment
will be deductible from their income taxes, in some cases up to the full
amount.

From the entrepreneur's point of view, the company will have deducted $96,000 from third year sales, which will reduce net profits after
taxes from $456,000 to $352,000. The value of the company after the
public offering, assuming the same price/earnings ratio, 17.5 times, will
be $6,160,000 versus $8,000,000 without the royalty deducted. The entrepreneurs will save the 33.3% dilution of the venture captial investment, and will own 50% of their company rather than 33.3%. Fifty percent of $6,160,000 is greater than 33.3% ownership of $8,000,000, and the
difference, although small, could be used to reward key employees.
One-half ownership has more clout than one-third, and the difference
may be worth much more in the future as the company grows. The entrepreneurs and the first-round investors have created more wealth
than had they raised the research and development captial by way of a
private placement of their common stock.

The trade-offs appear to work in favor of tax shelter financing, if the
yardstick is discounted cash flow of future wealth. But there are other
yardsticks to consider:

1. *Partner with a Deep Pocket.*   For entrepreneurs who select the
   tax shelter financing route, they forego the "professional"
   launch; that is, sidling up to an institutional venture captial fund
   that can provide capital contacts, advice, and sponsorship in the
   banking and underwriting community.
2. *Tax Loss Carry Forward.*   If the tax loss from R&D expenses is
   turned over to private investors, the company does not have it
   available to reduce its own taxes. It gets hit with the full brunt of
   the tax bite as soon as it become profitable.

3. *Expenses Associated with the Financing.*   Tax shelter financings are approximately three times more costly than venture capital private placements. Brokers charge as much as 15% of the gross proceeds for tax shelter financings versus the usual 5% for venture capital financings. An opinion of tax counsel is in the $25,000 to $50,000 range, whereas such an opinion is not needed in venture capital financings. An attorney must bless the private placement memorandum in a tax shelter financing, because the securities are being offered to individuals and the SEC's Rule 146 applies. To submit a business plan to private venture capital funds is not, on the other hand, a sale of securities and the business plan need not be reviewed by counsel. Of the various costs cited above, an entrepreneur should be prepared to eat a $25,000 bill if the tax deal aborts and much less if the venture deal aborts.

4. *Time Requirement.*   Tax shelter financings take more time at the front end in preparing the private placement memorandum and more time at the back end in rounding up all the investors in order to close. Venture capital financings should not take more than 90 days to complete if all of the information that the investors will want to see is prepared in advance. Tax shelter financings take at least 50% longer. This is true in other things when one deals with the masses and not the classes. The time difference narrows remarkably the fewer the number of investors in the tax shelter financing.

5. *Roll Up.*   At the time of the initial public offering, somewhere between the 3rd and the 4th year of the projections, the underwriter is likely to say to the company, "In order to take you public, you will have to roll up the R&D partnership. The reduction in net income from the royalty payments is too great." The company must then make an offer to the limited partners of cash, notes, stock or a combination of the three, and the offer must be acceptable to 50%–60% of the limited partners to effect the roll up. How much will it cost? Probably the discounted cash flow of earnings foregone, which in this case might be as much as the initial investment. It could eat into the proceeds of the public offering rather materially.

WHEN TO USE TAX SHELTER FINANCINGS

Tax attorneys are bright people and paid as well for their billfold surgery as cardiologists are for their heart surgery. Each year, it seems, there is a new "aggressive" tax shelter on the street. If it takes liberties with the IRS rules, it will eventually be closed down. But, if it is non-abusive, hundreds of copycats will come on to the market.

The following description of various tax shelter financing methods does not purport to recommend that you use them or does it say that the IRS has endorsed the use of them. These examples are taken from live offering circulars that came out on Wall, LaSalle, Montgomery and Spring Street in 1980 and 1981.

The Subscription Shelter

If you have wondered why so many new magazines are launched, the answer lies in the fact that magazine start-ups make interesting tax shelters. The usual objective in launching a magazine is to build a large base of subscribers, say 150,000 readers or so, who will fill an interesting demographic slot that certain advisers will enjoy trying to speak to. Advertising is sold on a cost per thousand basis, and the more thousands of readers there are, the more revenues to the magazine. It has been estimaed by magazine launch experts that it takes $30.00 to obtain one subscriber for a new magazine. Lots of analysis goes into creating the number $30.00, but for the magazine that needs 100,000 first year readers to sell enough pages of advertising to stay alive in year two, the publisher will have to raise $3,000,000.

It is extremely difficult to keep any decent equity ownership when you need $3,000,000 to attempt to find customers for a new concept—after all, what is a new magazine, but someone's concept of providing information on a regular basis to a given group of people. However, in the tax shelter format the entrepreneurs normally keep all of the ownership of the publishing company and nearly half of the income. What they offer to the investors normally is $2.00 of losses for every $1.00 invested in the first year and another $2.00 loss in the second year. In the vernacular of tax shelter financing, that is a 4:1 shelter.

Whereas the investors only invest $3,000,000 in cash or by guaranteeing bank loans, they assume the liability for fulfilling the subscriptions, or if you prefer, for delivering the magazine. That doubles the money at risk in the launch year and assuming no earnings in year two, the investor loses the amount of his guarantee then as well. In one recent magazine start-up, all of the investors were listed in the masthead as responsible to the subscribers to fulfill the subscriptions personally in the event of the financial failure of the magazine.

When a magazine fails, its list of subscribers is frequently sold to another magazine which then attempts to hold their interest for awhile and then puts on a full court press for renewals. Could the investors' liability indeed be an asset with marketability and transferability? If magazine tax shelters hold up in the view of the IRS, the seeming paradox will continue to exist.

And why would this not apply to other products that are sold on a subscription basis? Newspapers, book clubs, record clubs appear to be fair game. The same would apply to subscription-based businesses of the future, such as computer-game-of-the-month, wine of the month, cable television programs, food shopping services, and others yet unborn.

The R&D Tax Shelter

The continuing IRS assault on abusive tax shelters has heightened the popularity of R&D tax shelters because of the significant economic opportunities that investment in new product research offers.

Section 174 of the Internal Revenue Act provides that: "A taxpayer may treat research or experimental expenditures which are paid or incurred by him during the taxable year in connection with his trade or business as expenses which are not chargeable to capital account. The expenditures so treated shall be allowed as a deduction." The phrase "in connection with his trade or business" was clarified in 1974 when the Supreme Court held that a new limited partnership organized for the purpose of developing a new process or product is entitled to deduct research and experimentation expenditures. In other words, the investor need not be the manufacturer or in business in order to get the tax deduction on research carried out in his behalf.

Therefore an R&D tax shelter is usually organized as a partnership, and the research is usually conducted by a company under contract with the partnership. The same company is typically granted the option to license the technology developed and to manufacture products utilizing the technology. The partnership's remuneration is then tied to sales of the product that results from the research; but there can be no guarantee of remuneration or, for that matter, the repurchase of the technology from the partnership, for if that were the case, the partnership would not be at risk on the research.

Other expenditures in an R&D tax shelter may be treated differently. The costs of obtaining a patent, including legal fees, are deductible. Expenditures for the acquisition or improvement of land or property to be used in connection with research and experimentation are not deductible if the partnership acquires rights of ownership in the property. However, if the partnership acquires no ownership rights in the property, the entire cost of such property is deductible. The only property that the partnership should acquire an ownership right to is technology, for example, patents, designs, drawings, data, research, prototypes, formulas, trade secrets, processes, and know-how. The cost of acquiring patents owned by someone else is not deductible. Therefore, the research agreement should specifically exclude transfer to the partnership of patents, prototypes, production, or processes already in existence.

But, if the research is intended to improve on already existing technology, the owner of that technology can grant a nonexclusive license to the partnership for the term of the research agreement. The costs allocable to the acquisition of such nonexclusive license are also deductible. The cost of market testing, management studies, consumer surveys, inspection of materials, quality control, advertising, or promotions are not deductible.

R&D tax shelters that seem to be more frequently attacked by the IRS than others arise in those instances where the company that stands to benefit from the research lacks the wherewithal to produce and market the product that results from the research. Such a company might be in a start-up stage or merely lack the capital, or management, or operating history to commercialize the product that the partnership paid to develop. In these instances the IRS may argue that the purpose of the partnership was to achieve tax deductions and not to develop a product. Therefore R&D tax shelters are not recommended for start-up companies without operating histories. They are, however, appropriate for companies at the first stage of expansion which seek to broaden their product line or market share. For example, if a company is producing and selling one product, call it "EXP," and seeks to introduce "new, improved EXP." Another area that provides excellent opporutnities for R&D tax shelters is in biotechnology, where the Crick–Watson breakthrough in defining DNA in 1952 and the Cohen–Boyer discovery in 1973 of a means of recombining DNA have created billions of dollars of opportunities to develop new genotypes.

In structuring the royalty payment to the investors in the partnership, the entrepreneur should bear in mind that royalty income to the owners of the patent or technology is taxed at capital gains rates. These rates are substantially lower than rates on ordinary income, for example, 16%–20%, versus 50% or more. Thus a $1,000 royalty payment requires a $160 tax payment if the investor paid for the research versus a

$500 tax payment had he merely invested in the company's stock. Further R&D tax shelters are normally structured to lose the full amount of the investment in the first year, thus for an investor in the 50% income bracket, who invests $1,000,000 in an R&D tax shelter, his net investment is $500,000. If the entrepreneurs project that the product may generate sales of $1,000,000 to $10,000,000 per annum in years three through ten, a 6% sales royalty would return from $60,000 to $600,000 per annum. At the higher royalty level, the entrepreneurs would at some future date consider purchasing the technology from the partnership and saving the $600,000 annual payment. That figure would be more helpful to the company's common stock value on the bottom line.

The Licensee/Dealership Tax Shelter

A relatively new tax shelter that is particularly well suited to companies that are able to sell their products through regional stores, dealerships, or offices is the licensee/dealership tax shelter. Obvious examples include fast food and other franchises, but when the mind wanders a bit, other candidates come to mind, such as computer retailing, movie distribution, racquetball chains, weight loss and health care centers, and many more. The tax shelter to the investors in the partnership arises from the manner in which payments for the rights to the trademark, know-how, or system are paid for.

Let us assume that you operate a "wellness" clinic in a metropolitan area where people come to jog, play racquetball, stop smoking, lose weight, exercise, dance, and receive checkups. Further, assume that there are medical personnel, physical therapists, and physical education instructors on the staff, and they put the clients through a rigorous, systematic wellness program. The program, the personnel training, and the method of attracting clients and keeping them interested has been thoroughly documented in manuals. Additionally, the physical space, equipment, and layout have been tested to obtain the optimal results, as have the location in the metropolitan area and the hours of operation. In other words, the Wellness Clinic is a smoothly operating system.

You and your co-founders decide to open nationwide, but you want to maintain high standards of quality and service, which means tight control of the system. Following the time-worn axiom "you can't franchise quality," you find skilled managers to operate each regional Wellness Clinic from Maine to California on behalf of the investors. The original Wellness Clinic in its third year of operations has revenues of

$1,700,000 and net profits before taxes of $300,000. In the prior year revenues were $900,000, and there was a small loss; and in the start-up year revenues were $400,000, and the loss was $300,000. Further, it cost you the $300,000 loss plus $300,000 in equipment, leasehold improvements, and working capital to open the first Wellness Clinic, or an aggregate of $600,000.

If you want to open five new clinics next year, you will have to raise $3,000,000—an enormous, perhaps unrealistic target for a three-year old service company. The stock market does not bid up the prices of service company stocks as a rule, and private venture capital funds are frequently worried about companies whose "assets go home every night at 10:00 p.m."

Enter the tax shelter financing method. You can license a partnership to use the system for providing services as a Wellness Clinic operator in a specified territory and a predetermined number of years. A subsidiary of the licensor, which can act as general partner, can provide a variety of services to the partnership including site selection, hiring management, instruction in implementing the system, education, and advertising.

The partnership agrees to pay $3,000,000 per license or market—$15,000,000 for five regional licenses—which amount is roughly equal to the cumulative pre-tax earnings of an individual Wellness Clinic over the 12-year term of the license. Payment for the license is to be as follows:

	Annual License Fee	Percentage of Total License Fee
Year 1	$ 600,000	20.00%
Year 2	$ 600,000	20.00
Year 3	$ 10,000	0.33
Year 4	$ 20,000	0.67
Year 5	$ 30,000	1.00
Year 6	$ 40,000	1.33
Year 7	$ 220,000	7.33
Year 8	$ 320,000	10.67
Year 9	$ 330,000	11.00
Year 10	$ 340,000	11.33
Year 11	$ 210,000	7.00
Year 12	$ 280,000	9.33
Total	$3,000,000	100.00%

Naturally, if the private placement of limited partnership interests is for five licenses simultaneously, these numbers are quintupled: $3,000,000 in Years 1 and 2, $50,000 in Year 3, and so forth.

The method of payment of the license fee creates the tax shelter. The licensor company needs approximately $2,000,000 in cash to open the first two centers; thus it asks the investors to pay 33% of each of the first two years' obligations ($6,000,000), or $1,980,000 in cash and sign a note for the balance, or $4,020,000 plus a full recourse note for the balance of the license fee payments, ($9,000,000) over 12 years. Payments on the smaller note are deferred for three years and then retired, along with interest at 9% per annum, in three equal annual installments in years four, five, and six. These are the years in which there are small payments on the license fee.

The general partner agrees to manage the Wellness Clinics for an annual fee equal to a percentage of gross revenues, and the resulting income goes directly to the limited partners. The license agreement provides that the indebtedness to the licensor must be paid first out of the partnership's income, with the balance representing income to the licensees. The licensees may terminate the agreement at the end of any year, but they must retire the indebtedness by a fully amortizing note to be paid over five years.

As the income is received by the partnership it blots out the note, thus providing license fees to the parent of $15,000,000 over 12 years and income to the licensees after the indebtedness is retired. The partnership uses accrual accounting, thus enabling the limited partners to deduct the obligation to pay the first year's liability, $3,000,000, even though the cash payment is approximately $1,000,000. Hence internal leverage and a 3 : 1 tax shelter. The parent, or licensor, drops down a subsidiary that keeps its books on the cash basis, and records income only as received, so no income taxes there except on the $1,000,000, net of expenses.

This gets the Wellness Clinic $2,000,000, enough to open three of the proposed five new clinics. The balance comes from the parent's cash flow of $300,000, advanced to the subsidiary, along with a loan for $700,000, secured by the partnership's promissory notes, advanced to the subsidiary.

Section 1253 of the Internal Revenue Code sets forth the deductibility of certain payments made to effect the transfer of a "franchise." The term "franchise" is defined in Section 1253(b)(1) to include "an agreement which gives one of the parties to the agreement the right to distribute, sell or provide goods, services or facilities within a specified area." This also includes distributorships or other exclusive contractual arrangements under which the transferee is "permitted or licensed to operate or conduct a trade or business within a specified area." In the Wellness Clinic for example, the transferee receives a franchise within the meaning of Section 1253.

As to the means of payment for the franchise, Section 1253(d)(2)(13) provides for the deductibility in the year paid of a series of approximately equal payments. Proposed Regulation 1253-1(c)(3)(iv) states that such treatment is similarly available for a series of unequal payments over a period of the transfer agreement if no such payment exceeds 20% of such principal sum and provided that no more than 75% of such principal sum is paid in the first half of the period of the transfer agreement.

In the foregoing example, the partnership could defer two-thirds of the first two year's payments for the franchise. As an accrual basis taxpayer, the delivery of the note constitutes payment of a franchise fee, because the obligation to pay is firm and binding and not contingent on the productivity of the franchise. The investors in the partnership are at risk for payment of the full amount of the license fee, although they are to receive the funds with which to make payment from the income generated by the Wellness Clinics in which they have a proportional interest.

The licensee/dealership tax shelter is relatively complex to set up and requires sophisticated tax counsel. I have painted the preceding example with a broad brush to show how it might be applied to a service franchise. Numerous kinds of small businesses can raise money using this format, although caution and extreme care are required in setting up all of the necessary agreements and offering circulars, in this and other kinds of tax shelters, in order to stay within the strictest interpretation of the law. An entrepreneur should never attempt to raise money by way of the tax shelter route without tax and securities counsel and an investment banker.

The utility of tax and securities counsel is obvious, but why use an investment banker? There are two reasons: (1) he can place the limited partnership interests with sophisticated investors; and (2) he can structure the terms to provide a return on investment that is attractive to the investors, yet one that does not give away the store. The investment banker sees dozens of tax shelter proposals each year, and he can compare the risks and potential returns of your deal with traditional and aggressive tax shelters and advise you accordingly. In the case of the Wellness Clinic example, the investors "lose" for income taxes $3.00 for every $1.00 they invest for two years in a row. One would argue that their percentage return on investment in the future could be set very low. But how low? That is an investment banking question. Remember, inflation is the friend of tax shelter investors—over a 12-year period the $15,000,000 fixed franchise fee will become a progressively smaller percentage of overall income as inflation drives up revenues.

The Real Estate Tax Shelter

The most traditional tax shelter is the real estate tax shelter. In its simplest form, an industrial building is purchased by a partnership made up of high tax bracket individuals and leased to a small business. The partnership deducts the investment tax credit and depreciation on an accelerated basis, thus reducing income tax liability each year. The flexibility of this financing vehicle should not go unnoticed. If a building is worth $600,000 but the small business needs $1,200,000 in capital, the sale/leaseback is set at $1,200,000. The investors have to come up with more cash—presumably their bank will only lend 75% of liquidation value or around $400,000—but have more depreciation each year. The key to artificially raising the price of the building is the company's ability to pay the lease. It does no good to bury oneself in fixed monthly obligations if the cash flow is merely a projection and not realizable.

Because depreciation rates are relatively low percentages of the building's price—around one-fifteenth per annum—real estate tax shelters do not begin to approach the internal leverage features of the previously described shelters. They are conservative and more popular with investors. In scouting around for an investment banker to sell the partnership interests, it is easier to find one to manage this kind of tax shelter than a more aggressive one. Frequently, a wealthy individual might agree to take the entire investment and hire counsel to draw up the papers to suit himself. To find these investors, entrepreneurs can get some ideas from the regional Industrial Development Agency or Community Development Corporation Office.

7

RESEARCH AND DEVELOPMENT GRANTS

There are a variety of sources of grant money available to entrepreneurs, none of them particularly easy to obtain. The smallest research and development grants are those offered by the National Science Foundation (NSF). NSF awards $25,000 to an individual for the purpose of conducting original research in an area that it believes is socially useful. In recent years, the NSF has favored energy saving projects and alternative energy sources. The State of Connecticut offers grants of up to $350,000 for the development of a product that could lead to increased employment of scientists in the state. These kinds of grants are relatively narrow and small. The application for the $25,000 NSF grant is rather lengthy and can only be submitted in a brief period once a year.

The large and more interesting grants are those at the private foundation level: Ford, Rockefeller, Kellogg, Carnegie, and many of the other family foundations whose founders, like Andrew Carnegie, believed that their wealth should be held in trust for the benefit of the country. There are literally thousands of foundations in the country, and directories exist listing their assets, location, and key decision makers. It is important to determine if their assets are managed internally or delegated to a third party, but that can be done with a telephone call.

Grant money is part of an overall financing and is never the key ingredient. For example, assume that an entrepreneur has built a computer software company that produces custom and standard applications packages to run on a variety of machines. It is in its third year of operations with sales of $1,000,000 per annum and a good reputation in the marketplace. To maintain a base of programmers, who by their nature move from job to job with frequency, the entrepreneur decides to train retired persons in Florida and Arizona to be programmers. To accomplish this he needs capital to acquire equipment, for leasehold improvements, training costs, and working capital. Each training center costs $750,000 to launch, and the company requires research and development funds for new product development. In all, it needs more than $3,500,000.

The financing can be divided into four parts as follows:

1. SBA guaranteed loan of $500,000 to finance the computers and other equipment in the training centers.
2. Public offering of $1,500,000 to finance the opening of three centers.
3. R&D tax shelter financing of $1,200,000 to develop new products.
4. Grant of $300,000 to $500,000 to fill the gap.

The source of the grant funds in this example could be one or more of the family foundations that support adult education, or one or more of the national lobby or political action groups that represent retired people. Frequently they make funds available through universities, thus the capital is spent partially by the university and partially by the company.

Grant proposals are similar to private placement memorandums but stress the social utility of the project rather than the capital gain aspects. For example, retired people could make excellent computer programmers, would have enormous pride in their jobs, could work at home on microcomputers or terminals tied into a network, could set their own hours, and could rejoice in being a valid part of the economy and the high technology industry. This example, it should be pointed out, is taken from a live situation. ACS America, Inc., a New York software development firm, announced the first of its software training centers in Bradenton, Florida. Over 3,500 retired persons applied for the 36 positions available. Following a three-month training program, 35 persons ranging in age from 65 to 80 had become competent, dedicated programmers. Grant money has been offered ACS from several sources.

An extra step is required in obtaining a grant, but it easily justifies the cost. The entrepreneur must form a not-for-profit corporation whose objective it is to test or develop the socially useful product or service.

The grantor is not interested in achieving a capital gain on the money, but rather the development of the product or service. Many foundations support entrepreneurial endeavors with the interest and dividend income earned on their portfolios while leaving the principal intact. If a commercially viable product results from the research and development in the not-for-profit corporation, it can then be licensed to the for-profit corporation. Certain state-managed grant programs—the Connecticut plan comes to mind—seek to recoup the proceeds of the grant in the form of an income royalty for a fairly long period of time. These royalties should be very carefully examined, because they can eat into profitability to the overall detriment of the company. Although they may appear otherwise, grants are not free!

Federal grant programs have been around since 1862, when the Morrill Act provided aid to land-grant colleges. Then came the Federal Aid Road Act of 1916. Grant programs picked up speed under President Franklin Roosevelt and became a huge business under President Johnson in the 1960s. Under President Reagan, grant programs will probably shrink in size, because as Milton Friedman, a Reagan economic advisor and classical liberal economist said, "What valuable invention ever came about from a grant?" His views are shared by many economic advisors in the administration.

The Office of Management and Budget publishes semiannually a catalog of grant programs, and the 1979 edition listed approximately 2,000 assistance programs administered by more than 50 Federal agencies. Of these the Department of Education administered the most—nearly 300—as you may have guessed. Each of the programs has its own rules, regulations, application forms, and various requirements. The Federal Register lists revisions in these rules and requirements, which are published daily. The *Racing Form* for the eager grantsman is the Code of Federal Regulations, printed once a year and sold for $350. The Code of Federal Regulations synthesizes all rules and rule changes from the *Federal Register*.

In 1979 Federal grants totaled more than $70 billion, which represented nearly three times the 1970 figure of $24 billion. Approximately 25% of the annual grant figure is sponged up by the state and local governments, many of whom post permanent grantsmen in Washington. One of the more useful grant programs for entrepreneurs is the UDAG, an acronym for Urban Development Action Grant. A local government files with the Department of Housing and Urban Development (HUD) for a UDAG grant, the purpose of which is to create employment in the community by building a plant and/or related facilities—driveways,

parking lots, street lights, sidewalks, and so forth—for a business to occupy. The local community obtains the UDAG grant and then re-grants
it to the business. Some local communities loan it to the business at
nominal interest rates and long repayment schedules. There are a
number of small town mayors throughout the country who are exceptionally skilled raisers of UDAGs. A $1,000,000 UDAG grant to finance a
building saves more than $200,000 in annual debt service charges as
compared to conventional financing.

For the entrepreneur who is able to stick a plant virtually anywhere
in the country, small towns—many of them in the South—frequently
have city officials who know more about UDAGs and other unique ways
of raising grant money than the savviest investment banker. These mayors are adept at putting in new sewers, water treatment plants, roads,
and street lights and still have enough left over the for the plant that
was the stated purpose of the UDAG in the first place. Their argument
to HUD usually goes something like this: "I can't convince this business
to come to the town of Buzzard's Breath without better sewers, roads,
and lights. If you grant me the UDAG, I can build just the kind of plant
this company needs." Notwithstanding the recent cutback of Federal
loan guarantee programs, the UDAG program is alive and well with $450
million per annum in grant money.

8

PUBLIC OFFERINGS

Going public, or "hanging paper," as the sale of securities is sometimes referred to, is a feasible means of raising venture capital for start-up and first stage companies. In 1980, according to the monthly magazine *New Issues*, 237 companies raised $1.4 billion by way of the sale of newly issued securities to the public. The last previous bull market in new issues was in 1972 when 568 companies raised $2.7 billion. The year 1981 jumped off to a roaring start when, in the first quarter, 96 companies raised $658 million by way of new issues compared with 31 companies that raised $139 million in the first quarter of 1980. The new issues market ground to a halt by the middle of 1981 due to failures and fraud on the part of several new issue underwriters and because new issue investors found other less risky places to park some of their money.

There are three centers of underwriting activities in the new issues market: Denver, Jersey City, and New York City. The Denver underwriters appear to favor start-up companies and common stocks priced at 25 cents or less. These are commonly referred to as "penny stocks." One of the problems associated with penny stocks is getting them up to more than $1.00 where national investors become interested. In fact, Californians are restricted from buying common stocks having initial underwriting prices of less than $3.00. Investors in penny stocks have the mentality of slot-machine players in Las Vegas. When the stock they purchased goes from 10 to 50 cents, the tendency is to dump it. With this kind of resistance, it is difficult over the near term to get the price of the stock up to the range of decency even when earnings improve. For the entrepreneur, a penny stock issue certainly raises capital, but it may be years until any stock can be used to acquire other companies, attract key management, or be pledged as collateral or sold. Favorite issues of the Denver underwriters appear to be oil and gas related and high technology. There was a spate of penny stock offerings between 1979 and 1981 by Denver underwriters to back geologists in their search for oil. Fewer endeavors are as risky as oil exploration, but risk is apparently what the investors like.

Jersey City, New Jersey is a step up in quality of new issue underwritings. Although Jersey City happens to have a fair number of small underwriters, the name applies to a number of other regional underwriters in Albany, Philadelphia, and other towns near New York City. The basic Jersey City new issue offering is a common stock priced at one to 2 dollars per share. Whereas the Denver style is to authorize 20 million shares, issue 8 million to management, 4 million to Treasury, and 8 million to the public at 10 cents per share ($800,000 in gross proceeds), the typical Jersey City deal is to authorize 2 million shares, issue 800,000 to management and sell 800,000 to the public for two dollars per share ($1,600,000 in gross proceeds). The Jersey City underwriters prefer more quality, such as an operating history, or an initial investment by the founding entrepreneurs of $20,000 or so. The qualifications of many of the companies who flog their paper on an unsophisticated public are extremely weak, by many of the standards described herein (see Chapter 14, "Preparing the Business Plan"). Yet LTV Corporation, a New York Stock Exchange Company, began with Jimmy Ling doing a self-underwritten new issue from a booth at the Texas State Fair in the early 1960s. A handful of other successful companies raised their initial capital with a dollar issue through a small New Jersey firm.

Across the Hudson River in lower Manhattan is Wall Street where, it has been said, "gentlemen come to raise money." Most of the New York City underwriters who are inclined to manage new issues will not underwrite start-ups; but that rule is broken frequently. The venerable Allen & Co., early backers of Syntex, developer of the birth-control pill, raised $5 million for Codenol in 1981, a start-up laser development company. Goldman, Sachs & Co., investment banker to Ford Motor Company, the New York Times, and others, underwrote a new issue for Hybritech in 1981, a monoclonal antibody research and development company which had no revenues.

The Wall Street sponsored underwriting has a higher price per share—somewhere between five and twenty dollars—and the number of shares is correspondingly fewer, with the average offering producing approximately $5,000,000 for the company. Certain new issues can raise more capital if the problem that the company purports to be addressing is large, if the management team is extremely well experienced, or if there are promising aspects such as important contracts, numerous patents, or the blessings of important customers or suppliers. This was the case with Genentech, one of the premier biotechnology companies that manufactures interferon, a possible cure for cancer.

Why go public as a start-up or first-stage company? There are several good reasons, the most important of which to some entrepreneurs is to create wealth. Although shares of common stock of a public company cannot be sold for approximately two years after the offering, the Rule 144 requirement (except in a private transfer where the buyer is willing to hold onto the stock for the required length of time, which means he will buy them at a steep discount from market), some entrepreneurs enjoy or need to be "paper millionaires." It's a macho thing.

A second reason is that the public will generally pay a higher price for the stock of new companies than will private investors. This translates into more working capital. For the 18-month period ended September 30, 1980, there were 111 new issues, of which one-half were start-ups. The average size of the offerings was $2,130,000, or approximately twice the average size of private placements of early stage companies during that same period. Frequently half of the company's ownership is sold to the public, but many entrepreneurs regard that as a fair trade-off for $2,00,000 to test a business plan.

A third reason is to obtain currency. A common stock with a market value (although restricted in its transferability) is a form of currency, one step removed from complete illiquidity. It can be used to make acquisitions, attract key people, award bonuses, and be pledged as secondary or side collateral. For an entrepreneur with a boat manufacturing business who would like to acquire a catamaran manufacturing business, the stock can be offered to the seller in lieu of cash or notes.

We will examine the negatives momentarily, but first some mechanics. On April 3, 1979 the Securities and Exchange Commission (SEC) adopted Form S-18 Registration Statement as a means for smaller companies to file public offerings more easily and with less burdensome costs. The Form S-18 has subsequently all but displaced Form S-1, which is used by larger companies. If the size of the offering is less than five million dollars, Form S-18 is much easier to follow. It requires fewer disclosures and fewer number of years (two) of audited financial statements. The average length of time in registration (that is, the time required by the SEC to review the prospectus) for a Form S-18 offering is less than 60 days versus 90 days for a Form S-1. Regional underwriters have a strong preference for Form S-18. In the 18-month period ended September 30, 1980, 85% of all Form S-18 offerings were filed in a regional office. The average costs (not commissions) for a Form S-18 offering are approximately $65,000 for a start-up versus $100,000 for a first stage company. These costs* consist of the following:

	Start-Up Company	First-Stage Company
Printing costs	$14,069	$25,334
Legal fees	36,761	41,858
Accounting costs	10,136	26,537
Miscellaneous costs	2,649	4,653
Total issuance costs	$63,655	$98,382

What kind of companies raise start-up and first stage capital by way of public offerings? High technology manufacturing companies are clearly the most popular. In a recent survey it was shown that high technology manufacturing companies (SIC codes 281–384) represented 43.5% of the new issues, other manufacturers (SIC codes 200–399) 16.3%, wholesale and retail trades (SIC codes 500–599) 13.0%, and services (SIC codes 700–899) 13.0%. High technology issues are defined as having the following SIC codes: 281, 283, 289, 355, 357, 366, 369, 372, 381, 383, 384, and 343 (plumbing and heating equipment manufacturers, but only the solar energy equipment manufacturers).

Among the negatives facing an entrepreneur who goes the public offering route are the following: the costs, the dilution, the lack of invisibility, and the "to reveal or not to reveal" problem.

1. *The Cost of Search.*   Finding an underwriter that is interested in managing your public offering, who will follow the company after the offering, who has the credibility to put together a syndicate of underwriters who will be market makers in the stock and who will agree to a firm underwriting (as opposed to a best effort) is a time-consuming chore. It is best to visit underwriters in your region of the country, and if that region is Denver, Salt Lake City, Jersey City, or New York City you are fortunate. In a "hot" new

*Source: SEC, Form S-18 A Monitoring Report, March, 1981.

issues market, small underwriters are very busy and frequently cannot get to a new deal for several months. Finding a compatible underwriter capable of fulfilling the preceding criteria is difficult at best. An entrepreneur should reconcile himself to the fact that it will take about six months from start to finish.

2. *The Cost of the Offering.* The expenses of a new issue range between $65,000 and $100,000 on average. To this must be added the underwriter's commission of around 12%, plus warrants to buy as much as 5% of the company's common stock. In a $2 million offering, the net proceeds to the company will be around $1,700,000. Assume the company sold 40% of its equity to the public for the $2 million; after the underwriter's warrants, the give-up is more like 45%. The net valuation then is $1,700,000 for 45%, or approximately $3,800,000. This is still in excess of the price at which most private venture funds would value a start-up. The front-end costs of a public offering include the commitment fee to the underwriter, the down payment to the attorney to draft the prospectus, and the down payment to the accountants to audit the financial statements. A typical commitment fee is $10,000, and the total of the various other front-end costs is around $20,000, for an aggregate investment of $30,000. This amount, although small, is frequently difficult money to come by for the start-up company.

3. *Dilution.* In this example, giving up nearly one-half of the company's ownership in the first round can have deleterious long-range effects. For example, if the company has a three-person entrepreneurial team, 50% dilution reduces their ownership at least to 16.7% per person. If they need another round of equity in the future, say $5,000,000 for 33%, each entrepreneur will be diluted to nearly 10%. At some level of ownership, at least one of the entrepreneurs may lose incentive and go on to something else. When he pulls out, the company may become structurally too weak to survive. Private venture capital funds are very sensitive to this problem and rarely let the entrepreneurs feel that they have too little at stake.

4. *Lack of Invisibility.* For the company with a proprietary system in a test and development stage, a public offering may reveal more than the entrepreneurs would like. It is preferable to keep these kinds of experimental companies under wraps until the developments have been tested and proven. Larger companies

are prone to steal ideas if doing so provides them with a competitive edge.

5. *To Reveal or Not to Reveal.*   Presidents of small publicly held companies are constantly bothered by large stockholders and securities analysts for information about the company's near-term prospects. If the presidents do not reveal information that can positively affect earnings, the stockholders may dump the stock. If they reveal the information, they could jeopardize lead time on a new product. The trade-off is difficult to measure in the near-term: keep the stock price up or sacrifice the future. Presidents of small publicly held companies devote as much as one-quarter of their time to callers for information and to resolving this kind of dilemma.

9

PUBLIC SHELLS

A shell is a public corporation that has no operations, merely some assets, some liabilities, and some stockholders who in many instances are somnambulant about the investment. A "clean" shell is a shell that has some assets, no liabilities, and some stockholders. A "clean shell with cash" is a shell that has one asset—cash or cash-like securities—no liabilities, and some stockholders. When an entrepreneur seeks to obtain financing through a public shell, it is the clean shell with cash that is of interest to him.

Shells come about because eager underwriters take companies public before they have proven that they have a product to be manufactured or an idea for a business that can be implemented. If they find out that their business plan will not work before they have spent all of the public's money, the result is a shell. The company's management then begins to clean up the shell by paying off the liabilities and selling the assets for cash. The result is a clean shell with cash in search of the best investment that it can find in an emerging company. Normally, there is no urgency to invest, because all of the personnel are dismissed and the manager who is left to mind the store can easily pay himself with a portion of the yield on the cash that is invested in money market securities.

Public shells frequently advertise their existence in the *Wall Street Journal*. Occasionally they hire an investment banker or merger and acquisition broker. More frequently public shells are found either by shell merchants—people who buy shells for resale—or by aggressive entrepreneurs.

It is simple to buy a shell, the difficulty is negotiating the price. For example, let us assume Universal Solar Systems (USS) goes public by selling 40% of its shares of common stock to the public for $1,500,000;

that is six million shares at a price of 25 cents per share. Approximately $900,000 of the $1,500,000 is spent on the cost of the offering and on research and development for a new solar collector. The research indicates that a commercially viable product cannot be produced, and the USS board decides to fire everyone, pay all of the bills, sell the assets, and look for a strong merger partner that needs the remaining $600,000 cash and a public market.

Along comes a small company, Future Potential Corporation (FPC), that manufactures a proprietary product, that has $2 million in sales, $250,000 in net worth, and $75,000 in profits. Not exceptional in terms of its latest financial statement, but FPC's future appears promising, given a little bit of money to advertise or reach its market properly.

The goal of FPC's management is to gain control of USS's common stock to have free reign to spend the cash as it chooses. FPC management must present a convincing business plan to the USS caretaker and then to the USS board of directors. Once the USS side is convinced that its stockholders will do better with an investment in FPC than in other opportunities, the negotiation boils down to price. "Price" means how much of FPC's common stock will be acquired by USS in exchange for $600,000.

Many factors enter this negotiation, not merely the intrinsic value of FPC. For example, if there is a surplus of risk capital in the market and an active new issue market, then the FPC entrepreneurs will have several alternative sources of venture capital, and USS will end up with a smaller ownership position than FPC. If money is tight, the $600,000 in USS might purchase control of FPC. The ownership range in which the merger negotiations normally take place is between 30% and 50%, assuming that the cash on the table is less than one million dollars.

The mechanics that take place after USS board approval are the submittal of a proxy to the USS stockholders outlining the deal and describing FPC in order to elicit their votes. This is a formality when the board of USS owns voting control, but a requirement, nonetheless. Assuming that USS buys 35% of FPC common stock for $600,000, the next step is to reverse the deal, with FPC dissolving its corporation and USS changing its name to FPC. The FPC board then expands to take on a USS director or two, and the stockholders are issued new certificates relfecting the name change. Although the USS stockholders have suffered 65% dilution, they still own the same number of shares that they had before the merger. Usually the price of the stock moves up some, to a premium above the initial offering price, and FPC management begins to put the $600,000 to work as well as it can to create earnings. A dynamic management team that begins making acquisitions with the stock, or with cash and notes, and begins issuing press releases to chronicle its achievements and one that corrals brokers to become market makers in the stock can usually get the stock moving up to 35 or 45 cents per share. But, with close to 20 million shares outstanding, the story must have some substance to move the stock above one dollar. This is a prospect not unlike going public with a penny stock offering.

Finding a clean shell with cash is a systematic, time-consuming task, if one does not use a shell merchant. It requires going through the pink sheets (the daily listing of over-the-counter companies) and ordering Dun and Bradstreet reports on all of those with names that sound like they may be defunct and whose stocks either do not trade (no prices quoted in the pink sheets) or trade at subterranean prices like 1 / 16 or 5 / 32. Names that suggest industries that have fallen from favor, like solar energy, modular housing, or uranium mining, frequently make good shell candidates. The Dun and Bradstreet reports may have financial statements, and the financial statements may or may not be accurate. If the reports look promising, the underwriter who brought the company public can be contacted to determine the company's present interest in selling.

A shell merchant is part of an interesting breed. He builds an inventory of shells in the following manner. First, he contacts a shell's board of directors and offers them cash for their stock. Then he borrows the cash at his bank, buys the control stock at market or less, and repays the bank with the cash in the shell. For example, if a shell merchant got to USS before FPC did, a fair market price for the board's shares would have been 60% × $600,000, or $360,000. The insiders of USS owned 60% of the stock. However, since a bird in hand is worth dozens in the bush, the insiders probably would have taken a 20% discount, or $288,000, to be liquid. The merchant then has the keys to the vault. He pays the bank the $288,000 that he borrowed and he is sitting on a clean shell with around $300,000 in cash. If he then puts the $300,000 to work at 15% interest, the shell merchant can earn $45,000 per annum and pay himself that in salary while he seeks out a good investment. In some cases a shrewd shell merchant can get as good a deal for $300,000 as a less vigorous board can get for $600,000.

Shell transactions probably do not account for more than $10,000,000 of venture capital financing per annum. But they remain a stable and interesting source of venture capital.

10

GOVERNMENT GUARANTEED LOANS

What was a growing business in the 1970s—government guaranteed loans—has crawled back under a rock in the 1980s. There were three major guaranteed loan programs, two administered by the Department of Commerce known as the Economic Development Administration (EDA) and the Small Business Administration (SBA) and one administered by the Department of Agriculture known as the Farmers Home Administration (FmHA) Business and Industrial loan program. The EDA and FmHA programs have been stopped by the Reagan Administration, which pulls about $1.5 billion per annum of risk capital out of the system. The one remaining program is that administered by the SBA, which accounts for approximately $3 billion in government guaranteed loans each year.

An SBA guaranteed loan is available to a "small business," as defined in Chapter 4, in amounts up to $500,000 for a term of seven years, repayable usually in 84 equal monthly installments at an interest rate governed by Congress, but usually a few points over prime. The higher the interest rate, the more aggressive the lenders. The SBA guarantees 90% of the face amount of the loan, thus the entrepreneur must interest a commercial bank or an SBA approved lender such as a Business Development Corporation, to provide 10% of the loan. In fact, the lender puts the full amount of the loan in the borrower's bank account and either earns interest on the full amount of the loan or sells the guaranteed portion to a buyer of government guaranteed loans at a premium. The bank can earn a monitoring fee for processing the loan for the secondary buyer and a spread between the rate the borrower pays it and the rate it charges in the secondary market. The processing charge is usually around 1% per annum on the total loan, the spread is about half that amount. Couple these charges with its rate on the unguaranteed portion, banks that are active in the SBA guaranteed loan business can earn over 30% per annum on that portion of their loan portfolio.

Yet, relatively few banks have SBA loan departments, and those that do have fairly high standards. For example, the banks prefer to have fully collateralized positions, that is, at least $1.50 in assets to cover $1 in loans. But, because the bank is covered on 90% of the loan, it will give up one of its normal requirements—positive cash flow or earnings. This does not mean it will give up its requirement for personal guarantees. Even if the lender would be willing to forego personal guarantees, the SBA would not. That is the bad news. What is worse, the bank and the SBA will try to collect on personal guarantees if they have to.

It is this "belt, suspenders, and safety pins" attitude that makes the SBA guaranteed loan program relatively unattractive to entrepreneurs in terms of available alternatives. Why risk your business and your personal assets to finance your business? Isn't the belt enough to hold up the pants? Why wear suspenders at the same time?

The next most odious aspect of the SBA guaranteed loan program is that the SBA monitors the loan very tightly through the covenants that it insists on writing into the loan agreement. Growth is discouraged. Rewarding key members of management with salary increases and bonuses is discouraged. To swap collateral, sell an asset, buy an asset, or issue stock for cash or assets or to issue stock as a bonus must, in most cases, be approved by the SBA. These kinds of covenants infantalize management and do not protect the Government's position. More constructive covenants allow management to operate the business as it chooses, so long as certain negative covenants are not breached. These might include diminution in net worth or working capital, which are normal commercial banking loan covenants.

The third unattractive aspect of SBA guaranteed loans is the application itself. It is a relatively long, complicated application that asks quite a few irrelevant questions that are essential to the Government but a waste of time to the entrepreneur. Many entrepreneurs seek the aid of SBA loan packagers in filling out the form, but there are relatively few of these around because the SBA does not permit fees to brokers or consultants. The packagers' fees are frequently hidden as long-term consulting contracts.

Notwithstanding the difficulty in obtaining them, the restrictions in using them, and the usually excessive collateral required by them, SBA loans are in certain instances very attractive sources of financing. The best time to use the SBA is to build a chain of retail shops. The SBA understands retail businesses, those being its principal clients, and tends to be more accommodating in many respects. An entrepreneur can frequently open three or four stores with the SBA putting up nearly 100% of the financing before he has to go to other sources of venture capital.

Assume that an entrepreneur has an idea for a store to sell runner's supplies—shoes, sweatsuits, socks, and equipment. Assume further that the initial space requirement is for 500 square feet near a popular running area, about $35,000 worth of initial inventory, and $8,000 of furnishings and leasehold improvements. The entrepreneur intends to fix up the store pretty much by himself but needs another $7,000 for 90 days of working capital including rent, heat, light, power, and advertising. Thus the capital requirement is around $50,000.

The SBA has a myriad of booklets and pamphlets on operating businesses and financial ratios, one of which would show the entrepreneur that sales of $400,000 with a 50% gross profit margin is about tops for a store such as this one, let's call it "The Running Place." The entrepreneur projects sales of $20,000 per month in the first year, $30,000 in the second and $35,000 per month in the third year and thereafter.

As to the $50,000, assuming that the entrepreneur prepared a thorough business plan and met the other minimal qualifications for a loan, the SBA would be inclined to guarantee a loan for $43,000, everything except the working capital, which the entrepreneur would have to raise from savings, family, or friends.

Six months later, let us say the entrepreneur is breaking even with sales of $15,000 per month and overhead of $7,500 per month. A second location is found in a more popular area where a 1,000 square foot store and twice the inventory would be needed. Back goes the entrepreneur to the SBA with a request for a loan renewal from $43,000 to $135,000. A new business plan is prepared showing the projections for two stores. The SBA sees that the first store got into the black quickly and is making money. It goes along with the request, again fully collateralizing its position with inventory, fixtures, and leasehold improvements. The entrepreneur needs $14,000 in cash to cover the gap between the SBA's loan guarantee and the capital needed for the second store. From the first store's earnings he gets $5,000 and the balance from friends. Six months later with the first store earning $6,000 per month and the second store breaking into the black, the entrepreneur spots a location for a third store, goes through the same peregrinations as before, and rolls the $135,000 loan into a $230,000 loan, providing the equity from earnings and so forth until the SBA's limit of $500,000 is reached.

When The Running Place has five stores and has worked out many of its kinks, it is a $1,500,000 (revenues) business set for a roll-out to a significant regional chain by way of a venture capital financing. Its formation and development were financed as much as 90% through SBA guaranteed loans plus cash flow.

Normally, the SBA likes to see 20–25% of the capital requirement in the form of equity before it will provide financing. However, it is far more lenient in the case of retail stores because that is the industry with which it is most familiar.

11

ACCOUNTS RECEIVABLE, INVENTORY, AND EQUIPMENT LOANS

Although not of much use to the start-up company, secured borrowing is an extremely important source of capital to entrepreneurs in virtually every other stage of expansion. It is critical to know which lenders make asset-based loans and their criteria.

First, let us define terms. There are three kinds of institutional lenders in our capital markets: risk lenders, secured lenders, and no risk lenders. As we have seen, SBICs and MESBICs are in business to make risk loans. They usually do not ask for collateral, or if they do it is often not primary collateral, and they seek their return in two ways—interest or divided income and a capital gain from their ownership of the common stock of the borrower.

At the other end of the spectrum are commercial banks. They are no risk lenders. They seek protection in three ways: primary collateral, secondary collateral, and cash flow. If the borrower is a new company without positive cash flow, it is unlikely that a commercial bank would finance equipment or an inventory position. In certain instances, such as with an SBA loan guarantee or in concert with an equity financing, the commercial bank may provide a loan without positive cash flow. The reason for its reliance on cash flow is that commercial banks are simply not in the position of liquidating assets to repay loans. Rather, they look for repayment from cash flow and protection from the primary assets. The secondary collateral is a Linus blanket, but usually not easy to collect on. For example, personal guarantees normally take several years and considerable legal expenses to collect. Some lenders take a lien on the entrepreneur's house, but in a growing number of sun-belt states it is illegal to do that. Thus, if a borrower goes out of business, the bank first attempts to liquidate its collateral and then proceeds against the secondary collateral, such as the house or securities, or personal guarantee. Even an SBA guarantee, if called upon by the bank does not result in the bank's receiving cash; rather, the bank is issued government notes.

Even though a commercial bank can do very little to assist an emerging company financially, it is extremely important for an entrepreneur to develop as friendly a relationship as possible with his commercial banker. Emergencies can arise where an important favor is needed, such as meeting payroll when the company's funds are uncollected rather than good, discounting a purchase order, providing weekend credit against the float, and even permitting temporary overdrafts. Naturally, the bankers' patience should not be tried, and favors should be sought only rarely. In the main, keeping a positive balance and providing monthly financial statements and quarterly updates will enable the banker to keep an eye out. Then when he is asked by the potential venture capital investor to provide a reference, it will be positive.

The success of Silicon Valley in developing a climate that encouraged entrepreneurial spirit, that welcomed risk taking in high technology companies, and that catalyzed the formation of over 40 venture capital funds is frequently attributed to aggressive commercial banks. The leading candidates for the second generation of Silicon Valleys are Raleigh, North Carolina; Portland, Oregon; Boulder, Colorado; and Boise, Idaho. The communities with the most aggressive commercial banks will develop the most employment.

One last thought on the subject, commercial bankers are losing their autonomy. As banks grow larger and indeed begin to cross state lines, the branch officers begin to lose their lending authority. Decisions are made at regional credit centers. This, of course, is not as true for nonbranch banking states. Entrepreneurs generally do better with small town bankers than with invisible credit committees.

Who then are the secured lenders? They are called commercial finance companies, and their business is making asset-based loans. Because they understand the assets they lend against, and more important, know where to sell the assets if they have to and at what price, commercial finance companies will frequently make loans to companies that lack positive cash flow and that lack secondary collateral.

There are certain rules of the road in dealing with commercial finance companies. Their preference runs to the most liquid assets on the balance sheet—accounts receivable, finished goods inventory, and raw materials inventory. Commercial finance companies are not keen on equipment, unless that is a specialty of theirs—as it is with certain finance companies, or with real property or other nonliquifiable assets. Two other important rules exist: high interest rates and prepayment penalties.

Commercial finance companies do not have relatively inexpensive depositors' dollars to relend. Rather, they borrow from commercial banks and in the commercial paper market at interest rates that average a shade less than prime. The range of their charges for money is between prime + 4% and prime + 10%.

Commercial finance companies like to hold their borrower for at least a year. They understand that the borrower will leave them at the first opportunity to go with a less expensive lender. Therefore, commercial finance companies build prepayment penalties into their loan agreements. The penalty can be as stiff as one year's interest payments if the loan is prepaid prior to 12 months; or as lenient as two months' interest payments if the loan is prepaid prior to six months. In easy money economies, which have not existed since prime reached 20% for the first time in 1979, the prepayment penalty is either watered down or eliminated.

Commercial finance companies also ask for commitment fees to keep the borrower from shopping the commitment letter in order to improve the rate or terms. Commercial finance companies have a short fuse on their commitment letters—around 30 days, again to restrict shopping.

ADVANCE RATIOS

Commercial finance companies make loans up to the "liquidation value" of their collateral. For example, if their collateral is accounts receivable, they will exclude all receivables over 90 days old, all Federal Government receivables, all foreign receivables, some state and local government receivables, and all receivables due from individuals. These are habitual slow paying receivables; and in bankruptcy—that is when the lender has to collect on his loans—slow pay becomes no pay. Unless the accounts receivable have iron-clad guarantees, it is difficult to convince a commercial finance company to loan more than 80–85% of the under 90 days acceptable receivables. Receivables that are contingent on performance are also unacceptable. Finance companies are not in the service business.

If a commercial finance company cannot have the company's accounts receivable as collateral, it will not take the inventory. There is a simple explanation for this: inventory becomes receivables, and the finance company's collateral slips away with each sale to become the senior lender's collateral. Thus, if an entrepreneur has gone into business with a $300,000 SBA guaranteed loan with a "plaster lien" (all assets collaterize the loan) and needs to inject some capital because of expanded receivables, his first task is to get the SBA to release its lien on the receivables. Once that is done, the finance company can make a receivables loan. But if the SBA insists on holding the receivables, but releasing the inventory, the finance company will not make the loan.

A receivables loan from a finance company is actually a line of credit that permits draw-downs on a weekly basis based on that weeks' shipments. If the advance ratio is 80% of qualified receivables, then each week the borrower is entitled to pick up a check for 80% of its shipments. The finance company receives 80% of the cash collected from customers plus interest on the 80% advanced. Receivable financing can be on a notification or nonnotification basis. In the former case the customer pays the finance company directly. In the latter case the customer pays the company. If the company were to hold back on the 80% of collections that it owes the finance company, the finance company would hold back on advances. The checks and balances built into the system have a way of making it work out satisfactorily.

When an entrepreneur initially obtains accounts receivable financing, the company receives a large check, and it goes a long way to solving some financial problems. Four to six months later when the company is on more solid footing, but still toughing it out, being in bed with the finance company no longer seems like fun. It is at this point that the entrepreneur begins thinking about a new lender to replace the finance company and to offer a higher advance rate, qualify more of the receivables (perhaps to accept those under 120 days), advance against other assets, and lower the interest rate. It is because finance company borrowers have borrowers' remorse within 90 to 180 days after the closing that finance companies write stiff prepayment penalty clauses.

It is likely that a finance company will find acceptable the inventories of a company whose receivables it accepts. Certain kinds of inventory are more preferable than others, such as the finished goods inventory of a wholesale distributor. Auto parts, electronic components, and health and beauty aid wholesale distributors are popular customers of commercial finance companies. Their inventories are in large warehouses and in not too many locations, inventory control is usually computerized, the customers are corporations and not individuals, and the suppliers to the distributors do not get nervous when liens are filed on their goods. The suppliers may sell to the distributors on 90 days terms, thus for 90 days these inventories are "owned" by the finance company. In some industries the suppliers would not permit that, but in older, more mature industries every entity in the distribution chain survives on one another's obligation to pay, which they pledge to a finance company or, if they are strong enough, at a commercial bank.

The conventional advance ratio on finished goods and raw materials inventory is 35–50% of liquidation value. It should be pointed out that liquidation value is the price a buyer would pay for goods sold at auction or in a very short time, such as six weeks. Market value is the price a buyer would pay for goods sold over a reasonable period of time, such as six months. Replacement value is the cost of replacing a certain asset in the market that day. An asset-based lender deals with liquidation value only. It has neither the time for a reasonable selling off of the assets or the inclination to run the company. In some instances raw material inventory is quite valuable, such as when it is bought in commodity form and then stamped out or bent into various shapes. This is the case with brass or gold or aluminum ingots, which can be auctioned at any time in the commodities market. If these commodities are ordered pre-cut into specific shapes and sizes they immediately lose value to a lender, because they are not immediately liquifiable. Instead of liquidation value being approximately equal to market value, it is considerably less than market value.

Inventory loans are sometimes treated as draw-downs under a line of credit, and in other instances they are one-year loans that must be repaid or rolled over at the end of 12 months. In the former case, assuming a 50% advance rate on raw materials and finished goods inventories, the company submits its purchase order to the finance company, which writes it a check for 50% of the purchase price. When the goods are sold and become accounts receivable the Company receives 80% of the receivable thus generated and repays the finance company its 50% inventory advance plus interest. If there is a substantial markup from inventory value to receivable value, the net amount received by the company on the receivables loan is considerable. For example, if inventory is marked up from a $10 cost to a $20 price, then using these advance ratios, when the company makes a sale on terms, it receives a check in the amount of $16 with which it repays the lender $5 and reinvests the $11 in working capital. That is excellent leverage for the borrower. But, if the markup *is* considerable, over 100%, that indicates quite a bit of value added, which is precisely the kind of "customized" inventory that lenders fear. "Too much labor content," they say. "There's a service obligation in the receivables," they complain. As a result, more mundane assets have greater appeal to asset-based lenders.

As for equipment, some commercial finance companies like it as collateral and others do not. It depends on whether or not they have experience in liquidating equipment. If they do, they will loan against it; if they do not, they will recommend another firm. A typical advance ratio for equipment is 60–75% of liquidation value. An appraiser with experience in auctioning equipment is hired by the entrepreneur, after endorsement by the finance company, to visit the plant and appraise the equipment. The appraiser will always come in with a lower than expected value because he will build in an auctioneer's commission of 10% plus a margin of error to keep his nose clean for future business with the finance company.

Again, certain equipment makes better collateral than others. Fork lift trucks, band saws, lathes, and punch presses are readily convertible into cash. Customized equipment is harder to dispose of and represents poorer collateral. This kind of equipment includes complicated lines that pour, fill, cap, label, and package an item.

Equipment loans do not operate like receivables loans, which are essentially increased and decreased as volume expands and contracts. Loans that increase and decrease in tandem with asset changes are known as revolving credits. They automatically renew every 12 months if the lender and borrower are pleased with the relationship. Equipment loans are term loans, generally for five years, but occasionally for ten-year terms. They amortize monthly or quarterly, but frequently after a one-year grace period. Some term loans, like those guaranteed by the SBA, amortize monthly. It is more common for a term loan to amortize quarterly or semiannually.

What other collateral will commercial finance companies find acceptable? Frequently they will provide loans secured by the liquidation value of office furniture and office equipment. Typewriters, calculators, file cabinets, and similar assets are readily auctionable.

Patents, tools, jigs, dies, blueprints, and formulas are less likely to serve as collateral because they have "going concern" value more than marketability. Still, if sold as a package, a buyer of the equipment would be delighted to know what to manufacture with the equipment and how to manufacture it. A creative lender might be willing to place a small value on these assets. After all, they are not completely intangible.

Leaseholds may also have some value to a secured lender, especially if it intends to auction the assets as a block. If the owner of the building decides to find a new tenant, the lender must remove the assets first. Accordingly, the lender may provide a small amount of funds against the leaseholds.

An off-balance-sheet asset acceptable to many secured lenders is the company's customer mailing list. The names on the list are worth at least one dollar, and sometimes much more, if rented to companies in the direct mail business. Wholesale distributors tend to have value in the lists of customers to whom they mail their product catalogs. These customers frequently order by mail and receive delivery by truck or United Parcel Service. It is not unusual for an electronic components distributor to have 100,000 or more names in its mailing list. For additional cash flow it could rent the names to a direct mail broker for 5 cents per rental ($5,000 for the full list), and many lists turn 20 to 30 times each year. The value of the list is therefore $100,000 to $150,000 and not recorded on the balance sheet. A creative lender might advance up to 80% of the annual rental revenue of the list, or $80,000 to $120,000 in this case.

Commercial finance company lenders are for the most part quite entrepreneurial. They aggressively seek borrowers to whom they can sell money. Their attitude is almost always positive, and their style is exemplified by their most common sentence, as they peer gleefully over the balance sheet: "Okay, let's see how we can make this loan."

In instances where the finance company will make advances on inventory or equipment but such advances fall short of the necessary amount, it is possible for the lender to obtain loan guarantee insurance thus enabling larger advance rates. For example, if the borrower needs a $500,000 inventory loan on $1 million of inventory, but the lender will advance only $350,000, there exist insurance companies who, for a fee, will write a policy for the gap of $150,000. Their rate is normally 2% of the amount they insure. To interest them, the entrepreneur first sends them a listing of the inventory for a "desk appraisal" which is followed up by an on-site appraisal. The borrower nomally must pay the costs of the insurance company's visit. An insurance company that is interested in guaranteeing an inventory loan probably will be interested in equipment as well. Lloyds of London has for many years been the most aggressive provider of loan guarantee insurance, but its interest lies in large deals. There is a huge market for an entrepreneurial lender to provide loan guarantee insurance to small companies.

12

CUSTOMER FINANCING

The cheapest capital is customer capital. Many companies have been started by the checks sent in from customers responding to a mailing piece, or an advertisement or a new product release displayed in a magazine.

The inventor of a folding, lightweight portable satellite antenna, drove 500 miles to a home satellite convention in July 1980 and popped open his umbrella antenna in the parking lot. In comparison with the heavy, nonportable aluminum and fiberglass antennas in the lot that cost more than five times to manufacture than what his sold for, the inventor to his great surprise was immediately encircled by the television press, several national magazines, customers, potential dealers, and one man who whispered in his ear, "oil money." An Arab sheik asked for the rights to the Middle East plus a 30% equity interest for $750,000 (but he wanted management control). The inventor stood in the lot for one hour demonstrating the home satellite antenna system, and when he returned to his room later that day, he had $40,000 in checks stuffed in all of his pockets. He remembers someone asking, "What's the price?" And he thought he remembers answering "$750."

The inventor had driven to the show to see if there could be interest in his antenna. The prototype needed several months of engineering time and tooling at a cost of at least $25,000 to become a commercially viable product. The visitors at the home satellite show, while crossing through the parking lot, became the venture capitalists to the shy inventor.

The antenna invention is proof of the axiom that an inexpensive solution to a problem shared by many, demonstrated in front of the market, will always result in customer deposits. There are other documented customer deposit stories worth relating.

103

One of the most famous such legends is that of H. Ross Perot, founder of Electronic Data Systems (EDS), whose simple solution to a major problem resulted in his becoming a billionaire in less than five years. Perot's business idea has subsequently come to be called "facilities management," and it works like this: Perot, an ex-IBM salesman, would call on corporations with large computer installations. He would offer them a contract to operate their data processing departments, hire the people and buy the equipment (which he converted to leases), and deliver the required work at their budget. If he brought the jobs in for less than budget, the difference was EDS' profit. After two contracts were sold, Perot merged the facilities, selling off superfluous equipment and eliminating extraneous people. The profits became immense. Several contracts later, EDS became the fastest growing company in the country with sales of $36 million in three years. An underwriter agreed to take EDS public at 115 times earnings, and the stock moved up from there. I have left out some of the background music that fueled the stock. But one story among many made the small Texan seem Bunyanesque. Perot was negotiating an issuance of EDS stock with several underwriters in New York one cold winter day in 1968, while the snow fell in buckets and taxis couldn't move in the street. Unable to get a taxi, Perot walked from his uptown hotel to Wall Street, as the legend goes, and waited for the investment bankers to arrive. If he walks through snow, can he also walk on water? Of these things are myths made.

The story is also told of the starving photographer in England who had an idea for a male magazine similar to *Playboy*. He took a frontview photograph of a nude lady standing in the park and reprinted it on several thousand postcards that advertised subscriptions to a new magazine. He mailed most of them to young men but sent a few hundred to members of the clergy and temperance societies. The howl of invectives from the latter group made headlines in the newspapers and the demand for the new magazine, accompanied, of course, by payments in advance, was sufficient to launch what has become a major publishing empire.

The Holiday Inn story has been repeated many times, but bears another mention in terms of customer financing. Wallace Johnson and Kemmons Wilson, an innkeeper and a peanut vendor, had an idea for making Johnson's motor hotel more popular. They offered free lodging to children traveling with their parents. Business increased, and they repeated the formula and added some other features until they felt that

Holiday Inns had become an innkeeping system. They sold franchises to hundreds of small entrepreneurs who paid Johnson and Wilson for the right to use the name and the system. The franchise fees and monthly royalties provided Holiday Inns with sufficient capital to become the fastest growing lodging chain in the country. The company went public, and proceeds were used to buy back as many of the franchises as possible. This formula—franchise for initial capital, go public to buy back the territories—has been repeated by Kentucky Fried Chicken, McDonald's, and other chains and is a truly brilliant financing formula when done well.

One final example is the party-plan financing method done so skillfully by Tupperware and May Kay Cosmetics. Party-plan selling is in-home selling where a friend of the salesperson receives 10% of the gross sales of products to friends whom she has invited to her home. Tupperware has done it with kitchen apparatus, Mary Kay with cosmetics, Transart with decorative wall accessories, and Princess with crystal. The country is carved into districts and the districts into smaller units. There are commissions to the party giver, to the salesperson who brings the samples to the party, to the district supervisor who trains the salespersons, and to the regional head who manages the district supervisers. Commissions as a percentage of sales are in the neighborhood of 40%. The cost of the products might be 30–35% of the sales price, which leaves 35% for administrative expenses and profit. The salesperson collects the checks at the party and sends them to headquarters where the company, or should we say the bank, lets them mellow and in a few weeks time delivers the products. Not only do they bulge with cash, but party plan distributors build up huge customer lists, useful in renting to others. How about financing the sample kits used by the salespeople? The salespeople purchase them also.

Even simpler variations of customer financing are the self-actualization and weight loss seminar businesses. There are no products to deal with. Customers respond to ads in local papers to go to an EST meeting or Weight Watchers meeting. They pay hundreds of dollars for the experience and return again and again. The seminar leader is nicely paid, but the parent company really coins it. And what about dancing classes? I am told that the Arthur Murray Dancing franchisors have a business where net and gross income are practically the same. There are simply no assets involved. If a person wants to become a dance instructor and hang out the Arthur Murray shingle, he or she need only rent a hall, pay for the rights to the logo, buy the sign, and pay a monthly franchise fee. No equipment, no formulas for "finger lickin' good" fried chicken and no inventory to purchase. The franchisors, meanwhile, own a bank. If they want to make more money, they turn on the franchise tap. Make less: turn it off. What could be simpler?

There are three primary customer financing methods: (1) franchising; (2) facilities management; and (3) direct mail.

FRANCHISING

The franchisor raises money by selling exclusive rights in a region to a franchisee who pays an initial fee—the franchise fee—plus royalties based on monthly revenues. The latter might be tied to volume, and can range between 1 and 10% of revenues. Frequently, but not always, the franchisor agrees to purchase national advertising with a portion of the monthly fee. Some franchises begin with zero capital investment on the part of the franchisor. This results from very creative new business ideas. For example, the entrepreneur who founded the Wiks 'n Stiks candle shop chain, ran an ad offering to sell candle shop franchises. When someone sent him a check, he was in business, and busily created the logo and other appurtenances that would create value for the franchisees. The company was very successful from the beginning, partially because the admission ticket was a comfortably low $2,500.

Setting the franchise fee is not scientific. The price is equal to what the market will bear. For example, McDonald's currently charges in excess of $100,000; but it is able to document a large number of franchisees that achieve revenues in excess of $1 million per annum. A wide range of franchises are offered every Thursday in the classified section of the *Wall Street Journal.* Most of them are relatively new, hence their fees are less than $20,000.

Prior to the famous legal battle of the early 1970s known as the Chicken Delight case, a franchisor was able to force its franchisees to buy certain necessary products through or from the franchisor. This was not only profitable to the franchisors, but as was claimed by Chicken Delight's attorneys, necessary to control the quality of the product and provide a means of counting how much chicken was sold, hence giving a revenue count to the franchisor. Monthly royalties were then matched against the internal count. The court found in favor of the franchisees, stating they should be able to buy at the lowest price, so long as the standards were maintained. As a result, franchisors must be extremely careful not to step on their franchisees' toes.

Throughout the 1970s, the laws restricting the sell-now-deliver later axiom of the franchising business, have grown tighter and tighter. One needs skilled counsel to interpret the laws because they vary from state to state. Most franchisors find the most restrictive state law and follow it, in order to be covered in all of the states.

Notwithstanding legal fees and perhaps some logo design fees, the cost of launching a franchise-oriented business lies in creating the system. For example, let us say you start an automobile leasing business whose concept is offering a leasing business to all of the automobile dealers who handle a specific import brand. We will name the company Bemco Leasing Corporation. The justification to the dealers is that they can sell more cars, create a subsidiary or second corporation to shelter taxes by way of the investment tax credit, and tide them over rough spots in the economy when customers cannot afford to purchase and banks are unwilling to provide them with financing. Assume that the parent organization of the dealers blesses the leasing concept. The franchisors then obtain a credit arrangement to enable them to assign the leases to a third party and carry the paper once their net worth fattens up. It is not uncommon for a leasing company to have a debt to worth ratio of 10 : 1, with 6 or 7 : 1 closer to the norm. Bemco must also offer other features to make the franchise worthwhile, such as low cost insurance and national advertising. An automobile insurance company looking at the potential of thousands of policies that will come over its transom without its having to beat the bushes, is likely to propose a low flat rate. The final step is a national advertising campaign, which can be sketched out in draft form until enough franchises are sold to beckon the need for a national customer generating campaign. The Bemco entrepreneurs need also develop some on-site items, such as window signs, and outdoor signs, forms, and perhaps a file cabinet.

How do you price this franchise? One method might be the discounted cash flow of the income the dealer might make over 10 years, the method used earlier by the Wellness Clinic. A simpler method is to sell a franchise to the most highly regarded and best known dealer, perhaps the head of the dealers organization, and put him on the Bemco board, thus justifying a ground floor price of, say, $15,000. With his endorsement the price could be moved up swiftly to $25,000 for the next five, $35,000 for the next five, and finally to a tummy-warming $60,000. One note on greed. If the parent organization sees an interloper making an excessive profit from its dealers, it may block the scheme to keep the dealers' wallets full for their own purposes, or it may ask for either ownership in Bemco or a monthly royalty.

Assuming that a happy medium is reached, Bemco can project sales of perhaps 10 franchises per month in the first few months, increasing exponentially as word spreads to penetration of as many as 50% of the dealers, or about 500 sales at an average of $58,000 per sale. As soon as the system is installed at a dealership, Bemco can record the sales as income; but in the meantime it has already $3,000,000 in cash to operate with. Using conventional borrowing ratios, the company could borrow approximately $18,000,000 to buy cars. If the cars retail for around $18,000 each, it can have an initial portfolio of 100,000 cars earning the spread between lease charges and interest, overrides on the insurance, plus franchise royalties. As net worth builds, Bemco can increase its borrowing and begin to offer additional services to its franchisees as well.

Nothing is easy in business, even though these business examples may strike you as "Why didn't I think of that" simplistic no-brainers. However, when the steps are set down on paper and then followed one by one, new business financing becomes more systematic. In the Bemco example there are numerous glitches that must be overcome. For example, the parent organization would be loathe to deal with a fly-by-night franchisor. The officers and board would have to be impeccable, and Bemco's net worth could not be zero. Second, the dealers must be visited, courted, and the system carefully explained. There is likely to be a fair amount of resistance, as there always is to something new. Merely because customer financing is the least costly manner of financing a new business does not mean that it is the easiest. Car dealers are tough businessmen and not easily separated form their wallets. Entrepreneurs who elect to go this route must say to themselves, each morning, "I'm going to hear the word 'No' 50 times today but I'm going to keep marching forward."

FACILITIES MANAGEMENT

The essence of this business is to find a fair number of large organizations that share a similar problem and offer to deliver a solution at the price they currently pay for the problem. Automatic Data Processing did this magnificently with corporate payroll processing and Bradford Computer Systems did equally well with mutual fund data processing. EDS took over the entire data processing department and was rewarded with a meteoric rise in stock value.

One of the most popular areas to sell facilities' management contracts is in municipal services. The Scottsdale, Arizona fire department was taken over by a private contractor in the late 1960s. Several other cities followed. Municipal garbage collection has gone that route in certain instances as well. Venture capital funds, in raising capital from insurance companies and pension funds, are selling facilities management contracts of a sort: taking over the venture capital investment operation from these large organizations. For example if a two-partner venture capital fund raises $50 million from 10 investors, it is saving the administrative and analysis time of 10 people, and understandably doing a better job of investing the funds.

One might see wars fought in the future by companies hired by governments. Some of the oil rich countries in the world, not known for their skill at defending themselves, might be inclined to turn their defense budget over to a company of ex-Marines or the equivalent.

Milton Friedman, the most widely known free enterprise economist, in his book *Freedom and Capitalism*, suggests numerous government operated enterprises that could be better run by profit oriented companies. Included in the list are the Post Office (initially a private company in the Pony Express days, Dr. Friedman points out), school systems, sanitation, street cleaning and maintenance, and the fire department. *Freedom and Capitalism* was published nearly 20 years before the founding of Federal Express which appears to be well on its way to becoming our nation's private mail delivery service.

To launch a facilities management company, one must prove to the first customer the unquestioned ability to provide the solution at the price the customer is currently paying; that is, the cost of operating the department. The institutional food service companies have been successful in operating corporate dining rooms by solving a difficult assignment. Often the entrepreneur in facilities management companies worked previously for the first customer, or a close competitor. Once again, some assurance that the job will be done as promised, plus the endorsement of the people in the facilities management company, is essential to getting contracts. Frequently contracts are let on a trial basis whereby the entrepreneurs are given one or two aspects of the problem to solve before the entire contract is given to them. Of course, after two or three contracts are in process, the equipment can be merged and some of it eliminated, and there will be some people savings, as well. Assume that a new facilities management company wins three $2 million contracts in its first year and makes a 30% savings in equipment and people; its operating income, before overhead, would be $1,800,000. That is a comfortable base from which to launch a business.

DIRECT MAIL

There is no simpler business to launch a company on customers' advance payments than the newsletter business. The first entrepreneur to make money in a new industry is the newsletter publisher. The service he provides is to identify the problem that the new entrepreneurs of that industry are intent on solving. Frequently the newsletters grow into magazines, or branch into seminars, cassettes from the seminars, and conventions.

Many new markets are in need of a careful and frequent identification of their problem on a fairly regular basis. The womens' liberation market, when it was relatively new, and the identification of the problems created by male chauvinism was the function of *Ms.* magazine, a very fine, upbeat publication that indexes each month the problems, problem solvers, and solutions in the complex area of the changing role of women. *Ms.* creates the market, builds up a demand curve for liberating products, and sells books, tapes, and services into it. *Ms.* grew quickly to over 100,000 subscribers and with its strong cash flow entered the facilities management business. A large truck manufacturer paid *Ms.* over six figures to provide them with advice in the redesign of their cab to sell more women and team drivers. That fee had to be very profitable, perhaps equal to several months' profits at the magazine.

Electronic funds transfer systems (EFTS) is another market that is in search of more precise definition. Commercial bankers feel that if they do not begin to offer off-premises banking in stores, then the stores themselves or, heaven forbid, the less closely regulated Savings and Loan industry might do it. Sears Roebuck purchased Dean Witter, a stock broker, for $600 million in order to begin offering brokerage and banking services to its 21 million Sears credit cardholders. The checkless society is coming, but no one is quite sure how, why, when or where. A perfect scenario for a newsletter.

An eastern EFTS company called Payment Systems, Inc., acquired in 1975 by American Express Company on attractive terms for its founders, noticed quite early in its short business life that the banking industry had four levels of sophistication regarding EFTS or the "checkless society":

1. The largest group had heard or read about it and wanted to learn more.

2. The next largest group felt they should begin to see how they might implement different phases of EFTS, such as automatic tellers or debit cards.

3. The third largest group was ready to hire consultants to begin implementing one or two phases.

4. The fourth largest group was very well-informed about EFTS, had studied its costs and benefits, and wanted someone to install a computer-based system.

Since the market was pyramid shaped with the biggest dollars in group 4, among one or two banks, Payment Systems' job was to move potential customers up the pyramid. Group 1 bought a newsletter, group 2 attended seminars, group 3 hired the company for consulting, and group 4 engaged the company for facilities management of their EFTS facility.

The newsletter, however, provided the cash flow to support the other activities until the company matured. Thousands of banking institutions and computer peripheral component manufacturers subscribed to the newsletter. Their dollars subsidized the more sophisticated but poorer cash flow segments of the business.

Other markets come to mind as likely candidates for newsletters as a base for launching new products or services. The nutrition market, with follow-on nutritional products; the alternative energy markets; the genetic engineering market; the home computer market; the home video market; and others. The definition of a new market that will be of interest to entrepreneurs and venture capitalists is one with at least three newsletters.

Aside from the newsletter's ability to generate cash up front on a subscription basis or monthly on a newstand basis, a newsletter in and of itself is very inexpensive to initiate. You need a mailing list and a printer willing to prepare a lot of postcards. An optimistic, convincing publisher is able to convince the owner of the mailing list and the mail order printer to be paid out of initial subscriptions. The founders of *Psychology Today* launched their magazines on the strength of their initial mailings and with virtually no money in the bank. Their success is a matter of recorded fact.

Direct mail and mail order selling of products other than newsletters has become an increasingly popular method of financing a new company, given the proliferation of credit cards and the growing reluctance to drive to the mall to make purchases. The necessary ingredients for the launch are a consumer product, a high gross profit margin, and a retail price of less than $50.00. The direct mail method involves heavily advertising the product and soliciting orders by way of mail order (advertisements in newspapers or magazines), direct mail (to rented lists of names), or other media, and then applying the receipts, net of selling expenses to produce and deliver the products that are ordered. The primary examples of the direct mail method of financing a new company are the "Oldies but Goodies" record publishers. In most instances, the albums advertised on television have not been produced at the time of the advertisement, but will be upon receipt of the thousands of small checks that will pour in following the advertisement.

You have probably read the direct response advertisements of Joe Sugarman, the Northbrook, Illinois entrepreneur who founded JS & A. JS & A's advertisements in airline magazines and financial journals for small electronic gadgets are, in a word, masterful. More important, they work. For entrepreneurs who have developed consumer electronic products that can be produced to sell for around $50 or less, and yield a healthy gross profit, JS & A and comparable mail order companies will market the product. Their share of the pie varies from 35% to 50% of selling price.

American Express, other credit card companies, oil companies, and department stores that offer credit cards to their customers, will offer a product to their customer lists in their monthly billing envelopes (called "stuffers"). This is a widely used means for selling small appliances, giftware, housewares, decorative accessories, and art prints. One of the typical pricing methods is for the credit card issuer to incur all of the marketing costs in exchange for 50% of the retail selling price. For art prints that are marked up about 800%, the value of a Sears mailing to 20 million Sears credit card customers is extraordinary. Assume that an artist charged you $10,000 for a drawing and that you could reproduce them for $5.00 apiece and sell them for $40.00. Assume further that a department store stuffed your offer into 2 million envelopes and that 1% of the recipients (20,000) ordered a print. Your revenues would be $800,000, of which the department store would keep $400,000. Your costs would be $110,000, for a net profit before taxes of $290,000. Even at a one-half of 1% response you would come out handsomely.

The direct mail method of financing a new company assumes that you are able to produce and deliver the product within about six weeks.

After that period of time the customers will be getting anxious about the product. Failing to deliver a product for which an entrepreneur received cash in the mail is mail fraud, a serious felony. The entrepreneur must return the money or face serious consequences. Very few entrepreneurs are larcenous; but those who have defrauded the public by failing to deliver a product have cast an aura of foul play over direct mail, in general, mitigated in large part by the fine firms that are increasingly entering the business.

=== 13 ===

JOINT VENTURES
AND LICENSING

Joint venturing is a frequently overlooked source of seed capital and method for launching a new company. A joint venture is a partnership of two or more entities formed to undertake a certain project. A joint venture opportunity exists when each partner brings to the project a property that the other partner (or partners) does not have, but regards as integral to the success of the project.

An entrepreneur in search of seed capital must honestly confront the fact that he needs more than money to launch his new company. Although his project may call for manufacturing or distribution of a certain product, it is not always so that merely by obtaining capital, the entrepreneur will be the most efficient manufacturer or the most successful distributor of his product.

For example, assume for a moment that you invented a solar car. It looked like all other standard cars, except that most of the roof was clear, nontinted glass with an aluminum plate underneath it and the area that normally was occupied by a gas tank in your car was occupied by a bed of lightweight storage material. In addition, there was some duct-work linking the solar collector (roof) to the storage area. The principal economic justification of the solar car is that it has a zero fuel cost; the driver never has to put gas in it. In the event of prolonged grey skies, say two straight weeks without sunlight, the car's redesigned battery could provide alternative fuel for a short time.

Further, assume that the average annual fuel savings is $1,400: 20,000 miles of driving per year, an efficiency level of 20 miles per gallon of gas, and a gasoline price at the tank of $1.40 per gallon. The savings to the customer would be $4,200 over the three-year average life of the car, excluding the following kinds of savings:

1. Elimination of time-consuming stops to buy gas.
2. Cost-savings of approximately $500 to have an air-conditioner installed.
3. Elimination of need for indoor garaging, which could result in several hundred dollars per year, depending on whether or not the car is driven to work.
4. Possible long-term reduction in insurance rates, as there would be no gasoline fires to worry about or vandalism problems relating to running out of gas and temporarily abandoning the car.

The cars cost $3,000 to manufacture in runs of not less than 10,000 per month but cost $10,000 to manufacture in runs of only several thousand per month, a not unlikely assumption. To have a successful venture, the solar car entrepreneur would be required to create product identification and image, not unlike other automobile advertising. Finally, a large service organization would have to be launched in order to serve distributors properly—some new tooling and mechanic training may be required—and to provide customers with confidence that their "risky" purchase and contemplated dollar savings will not come back to haunt them as a lemon.

Given this overlong background it is clear by now that the "father of the solar car" is going to need some big linemen to create holes in Detroit's and Tokyo's defensive line. Where does the entrepreneur go for assistance? The needs are manufacturing and distribution. If a major partner or partners joins the entrepreneur as manufacturer and distributor, money should be fairly easy to raise; even the partners should be willing to commit some money or at least loan guarantees, depending on their level of involvement, that is, strictly a license to generate income, or a license plus equity involvement.

Where does the entrepreneur look for joint venture partners? Anybody can make a product, but the key to success is marketing. In other words, in most cases, the most critical area for any new company and product is marketing. Let us examine the alternatives.

The distribution partner must have the following:

1. At least 500 locations nationwide.

2. Locations similar to new car dealerships, with inside and outside showrooms and service areas.

3. An automobile related product or service.

The joint venture candidates include: (1) new car dealers, (2) farm equipment dealers, (3) truck dealers, (4) tire dealers, (5) muffler shops, and (6) gasoline stations.

The first and most likely candidate, new car dealers—particularly a company much smaller than the big three—is the place to shop first, because they have obvious manufacturing expertise, plants, designs, and less downtime in getting the project underway. American Motors or one of the foreign car makers might jump at the chance to become the Moses of the enslaved car driving public who leads his people out of the chains of bondage of the cruel, tyrannical Pharoah, named "Energy Crisis," into the land of solar power where fuel is free and pollution mitigated.

The second best alternative would be either farm equipment or truck manufacturers, who may be more excited about getting a piece of Detroit's action and flattening their intensely cyclical curves than about saving the consuming public from rising gasoline prices.

The other candidates are less attractive because of their lack of automobile or vehicle manufacturing ability, and no matter how attractive or remunerative the project may be, boards of directors can all too easily kill it with "What do we know about cars? Our business is tires!"

Joint venturing ideas come to large industrial corporations every day by the sackful. The Vice President of Corporate Planning for American Hospital Supply Corporation has stated that he receives as many as five inquiries per week seeking a distribution partner for a new drug or medical service.

The best way to approach the large corporations is through their corporate planning officers. These people are responsible for acquisitions, divestitures, joint ventures, and, in some cases, developing new products and overseeing research and development activities within the firm. As a general rule, vice presidents of corporate planning are among the most creative officials within their corporations, and they are interested in new ideas. Their vertical movement within the corporation can be accelerated if they seize new opportunities and convert them into new profitable markets.

Corporate planning officers in some instances provide the only excitement at board meetings. A director of one large pharmaceutical company once described his hypocritical function at board meetings as: "Approving new acquisitions and joint ventures, because the security analysts expect us to use our high priced stock and cash flow for something; and then a year later voting to dump the mistakes made by our acquisition and venture teams." The point is, there is a lot of activity at the corporate planning department levels of major corporations, and a carefully, professionally written letter to the vice president of corporate planning should be sufficient to obtain a meeting to discuss a joint venture proposal.

Not dissimilar from joint venturing is licensing a large corporation to manufacture or market a product. A manufacturing license is generally granted when the new company is unable to produce a product as cheaply as a major company is able to. For example, Polaroid is a research and development and marketing company; all manufacturing is contracted outside of Polaroid. In addition, the new company may be marketing oriented in terms of entrepreneurial backgrounds and experience, and not confident of its ability to build a plant, staff it, and turn out product.

International Water Savings Systems, Inc. (IWSS), a company founded by a 76-year-old entrepreneur, owns the patents, tooling, and designs for a one-quart toilet; that is, it operates on one quart of water rather than the conventional five gallons used to discharge human waste in most standard home toilets. A companion product for boats was sold outright for $1.6 million plus a royalty to recoup development costs. The home toilet can be manufactured for less than $200, which, if it sells at retail for the $600 to $700 price of American Standard and Crane toilets, should permit sufficient manufacturing and distribution profits.

Toilet manufacturing is easy for American Standard and Crane who have highly skilled production managers and efficient machinery and labor. For IWSS, which must add a patented mascerating device and some electronics to its toilet, the job is not so simple. IWSS was founded by Walter Heinze, a marketing entrepreneur who brought us the Playtex "Living Bra" and STP, the oil additive, commercialized successfully by co-founder Andy Granitelli. Heinze's skill is product positioning, developing a sales force, and penetrating markets. Naturally he should license the manufacture of the product, which he intends to do.

However, there is more to the story. Saudi Arabia which needs more water than it can produce, has been seeking innovative means to generate or save water. It has been unable to float an iceberg efficiently from Antartica to its doorstep. It uses 36 billion gallons of water per year flushing toilets, and it does not have 36 billion gallons of water in a year. It is water short, and some people must discharge waste without toilets, which leads to epidemics such as typhus and cholera. Countries such as Saudi Arabia have been approached by IWSS not just for the granting of manufacturing licenses, but for the exclusive rights to sell the toilets in their markets. The price for this privilege might be more than a $1 million down payment and minimum royalties for each of the next 10 years in the range of $1 million per year. At a royalty to IWSS of $50 per toilet, that could represent minimum sales of 20,000 toilets per year in the Middle East.

An ideal licensing situation is one in which you can sell off an exclusive product or territorial right, like the IWSS example with its boat toilet or in the Middle East, and use the proceeds therefrom as capital to finance the development of the major activities of the company. This type of opportunity exists principally with multimarket proprietary products, but perhaps surprisingly, with commonplace products as well. Looking back at the direct mail example with framed art prints put into credit card stuffers, those same framed art prints could be licensed to a catalog, premium or direct mail firm, or to a publisher for inclusion in a book, and so forth. The computer software industry is another area where licensing is the norm rather than the exception.

Licensing has a myriad of ramifications. In terms of raising venture capital, however, one should think in terms of the following:

1. Is there a submarket for my product willing to pay a premium for it because of a serious problem that my product solves?
2. Is there an entity in that submarket that can manufacture and market my product?
3. Is it large enough to pay me a substantial down payment and to guarantee the payment of future minimum royalties?
4. What is the potential size of that submarket in terms of number of units (dollars) per annum?
5. What is the highest level contract that I can establish with that entity? (An introduction through an investment or commercial banker is preferred).

The optimal licensing arrangement involves a substantial down payment by the licensee and relatively high annual minimum sales goals. For example, $50 per toilet and 20,000 toilets per year for 10 years would be a handsome consideration in exchange for the exclusive rights to market the toilet in Saudi Arabia.

14

PREPARING THE
BUSINESS PLAN

There are two presentations made by entrepreneurs to raise capital: the oral presentation and the written presentation. The former occurs after the written presentation has been received. The written presentation, called many things but generally referred to as the business plan, is designed to carefully *explain* the business, its objective, and methods of reaching its goals. The oral presentation is the entrepreneur's opportunity to *sell* himself and the deal to the investor. These two presentations work hand in glove, and both must be successful to obtain financing. If the entrepreneur contradicts orally a statement in the business plan, it is unlikely that the investor will consider him credible.

The sequence of events that leads up to an entrepreneur-investor meeting are as follows:

1. The entrepreneur (or his investment banker) telephones the investor and outlines the business plan. He offers to submit the plan for review.
2. The business plan is delivered to and reviewed by the investor.
3. The investor is recontacted to determine his interest in meeting the entrepreneur.
4. Either the meeting occurs or the business plan is returned with a turn-down.

For an investor to respond favorably to the first qualifying call, the deal must meet his general area of investment interest. Offering a tax shelter to a private venture capital fund or a loan guarantee to a tax shelter investor is a serious waste of time. So imperfect are the risk capital markets that a large portion of every day is spent by venture capitalists and lenders in directing traffic: rerouting deals to places where they might obtain a more favorable response.

Venture capitalists do not make themselves too accessible. Citicorp Venture Capital once had a street location, but they had so much walk-in traffic from incurable inventors and kooks that they could not get any work done. To avoid having their time wasted as much as possible, serious venture capitalists assume a low profile and place the burden of locating them on the entrepreneur.

The qualifying telephone call should cover three things: market, product, and management. Most venture capitalists will ask to see the business plan if the qualifying telephone call convinces them that the market being addressed by the company is large and growing rapidly, if the product or service solves an important problem in that market or has created a niche for itself, and if the management team assembled by the entrepreneur has at least some of the key functional areas (marketing, production, engineering, and finance) covered by experienced people. If the market size and product factors are overwhelmingly positive, the investor might be willing to help build the management team by adding qualified people known to him from other deals. In fact, start-up specialists are skilled at bringing entrepreneurial opportunities to managers who they backed previously. Nolan Bushnell, the founder of Atari, a computer games manufacturer, was backed by some of the Atari investors in Pizza Time Theatres, an operator of games parlors. When David Lee, one of the engineers who developed the Diablo printer, wanted to start Qume a new printer manufacturer, his venture capitalists, Sutter Hill Management Company, brought in Robert Schroeder, an Executive Vice President from Cummins Engine Company. When Bill Poduska, a co-founder of Prime Computer, wanted to launch Apollo Computers, the marketing partner selected for him was Charles Spector of Digital Equipment Corp. The examples go on and on until they begin to sound like the annual yearling sales at Keeneland: namely, so-and-so out of such-and-such, sired by what's-his-face. But in fact, if the entrepreneurial team has among its members former successful entrepreneurs and managers involved in company launching, the price of their stock will be valued much higher than that of a similar company launched in a garage by a first-time entrepreneur.

For the entrepreneur who has not been blessed by previous company launching successes, plans should be made early to hire people with proven track records in the missing link areas. In so doing the entrepreneur is exhibiting his most important skill: judgment. Entrepreneurs must do the right thing. They can hire people to do things right.

The qualifying telephone call identifies interested reviewers of the business plan. The business plan must answer the five following questions that all investors ask:

1. How much can I make?
2. How much can I lose?
3. How do I get my money out?
4. Who says this is any good?
5. Who else is in it?

HOW MUCH CAN I MAKE

The essence of the business plan lies in the answer to this question. The investor is interested in knowing how much money the entrepreneur projects that the investor will make in three to five years on his investment. In financial terms, this is known as a rate of return on investment or ROI.

Most venture capital investors have a target ROI of 45–60% compounded per annum over a 3 to 5 year period. For start-ups, or riskier deals, the target is closer to 60%. For first stage investments, or less risky deals, the target is closer to 45%. Investors convert the ROI percentage to four to five turns on their money in three years or approximately 10 turns on their money in five years. They assume that the company will achieve a public market for its common stock within three to five years or sell out for cash or stock, thus producing the return. These rates of return may strike you as overly ambitious, pie-in-the-sky, unrealistic, and as false targets thrown at naive entrepreneurs to make them shelve their business plans and go back to their jobs. Not true. Some of the old-line private venture capital firms achieve these ROIs in 8 investments out of 10. By picking companies with favorable product niches in huge markets with good people, even those that do not make it can be peddled to large corporations at prices in excess of the investors' cost.

The first section of the business plan that investors read is the three-to five-year operating statement projections. They look at the third year's projected earnings and multiply by an appropriate price/earnings ratio for similar companies, say 10.0 to 12.0 times. Then they multiply the amount they are being asked to invest by 4 or 5 and divide the resulting number by the first sum to determine the required percentage ownership. If it is too high, then the projections are too low, and the deal will be turned down. If the required ownership level is too low, they will ask if there is pricing flexibility and a willingness to negotiate before they go forward.

Operating statement projections are known as hockey sticks because most of them take the shape of a hockey stick. The company's earnings are at the base of the hockey stick, but if it receives venture capital, they will move up to the handle.

In the hockey stick in Exhibit 5, the Company projects third year net profits after taxes (npat) of $2,000,000, or a market value at that time of $24,000,000 using a p/e of 12. The investor multiplies $1,500,000 by 5 and divides the resulting value $7,500,000 by $24,000,000 to see how much ownership his $1,500,000 should purchase; about 31% in this case. If the business plan offers him an ownership percentage of about that amount he will read the business plan in more depth. The valuation formula once again is as follows:

$$\frac{\text{investment} \times 4 \text{ or } 5}{\text{third year npat} \times 10 \text{ or } 12} = \begin{array}{c}\text{ownership level necessary} \\ \text{to achieve target ROI}\end{array}$$

Referring to Exhibit 5 the valuation formula translates as follows:

$$\frac{\$1,500,000 \times 5}{\$2,000,000 \times 12} = \frac{\$7,500,000}{\$24,000,000} = 31.25\%$$

There are two red flags in this formula that could result in a quick turn-down, and they have to do with proportionality. If, in the case of the above example, the company claimed that it could achieve the $2,000,000 earnings level with a small amount of capital, say $150,000, the deal would sound too unrealistic and too optimistic. It would not appear reasonable to the investor that a fairly dramatic surge in earnings would result from so miniscule an investment. The steeper the earnings ramp, the greater the fuel requirement at the base. "Why surely you would not want to give this investment opportunity to a per-

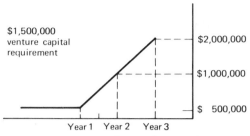

$1,500,000 venture capital requirement

$2,000,000

$1,000,000

$ 500,000

Year 1   Year 2   Year 3

EXHIBIT 5.   The Hockey Stick

fect stranger," would be the investor's initial reaction. Or, "What's wrong with this deal that so little investment can create $24 million in market value in three years?"

Earnings in the third year are multiplied by 10 or 12 to determine the company's market value. The investor's capital is multiplied by 4 or 5, and the first sum is divided into the second to determine the investor's required ownership position. If indeed the investor asks for that owner- ship position (the entrepreneur may initially offer less), he will make 4–5 times his investment, a 45–60% compound annual ROI (before capi- tal gains taxes) if the projections are met.

On the other hand, assume that the $24 million of market value re- quired an initial investment of $6 million to achieve $2 million in third year earnings. Four times $6 million equals $24 million, and the in- vestor would have to buy all of the company to justify the investment. Or, the projections should perhaps be extended a few more years at which point they may begin to grow more vertically and create a more attractive rate of return in the fifth year. There are a number of deals that require years of laying pipe before the oil is pumped. MCI Commu- nications took three rounds of financing, Federal Express, which raised $96 million on its first round, needed two more massive financings be- fore it began to generate income. Apollo Computers raised $1 million at $1 per share in January 1980, $1 million at $5 per share in December 1980, and $2 million at $25 per share in July 1981. The investor might also look behind the $6 million to see if some portion of it might be done with debt to reduce the equity investment and increase the re- turn on investment.

Venture capitalists are extraordinarily busy people for whom time is unusually valuable. Not only must they devote a big slice of each day to reviewing new proposals, but they have portfolios to monitor, board meetings to attend, tasks to do for portfolio companies—and in recessions most of their time is spent playing Red Cross nurse to their port-folios and not reviewing new proposals—and finally, making on-site in-spections of new deals. Therefore, when a new business plan floats in the door, the first areas reviewed are the hockey stick, the amount re-quired, and the management team. If the hockey stick suggests the kind of ROI they are interested in, they will read management's track record to see if the projections were prepared by qualified managers or merely good hockey stick artists. If the former, the package will get a thorough reading. If the entrepreneurs have short track records, the other as-pects of the business plan must be extremely interesting, including the ROI, market size, growth rate and product niche. Venture capital firms are increasingly hiring former entrepreneurs, hence the product de-scriptions in business plans are subject to more scrutiny than ever before.

A similar ROI calculation is done by tax shelter investors and under-writers, although less systematically. The tax shelter investor requires a lower ROI, somewhere in the 30–45% per annum range because he is receiving an annual return in the form of royalties, and it is not subject to the viscissitudes of the public market or a third to fifth year buy-out.

The underwriter's required ROI is somewhat less than the venture capitalist's also, say 25–35%, because the investors he will approach will have complete liquidity—they can sell the investment if they are displeased. But for the tax shelter investor, the underwriter, and the professional venture capitalist the hockey stick, or operating statement projection, is the key to making the investment.

Credibility of the Projections

What makes projections believable? Normally it is the credibility of the projection maker in concert with the facts he is dealing with. Lee Iaccoca had a combination of experience and management skills, plus bubbling enthusiasm, to convince the Federal Government to guaran-tee $500 million of loans to Chrysler Corporation in 1980. John DeLorean, who had previously run the Chevrolet division of General Motors, convinced two governments, the United States and Ireland, to guarantee close to $50 million in loans to launch a brand new automo-bile manufacturer. Up-start Storage Technology Corp., a computer pe-ripherals manufacturer, raised $50 million in 1981 in R&D partnerships to develop computers to compete head-to-head with IBM. Fred Smith, at the age of 29, on the strength of a paper he had written at Yale and no previous business experience, raised $96 million in venture capital and joint venture funds to launch Federal Express. Jeffrey Roloff, at the age of 23, raised $600,000 of venture capital from two funds and $600,000 in Industrial Revenue Bonds to expand Central Data Corp., a computer manufacturer that he began at the age of 19. The task of each of these entrepreneurs was to convince lenders, guarantors, and investors that the projections would be realized.

Let us begin with the key line in an operating statement projection—revenues. How is it derived? Why do sales increase each year? These questions may seem naive, but they must be answered at some point in the business plan.

One of the most ridiculous business plans I ever saw was for the Bunny Hutch, a proposed chain of fast food restaurants offering bunny burgers. It began with the following memorable sentence: "Assume each person in America eats one bunny burger one night per week: at $1.00 per bunny burger, that's $120,000,000 per week." One does not base revenue projections on a sweeping assumption such as the change in taste and frequency of eating out of 100% of the American public. To launch the Bunny Hutch, you begin with reputable market research regarding the taste preference for rabbit meat and locate restaurants near centers of those taste preferences. Appendix 2 includes a business plan that applies to a retail chain launch.

Many successful entrepreneurs have used third year percentage market penetration as the hook to hang the revenue hat on. Then they ramp the first three years' sales up to that point. Appropriate language must be the following: assume that the market for energy saving motor controls is $150 million per annum, in the base year (the immediately prior year) as measured by Frost and Sullivan, Stanford Research Institute, or a similarly reputable source. The source also projects growth to $750 million by 1985; and, if possible, that growth rate is confirmed by another source, possibly a brokerage house research report. The entrepreneur assumes in the business plan that funding will occur by late 1982, and the beginning of operations by early 1983. There are 12 quarters in a three-year projection, and the entrepreneur assumes that the company is ready to sell product by the third quarter of the first year—Q3. He further projects, that the company will achieve a 5% market penetration by the twelfth quarter, Q12, that sales will be at the "annualized rate" of $37 million; that is, Q12 sales of approximately $9,375,000.

The plan for achieving those sales must be carefully thought out and expressed in the business plan. If the company is manufacturing a product, the method of reaching customers can be through direct salesmen, wholesale distributors, dealers, marketing representatives, a licensed marketing organization, co-owned stores, co-franchised stores, direct mail, mail order, leasing, party plan sales, renting, metering (like Xerox machines), or a combination of the above. The marketing plan must be carefully explained to the reader and the reason for selecting that particular plan, as well. An examination of what competitors or similar companies are doing is useful. The courage of Xerox Corporation to sell copiers on a metering or pay-for-use basis, a brand new selling method, is one of the best business primers of entrepreneurial guts.

A classic error made time and time again by overanxious entrepreneurs is to develop the orders for a product without being in a position to deliver. For example, a small business may raise just enough initial capital to open a manufacturing plant and establish a production capability. It may then place an advertisement or a new product release in a trade journal. If then 300 inquiries are generated, how does the new company proceed to follow them up? What then follows is a slap-dash effort to raise $500,000 from venture capitalists who want to know how the marketplace responds to the product. But if the company is unable to ship product to an apparently interested market, the venture capitalists will probably turn the deal down or invest only if they can put in a chief executive officer who knows better than to sell hard before the production process is ready.

There is a time-tested method of avoiding glitches of this kind and many others as well, known as the PERT chart. PERT stands for "program evaluation and research tool," and it is an outgrowth of the operations research craze, of the post-Sputnik era. The systematic thought process of operations research, when applied to launching or expanding a business, can frequently obviate serious and costly mistakes.

A PERT chart is a little like "sentence diagramming," an old-fashioned method of learning grammar in elementary school. Each step is interconnected to another step along with a time axis, and then costs are applied to the steps. One may think of a PERT chart as events plotted against time with costs assigned to the events. A simplified PERT chart appears in Exhibit 6.

By studying the PERT chart the entrepreneur is able to see the effects on all of the other activities when one of the activities is delayed or fails. For example, if the prototype takes an extra two months to become

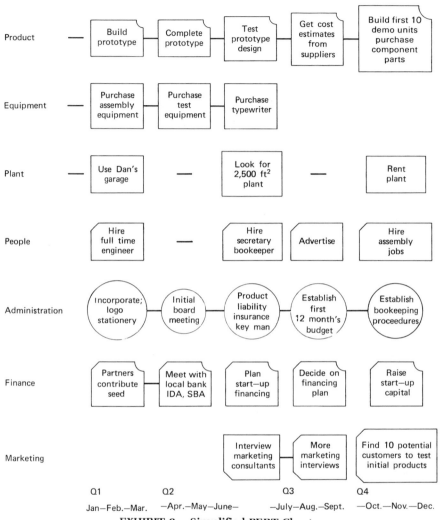

EXHIBIT 6. Simplified PERT Chart

operational, the company will need extra salary expenses, extra rental expenses, and face a delay of two months in other activities. Experienced entrepreneurs anticipate delays of this nature and build time and financial cushions into their projections. Some entrepreneurs call this "negative planning" or "risk aversion." It is a process of continually asking oneself, "Now, if that doesn't occur, what can I do to cover the shortfall?" Tim Hay, president of the highly regarded Security Pacific Capital Corp., Los Angeles, likes to back entrepreneurs who were raised on farms, because "they are used to receiving immediate feedback to their actions and then taking another course of action." Venture capitalists who are experienced in funding start-ups, allow for mistakes up to 100% in time. For example, one New York venture capitalist who specializes in high technology start-ups estimates that each dollar he invests will require another dollar because the company will be delayed twice as long as it thinks it will in climbing onto the hockey stick.

His philosophy of venture capital investing, shared by others as well, is that investments go bad for one or several of four reasons: (1) concept; (2) valuation; (3) management; and (4) timing. In most cases, these reasons appear together or in pairs.

Concept.   It is rare that the failure of a business results from bad fortune. It should be almost equally rare that the initial business concept is completely faulty. Diligent and detailed investigation and common sense should preclude most failures of this kind. Since two people are less likely to be seduced by an attractive but flawed concept, venture capital funds usually have at least two experienced people to investigate each investment. They also prefer to invest in conjunction with good partners.

In evaluating an investment there are three basic essentials—product (or service), market, and management. Venture capitalists attempt to take a significant risk on no more than one of these elements. It is not often that the venture capitalist can avoid all of the three. But whatever the advantages and risks of a specific investment, the venture capitalist attempts to commit himself to a dispassionate and factual analysis. Most experienced venture capitalists have well-developed instincts that they trust and are willing to use in conjunction with logic.

Much more common reasons for failure are mistakes in valuation, management, and the timing of the sale.

Valuation.   Proper valuation is extremely important. The venture capitalist must often assume the risk of the failure of the enterprise; he cannot, therefore, also afford to assume substantial market risk. The long time horizon and limited liquidity make the indefinite perpetuation of high stock price multiples unlikely. The venture capitalist should plan on achieving a sufficient enough profit at a low multiple to compensate him for the risk. Mistakes of valuation resulting from the limited success of the enterprise can be mitigated, if not avoided entirely, by structuring investments into fixed denomination securities.

Management.   Active involvement in overseeing the conduct of the enterprise and a willingness to assume the burden and risk of changing management are essential. The risks of inaction tend to be considerably greater. The venture capitalist should not make the mistake of trying to manage his investees. Any such necessity is a sure sign of management failure. While the review of management performance is the single most important function of the venture capitalist, it is also essential that he be able to achieve a good working relationship with the entrepreneur. While often unavoidable, conflict between the investors and management is neither pleasant nor profitable.

Timing.   From the inception of the investment, the venture capitalist must know to whom he believes an investment can be sold, whether or not successful. Equally essential, he should have an understanding on this issue with the entrepreneur; even then conflict is often unavoidable. But by acting early, when the venture is still well financed and its prospects only diminished, loss can often be avoided by selling the enterprise to a larger entity that can use its product or other capabilities.

More important, once an investment is successful and the venture has accomplished its initial business plan, the venture capitalist must press for liquidity. At a minimum he should recover his initial investment at the earliest opportunity. Often the risk of a venture will increase as the enterprise grows larger and more successful and begins to reach the limits of its business concept and the capability of its entrepreneurial management.

Thus, as the entrepreneur puts costs on the items in the PERT chart, he should overestimate both the costs and the time it takes to accomplish the tasks by at least 25%. This should provide the company with enough cushions to fall back on in the event of unexpected delays.

The first 12 to 18 months of a start-up operation are usually a period of net cash outlays. Funds are spent developing a product, hiring people, purchasing equipment, setting up a manufacturing procedure, and building test and development products. As sales develop slowly while customers experiment with the product before committing to it, the monthly cash outlay becomes smaller. In time, the company begins

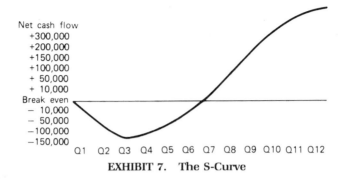

EXHIBIT 7.   The S-Curve

to operate at or near break-even, and, if the product indeed solves problems for its customers, the company moves into a positive cash flow position. This series of events is called an "S-curve" because it takes the shape of an "S".

In the Exhibit 7 example, the company reaches its peak cash deficit in Q4 at ($150,000) and then begins to improve steadily until it crosses the break-even point in Q7. To determine the amount of capital that the company needs, the entrepreneur accumulates its net cash deficit quarters, and that sum plus a cushion of another 25% is its start-up capital requirement. The amount of start-up capital required in Exhibit 7 is calculated as follows:

Cumulative Quarterly
Net Cash Deficits

Q1	—
Q2	$ 25,000
Q3	100,000
Q4	150,000
Q5	125,000
Q6	50,000
Q7	15,000
Subtotal	$465,000
+ 25%	115,000
Total	$580,000

The initial capital injection should be $580,000. If the capital or part of it is raised by way of a bank loan, an additional sum should be raised to cover annual interest charges of at least 20% of the principal amount of the loan.

Returning to revenue projections, we consider the crucial issue of product pricing. This subject is extremely complex because there are many pricing methods and formulas. Polaroid, for example, very brilliantly priced its camera at a slight markup over cost and applied a substantially higher markup to its film. Xerox metered its product, like a toll booth on a highway. In productivity-improving manufactured products—those sold to industrial customers—a rule of thumb is to mark up the product 2.5 to 3.0 times above the sum of materials and labor, in small quantity runs. Thus, if the sum of material and labor costs in $3,275, the price to the customer would be $8,187.50. Then, when the customer asks for quantity discounts, 20% can be taken off of the retail price, bringing it down to $6,550.00 per unit, which still leaves a 2.0 times markup and a 50% gross profit margin. Further, if the company must sell through dealers, distributors, or representatives, commissions or discounts of 15–30% can be applied without seriously impacting profits.

Price decisions must also take into consideration competitive prices for similar products. It is important to price the product aggressively, rather than at a steep discount from the competition. If the product has a price lower than its competitors, it may be deemed to be of less quality. Malcolm McLean introduced container shipping in 1962, a method of shipping a product in a truck body where the truck body is lifted up and into a honeycomb onboard the ship and then lifted back on to a truck at the other end of the voyage. Liquor companies were losing almost one-fourth of their cargo of barrels at the dock with conventional shipping. McLean encouraged the liquor companies to try his method, because all of the liquor would stay inside the truck bodies. He held the price constant and eventually took all of the business for McLean Industries.

To complete the answer to the question "How Much Can I Make?" the operating statement projections must be carried out the full 12 quarters. Companies with longer start-up periods—a deeper well in the S-curve—may have to go out five years in their projections to show attractive profits. The PERT chart should be extended from 12 to 20 quarters so that all of the expenses of building the business can be properly accounted for in the quarter in which they occur.

The ramping of revenues is tied into a number of factors including achieving a target percentage market penetration, a reasonable level of achievement for the marketing staff or dealer network, and a comparison with other similar companies.

One method of testing revenue projections is to divide sales by the number of sales people to see if it is reasonable for the sales staff to achieve those goals. Then, take one salesperson's compensation and determine if he is making a living wage or, conversely, being overcompensated to the point of becoming too relaxed.

The manufacturing costs are subtracted from revenues, and the operating expenses are taken from the PERT chart on the month or quarter they occur and subtracted from gross profit. Samples of three-year operating statement projections with a list of assumptions appear in Appendix 2.

HOW MUCH CAN I LOSE?

The answer to this question lies partially in the structure of the financing and partially in an assessment of the riskiness of the deal. In regards to financing structure, the weakest instrument an investor can purchase is a limited partnership interest and the second weakest is a minority common stock position. A senior common stock or preferred stock position is the third weakest, providing only preferences to the investor in liquidation and in receiving dividends prior to any dividend payments on the common stock. The fourth weakest instrument is an unsecured loan, usually referred to as a subordinated debenture, and finally, the strongest instrument is a secured loan.

In all of these securities the investor and the entrepreneur can enter into agreements that spell out how they will treat one another over the course of the relationship. But the investors can enforce their position if they must if their investment vehicle is strong rather than weak. The purchase agreement entered into between the company and the investor at the closing contains a litany of the things that the company must do ("positive convenants") and the things that it must not do ("negative convenants") to and for the investor. Failure to comply places the company in default, and the remedies in the event of default are the determining factor in measuring the risk of loss of the investment. One of the remedies that is useful in protecting an investor's principal is the ability to take control of the company's board of directors. This permits the investor to bring in new management to try to turn the company around.

Other remedies, which may include demanding immediate repayment of the investment, are difficult to enforce on strapped companies but serve as a threat of the lengths to which the investors will go in order to protect their principal. Tax shelter investors rarely have remedies such as these.

The second measure of the downside of a deal is a calculation of the inherent risks. There are three major risks in every early-stage company, and they are as follows:

1. Production—Can the product be produced?
2. Marketing—Can the product be sold?
3. Management—Can the product be produced and sold at a profit?

Naturally, in R&D tax shelters and development stage investments, you must add the fourth risk: Research—Can the product be conceived and developed?

For going concerns operating at a profit, all three risks are relatively small, and the investor has only internal risks to deal with such as liquidity and marketability. For example, there are many profitable nursing home management companies seeking expansion capital, but many investors are unwilling to put money in that industry because of its publicity-attracting ability. Politicians love to kick the daylights out of nursing home owners prior to election. Some deserve it, but many do not. Therefore, it may be difficult to sell an investment in a nursing home management company at a profit. Thus the venture capital industry has the "closed" sign out for this industry. The same may be said of other industries that may have lost their allure or sparkle. Naturally, this means they can be picked up more cheaply, which does not mitigate their risk, rather, enhances the ROI. To quote the overworked investment motto attributed to one of the Rothschilds: "Buy when blood is running in the streets. Sell when the fatted lamb is lowing in the fields." Only the Rothschilds apparently follow this dictum. The rest of us, alas, are too frequently rather ovine in our investing habits, following trends and looking for hot buttons and key words.

The existence of the major risk areas—production, marketing, and management—indicates to the investor the probability of losing his entire investment. However, of these three areas, the most serious is the management risk. So important is the entrepreneurial team to venture capitalists that investors will build companies to fit the right entrepreneurs.

Tandem Computer Corporation, the creation of the venture capital firm of Kleiner, Perkins and Company and James Treybig was one of the first created in a laboratory setting. Treybig was plucked out of Hewlett-Packard by Kleiner, Perkins and incubated at the venture firm for a year while he reviewed business plans, met entrepreneurs, studied the company-launching process in depth, and finally produced the business plan for Tandem.

Kleiner, Perkins has sculptured other Michangelos out of raw stone including Genentech, Tandem, and Hybritech. It concentrates on state of the art technology venture capital investments at the start-up stage, with a preference for West Coast deals. In its last fund-raising effort, Kleiner, Perkins raised $50 million in less than 30 days from insurance companies and pension funds. Most venture capital funds require six months or a year to raise that much money. The point of the Kleiner, Perkins story is that certain investors who are experienced in dealing with raw start-ups at a research and development stage are comfortable with that level of risk because they have selected, in their opinion, the right people to back. Their entire investment may be lost with each check they write, but they have a fat Roll-O-Dex of names and entrepreneurial managers to call on for a bail-out should their investment be turning sour.

In preparing the business plan, the entrepreneur should spell out his achievements in other capacities such as:"From 1976 to 1980 Mr. Smith held positions of increased responsibility at ABC Corporation, culminating with the position of Vice President—Marketing, where he was functionally responsible for sales to industrial customers. Approximately 15 salesmen and more than 100 representatives reported to him. He handled 30 corporate accounts personally. While in this capacity, sales increased from $42,500,000 to $180,000,000, whereas personnel increased by less than 50%. Mr. Smith was given six raises in a three-year period and bonuses equal to 10% of salary."

Every business plan should have a "Use of Proceeds" section which explains how the money will be spent. Merely to say "working capital" is insufficient. The investors are entitled to know item by item how their money will be utilized. All of the facts are on the PERT chart, and the low point of the S-curve provides the working capital figure. Following is the Use of Proceeds section of a business plan for a computer systems firm that raised venture capital primarily to open national sales offices:

Use of Proceeds
of the $700,000 Financing

To open, stock, and staff additional retail branches at the rate of one per month until positive cash flow is achieved	$ 200,000
Marketing and advertising expenses, including national advertising to support branches and dealers	150,000
Additional inventory buildup to support expansion	150,000
Salaries of programmers engaged in product development and enhancement	55,000
Working capital reserve	100,000
Legal and investment banking fees and financing expenses	45,000
Total use of proceeds	$ 700,000

HOW DO I GET MY MONEY OUT?

The normal means of achieving liquidity in a venture capital investment are by public offering or acquisition by a larger company for cash or stock.

The business plan should indicate that the entrepreneurs are indeed interested in arranging for an exit route such as this for the investors. If they have another means in mind of achieving liquidity such as participation in earnings, this too should be mentioned, but it is rarely as attractive as selling out at a high p/e ratio. Large industrial corporations for whatever reason, are not successful developers of new products. Their research and development efforts over the years have been poorer at generating valid new products (except in the pharmaceutical industry), than has the entrepreneurial process. Thus, they continuously acquire entrepreneurial success stories and they do so at prices that will make an entrepreneur turn his head abruptly.

WHO SAYS THIS DEAL IS ANY GOOD?

Investors like endorsements and testimonials. Professional venture capitalists will call dozens of references before investing—customers, suppliers, and personal references. "Why did you buy the product? What do you think about it? Will you buy more? How was the service?" are a few of the typical questions asked of customers.

Personal references include bankers, previous employers, and previous co-workers.

The reference checks on entrepreneurs are not always glowing. Burt McMurtry, a specialist in high technology start-up investments, says:

> Quite often when I check on a prospect, his former subordinates say they worshipped him. He was dynamic, the high-energy type. His peers, however, were often irritated with him because he was something of a prima donna, always trying to get his project funded first. And his former bosses? Some of them will say they like what he accomplished, but he nearly drove them crazy. Didn't take no for an answer easily, and had zero grasp of corporate politics.*

Some venture capitalists ask for seven personal references—five good ones and two bad ones. The business plan should offer to make these available, but they should be referred to only and handed out at meetings with interested venture capitalists.

Business plans are supposed to be confidential, but occasionally an investor will ship the plan to the unknowing company's competitor. The use of an investment banker can mitigate this problem.

The business plan should include many of the endorsements received by the product in trade journals, letters from customers, and customer responses at demonstrations and trade shows. Investors should be given a hands-on demonstration of the product or service by going to a trade show, visiting the company at its plant, or, at a minimum, through product photographs. In attempting to convey enthusiasm about a business to an investor, the entrepreneur should bear in mind the plight of the first person who ate a lobster and tried to con-

*Forbes, August 3, 1981

vince others that it was good. "You mean you ate that strange thing that crawls on the bottom of the sea?" they were likely to ask. "Yes, and let me explain why it was good." Clearly, the lobster eater could have used the endorsement of others who ate it and did not die.

Following are samples of possibly useful descriptions of products and opportunities, each of which attempts in its own way to quantify the market size potential of the product.

Description of a Computer Software Product

Market Size.   There are, according to the U.S. Department of Commerce 23,000 home improvement centers in the United States and an estimated 120,000 locations. The geographical distribution of these retail outlets is fairly even as may be seen in the following list*

	Number	Percent of Total
New England	1,309	5.7%
Middle Atlantic	3,501	13.2
East North Central	4,321	18.7
West North Central	3,470	15.0
South Atlantic	2,875	12.5
East South Central	1,542	6.7
West South Central	2,921	12.7
Mountain	1,254	5.9
Pacific	2,319	10.1
Total	23,512	100.0%

The problems confronting the managements of these stores are fairly standard and common to many retailers who have recently begun to "computerize." The most important problem is that their costs have risen rapidly to the point that they must squeeze their inventories to minimum levels while holding their out-of-stocks to less than 10% to maintain satisfied customers—many of whom are contractors in the middle of jobs—who will simply go elsewhere if the store is out of stock on important items. The stores are larger than ever and stock a greater number of product lines and broader lines as well. Home improvement centers have lumber and hardware departments, of course, but many

*Source: U.S. Department of Commerce, Census of Retail Trade, 1980.

have broadened into decorating centers, "energy corners" (wood burn-
ing stoves, flu dampers, fireplace converters), solar equipment, burglar
alarms, energy cost savers, and other lines. It is increasingly difficult to
manage these stores on a manual inventory control basis. Payrolls have
expanded, sales taxes have grown in complexity, and credit customers
take longer to pay their bills, all of which beckon the need to introduce
data processing to lumber yards.

The company believes that at least 10,000, or 45%, of the home improvement centers are large enough to consider data processing, of
which perhaps 10% have already installed systems. That would leave
9,000 additional customers with as many as 30,000 locations, which at
the price the company charges for its system, $60,000 per location, sug-
gests a total market size of approximately $1.8 billion.

The Product.   The company's system known as the Home Improvement Center Management Systems, or HMS, provides the following applications to the user:

1. General ledger
2. Payroll system
3. Accounts payable
4. Accounts receivable
5. Inventory control

All of the applications are designed around the interface between the
customer and the sales clerk at the point of sale. The customer tells the
clerk what she/he wants (if its in the yard) or comes to the counter with
purchases if in the store, or more likely some of each. The sales clerk
queries the terminal for out-of-stock inventory, and if out of stock, for
next availability. If the customer is buying on credit, the clerk queries
the terminal for his credit limit. Inventory by stock number is maintained in memory and continually updated as transactions occur. All
prices, discounts, and taxes are in memory for rapid retrieval and calculation. The invoice is printed, and the transaction time is less than
with present manual methods.

Moreover, the computer in the accounting department records the
transaction and all other transactions and automatically generates reorders, invoices for credit customers, payables to reflect reorders,
payroll records, and a general ledger of the store for the day, week,
month, or year.

Some markets are much newer than home improvement centers, hence must be carefully defined before showing how the product solves a problem in that market. Earth stations comprise just such a market.

Description of the Home Satellite Television Antenna Systems Market

Definition of Earth Stations.   Home satellite television systems or earth stations (also known as TVROs, for television receive only) are packages of equipment wired into standard television sets that enable receivers to select from more than 60 channels of programming. The equipment consists of a parbolic or spherical dish (antenna) to gather the signal that is reflected off the satellite 22,300 miles in space, a low noise amplifier (LNA) to boost the weak signal, and a special microwave receiver to tune in the pictures and sound.

There exists a magazine like *TV Guide* to assist the viewer in selecting a satellite at which to point the antenna. Once aimed at either Comstar 1,2, or 3, Westar 1 or 2, Satcom 1 or 2, Intelsat, or Anik 1, 2, or 3, the existing satellites in the Western Hemisphere, the viewer then tunes the receiver to any of the channels on that satellite. Programming includes a 24-hour sports network, religious networks, several major independents (WOR-TV New York, WGN-TV Chicago, and KTTV, Los Angeles), the House of Representatives live, Spanish language entertainment and news, first run movies, variety shows, and other programs.

The price of earth stations to consumers, depending upon the size of the dish, degree of noise interference with the picture, and the number of extras, ranges between $4,000 and $7,500. Since the signal from the satellite shines down on earth like a flashlight, it can be picked up anywhere in the country as well as in parts of Mexico, the Caribbean, and Canada. An earth station is as easy to install as a stereo set. It can be installed outdoors, on the roof, or in greenhouses. An antenna will withstand normal heat, rain, ice, and snow for about 5–10 years before maintenance is required.

Mechanics of Satellite Communication.   In 1962 Telstar, the first manmade orbiting satellite to relay television pictures, was lifted into orbit around the earth. In the 1960s, many of the rocket-placed communications relay stations orbited no more than 100–150 miles above the earth's surface at their closest satellites (perigee) point. This was so because technological sophistication was lacking to lift a "heavy weight" relay device and the control systems to maintain it in orbit. To transmit and receive electronic messages between the satellite station and the earth, ground-based stations required an antenna that could track an orbiting satellite as it passed overhead. Because the orbiting station was moving constantly, the ground-station antenna could follow for only small portions of its journey around the earth before it disappeared again below the earth's horizon.

The Hughes Aircraft Company experimented with a new concept called SYNCOM and in 1963 placed an orbiting station approximately 22,300 miles above the earth's equator (the earth's point of maximum gravity). They orbited the SYNCOM satellite in a direction identical to the direction of the earth's rotation on its axis, and something called "geostationary orbit" was achieved. By this it meant that the orbiting satellite moved at the same speed as the earth's rotation, thereby appearing to hover in the sky above one ground location transmitting and receiving station. This technological breakthrough effectively ended the tracking of satellites that were only useful for telecommunications during certain portions of the day.

The modern satellites, such as those dealing with television service, weigh between 1,800 and 4,000 pounds and are very complex systems. They create their own power by way of the banks of solar power cells they carry. These power cells must always point toward the sun to collect its rays for conversion to operating power. The satellite has batteries to store power, as well, which come into use during the occasional periods when the earth moves between the satellite and the sun and causes a several-hour eclipse. The satellites adjust themselves to constantly changing gravitational forces and the press of solar winds through the use of miniature rocket thrusters on their surfaces that fire on command and gently angle them back into the correct orbiting position. They contain a series of radio/television receivers to pick up earth transmissions (this is called the "uplink"), frequency converters that change the uplink signals to new frequencies for the transmissions back to earth (or the "downlink"), transmitters to boost the downlink signals, and a set of complex transmitting and receiving antennas.

Market Size for Earth Stations.   It has been estimated that nearly five million American homes have no television reception whatsover. An additional 10–15 million American homes are believed to be "hardcore" television watchers—they own or intend to own video recording devices and/or large screen projectors—interested in the capability of viewing more than 60 channels of programming. And an estimated 10–15 million bars, clubs, cocktail lounges, hotels, motels, restaurants, and gathering places represent potential customers for each station. Smaller markets include Mexico, where U.S. television would offer a broader variety; Canada, Alaska, and Hawaii, whose reception is very poor; and homes in areas serviced by cable television but too remote to have the cable connected; as well as offshore drilling rigs, the Caribbean Islands, and Puerto Rico.

In addition to entertainment, information can be transmitted by way of satellite faster and more cheaply than by virtually any other means. Several multilocation companies and institutions have announced their intention to "teleconference" with their branch locations by way of satellite. The Mormon Church, in fact, rents a transponder on the Westar satellite.

Before accounting for the international market, the North American market for earth stations is probably in excess of 20 million units at a price range between $4,000 and $7,500 per unit, hence, a North American market size of an estimated $100 billion.

Description of a Symbiotic Product and Its Niche

Some products are symbiotic to a major product, as blades are to razors, films to cameras, and so forth. Here is a sample product description for those kinds of businesses. The company designs, develops, and markets software games for personal computers. Its product line currently includes 10 games for each of three popular personal computers. The company's product is produced on disks or cassettes, packaged in a rigid four-color box with a detailed printed manual, and sold to retailers and distributors that sell the most popular brands of personal computers. To date the company has sold and delivered approximately 150,000 packages to approximately 70,000 customers for a penetration of approximately 7% of the estimated installed base of one million personal computers. The company's products accounted for approximately 6% of the software packages made in 1981 by software publishers independent of the hardware manufacturers.

The company is seeking long-term capital in order to significantly broaden its line into educational software and sports-based packages.

Market Size. A 1980 study of the computer software industry by the Association of Data Processing Service Organizations (ADAPSO) projects the growth in software products from $1.08 billion in 1978 to $8 billion in 1985. Of that amount, they see applications software capturing one-half. *Consumer Electronics*, March 1981, estimates that retail sales of packaged software will be double from 1980 levels as the installed computer base reaches 1.5 million units by the end of 1982. *Business Week*, September 1, 1980 ("Missing Computer Software"), reports that

> Doubts are rising about whether the industry can meet the soaring demand for software in the years ahead. . . . So fundamental is this software squeeze that is has led to the rise of a brand-new industry—the independent software business. Barely in existence 10 years ago, the software industry is exploding now.

The Product. The company publishes some of the most highly regarded and widely used personal computer software in the market. It has 150,000 packages in the field and a customer list of 500 retailers and distributors. There are an estimated 1,400 computer retailers in the United States, Canada, and abroad. The company's customers (endusers) have an average reorder rate of 3.5 times following the initial order. Because of its popularity and reputation, the product line is believed to have "pull through" ability for future products. The management has applied the company's limited resources to developing highly commercial products and selling them at a continually increasing rate.

Future Prospects. Company management perceives an opportunity to obtain a significant market share of the educational software and business games software markets by broadening its line and diversifying beyond computer games.

WHO ELSE IS IN IT?

Investors like to have company in a deal. They want to know that other institutions or corporations are involved with the company in either a risk taking capacity or as lenders, suppliers, or customers.

When Fred Smith raised $96 million to launch Federal Express, he first got General Dynamics excited about selling him hundreds of Falcon jets. Then he hired an investment banker to endorse the business plan and himself. Then he showed that he was investing all of his net worth. Then he got Prudential Insurance to say they would supply a middle tier of long-term financing subject to the venture capital being raised. Then he went back to General Dynamics and improved the terms of their deal to signify to others an improved and improving relationship.

The investment bankers needed $26 million of venture capital to support the debt structure, and they landed some important names first: First National Bank of Chicago, Allstate Insurance, and Citicorp. The rest of the financing came together quickly because of the endorsement factor. Endorsement makes the difference between the Masters Tournament and the local pro-am. Further, in the event that the company needs more capital in the future, there will be more than one person pulling the oars.

The business plan or the investment banker's cover letter should indicate what other institutions or corporations are financially involved with the company. Endorsements are very important in the rather small world of business where with a few telephone calls an investor can check out the credibility and integrity of an entrepreneur.

15

QUESTIONS
AND ANSWERS

There has been a good deal of data set forth in the preceding chapters, and some of it may have been presented too pedagogically to make a lasting impression. So it is probably a good idea to stop here and deal with questions frequently asked by entrepreneurs as they relate to specific companies. These questions come from live situations, although I have liberally disguised them to protect the companies.

1. Q: I am a 25-year-old engineer with a major electronics firm. I have developed a patentable instrument for my employer, but they do not want to manufacture it, and they have given me the opportunity to file the patent in my name as long as I assign them a nonexclusive right to make, use, and sell it. I have estimated my capital requirement to start a company to produce the instrument at $80,000. The capital will be used as follows:

Technical equipment	$ 41,500
Benches, lights, tools	1,785
Beginning inventory	16,200
Technician's salary for 6 months	12,400
My salary for 6 months	6,000
Legal fees, incorporation, and patent	2,115
Total	$ 80,000

I need very little salary. My wife makes $15,000 a year teaching, and she can help with the bookkeeping in the afternoons and evenings. In six months I should have enough sales to begin operating profitably. What is the value of my company? How much ownership should I given away to friends and relatives for $80,000?

1. A: To answer the question of how much the $80,000 is worth, I must make one or two assumptions. First, the product is probably an interesting and useful piece of electronic instrumentation, but your employer does not perceive it as having a sufficiently large market size to build a new product line around. So, it might make a $20 million (sales) company in five years, but that is too small for your employer. Further, you perceive that the right you are giving to your employer is modest and that by the time they get around to making their version of the product, if they ever do, you will have modified and improved your version of it. Third, you perceive additional applications and markets for the instrument beyond those determined by your employer and a substantially larger market size for the product.

The assumptions are probably true, for if they were not, your employer would not let you leave with the product so fast. Large corporations have a habit of allowing good things to slip out the door. It is rumored that Itek Corp., a company formed by ex-Eastman Kodak officers, stands for "I took Eastman Kodak."

The first $80,000 is pure risk money, sometimes called "crapshoot" money. There is a product idea and a talented engineer, but no business plan, management team, manufacturing capability, or demand curve. All of the risks are prevalent: Can the product be made? If made, can it be sold? If sold, can it be sold at a profit?

You obviously believe in the product and in your ability to produce it, to develop orders for it, and to build a company from it. You are taking a career risk, a financial risk, and asking your wife to make significant sacrifices. I assume that you are rational and that the decision to leave your job and start a new company has been carefully thought through and discussed with your wife and perhaps one or two other people whose opinions you respect.

Given that the above scenario approximates the actual circumstances, the issue of valuation can be dealt with systematically. Your new company will either fail; operate as a small, one-product company for many years without producing wealth; or succeed, that is, create wealth. If the investors are willing to put in $80,000, their goal is to achieve wealth, most assuredly, but also to help you get started. The risk associated with backing you is about 50 to 1 that they will achieve a venture capital type rate of return and about 25 to 1 that a going concern will result and perhaps pay them back through dividends. If you had a business partner that had managed a growing company then the odds could be cut in half. But you are all alone.

It is not likely that your company will be able to grow beyond sales of $250,000 per annum without additional capital. You will need larger facilities, more inventory, more people, more production equipment, and capital to carry receivables and to support larger shipments from suppliers. You will need advertising dollars at some point, a seasoned marketing executive, and a sales force or representative organization. And finally, you will need more engineers to launch an R&D effort to add complementary products.

Let us assume that the additional dilution for capital and key people will be in the neighborhood of 50%, as follows:

Head of marketing	10%
Heads of production, finance, and other key employees	10%
Second round venture capital financing	30%
Total additional dilution	50%

Following that stage of development and the addition of very capable members of management, let us assume that you grow the company with some success in five years to sales of $18,000,000, earnings of 7.5% after tax ($1,350,000), and that the next stage of expansion requires a larger plant, modern automated assembly operations, a second plant in Europe, and more people, all of which comes to a bill of $3,000,000, including repaying some debt accumulated along the way. The underwriters are willing to value the company at a p/e of 15, or 15 times $1,350,000, or slightly more than $20,000,000. To net $3,000,000, you raise $3,500,000, and the dilution is another 17.5%. Therefore, assuming a pattern of successful growth, you may expect five separate dilutions.

Let us back up to the practical issue of pricing the deal for the $80,000 investors. Let us create three valuations: $500,000, $750,000, and $1,000,000 (see Exhibit 8). In the first instance, the $80,000 would own 16%, in the second instance 10.7%, and in the third instance 8%. In my opinion, the range of values of the new company is between $500,000 and $1,000,000. I will get to that in a moment, but let us examine at this

**EXHIBIT 8.   Resulting Wealth to Founder After Five Years
Given Four Different First-Stage Valuations**

Initial valuation	$160,000	$500,000	$750,000	$1,000,000
Initial equity give-up	50%	16%	10.7%	8%
Total dilution for venture capital, key management, and public offerings	67.5%	67.5%	67.5%	67.5%
Resulting Ownership to Founder	23.4%	39.3%	41.8%	43.0%

point whether the risks and hard work are worth it for you after five dilutions. Assume that the $80,000 costs you 50% ownership on the one hand and then between 8% and 16% on the other.

On the low side you stand to own 23.4% of a $20,000,000 company, or wealth of about $4,000,000 after capital gains taxes; on the high side 43% of $20,000,000, or slightly over $8,000,000.

The $80,000 investors would have the same wealth as you in the first instance, $4,000,000, or a rate of return of 50 times in five years. If they bought 8% of the equity, they would own 3.7% of the company after five years and have achieved a rate of return of $300,000/$80,000 = 3.75 times. That is at the relatively low end of acceptable returns for the level of risk.

My own instincts support an ownership level of 10.7%, that is, an initial valuation of approximately $750,000. My reasons are several. On the one hand, 10.7% dilutes to 5%, or approximately $400,000 valuation in the fifth year, a compound ROI of 37% per annum, which is a higher ROI than the average annual performance of the private venture capital funds.

Second, the initial investment of $80,000 was relatively small, in fact too small to do much except launch the company, and most assuredly will lead to further dilution in the future, primarily in the event of the company's success. Third, the initial investment could have been lost entirely without seriously affecting the net worths of the investors. It is "friendly" money, and there would be no bitterness or conflagration if the money went down the rathole.

Further comments on this question would lead me into numerous stories of bright young men and women being "helped" by family and friends who invest a little bit of money for 60–70% ownership. Not only is this level of ownership unwarranted by the business plan, but also it dilutes the founding entrepreneur to a level of disincentive. There is an ownership level at which an entrepreneur will refuse to come up for air the proverbial third time. This is a hard lesson for many novice investors to learn, but the entrepreneur must have enough equity ownership to justify toughing out the hard times. If he has 20% ownership at the beginning, and if there are three rounds of dilution, each of 20–30%, then if a problem arises that requires the entrepreneur to work around the clock, night and day for six weeks, he may decide that the effort is not justified by the ownership level. If he then walks away from the company, the investors have no one to thank for their imminent write-off but themselves. I have found that more experienced venture capitalists are more aware of the need to incentivize the founding entrepreneurs.

2. Q: A friend and I want to begin a fast-food restaurant chain. I have a real estate background and about $200,000 to invest. He has five years' experience with McDonalds at the store operations level, but he has no money to invest. How do we divide the pie?

2. A: The manner in which you split the initial ownership should be a completely voluntary contract between the two parties. You will have to live with each other through many nightmares over a five-year period, and if either person bares a grudge about the initial ownership percentages, it will split the relationship irreparably. Therefore I would avoid the interference and recommendations of lawyers, accountants, bankers, and the like, whose advice, although advertised as objective, will probably favor the partner who is investing the money rather than the other partner.

The McDonald's-trained partner could raise $200,000 on the strength of a business plan for a new fast food chain, borrow $500,000 from the SBA, and launch two or three stores without giving up control. He could hire a real estate person to spot new locations and not yield any equity for that skill. Franchises could be sold for additional cash, or tax shelters or, indeed, a private placement with SBICs could be undertaken for expansion capital.

The real-estate-trained partner with the $200,000 would have more difficulty launching the fast-food chain on his own, and indeed, would have to give away equity to someone with operations skills. He may or may not know anything about location selecting for fast-food chains. He probably knows a good deal about banking relationships and probably has dozens of banking contacts to draw on—this helps any business, but is critical in the restaurant business, which is heavily leveraged.

Thus one partner brings the "product" and management and the other partner brings money and finance-administration skills. Under the circumstances, and if both partners agree to guarantee bank loans jointly and severally, to take the same salary and perquisites, and to invest the same amount of time, I would recommend a 50-50 split.

Great restaurant chains do not happen because of the availability of seed capital, banking contacts, or real estate development skills. They are highly reliant on the food, service, ambience, and feeling that the customer gets at the restaurant. I could make an argument for the McDonald's trained partner getting more ownership than the other partner. However, true partnerships are 50-50, and there is a greater wholesomeness to that arrangement.

3. Q: I have invented an alternative energy source that is cost free, yet can provide enough power to electrify the entire country, or at a minimum, provide lighting for streets, office buildings, and homes. In my plan, streets and sidewalks are replaced, not entirely, but at intervals within a city, by strike plates. When walked or driven on, the strike plates depress a hydraulic device that turns a lever, the lever rotates a rudder suspended in a water tank situated above and alongside the street and turns a turbine to produce energy. I have received a patent for this invention. A small underwriter is willing to take me public: $1,500,000 for 40% ownership in a penny stock offering. Do I take the deal?

3. A: It is quite a leap, mentally and practically from a patent to a public offering. Where is the PERT chart, the business plan, the production model of the device to see if it will work, and what are the energy trade-offs?

Alternative energy start-ups are one of the staples in the venture capitalist's morning mail. We can count on several deals of this nature every day with some regularity, thanks to OPEC. Solar, windmill, methanol, ethanol, alcohol, wave-power, and sidewalk-street strike plates seem to be the most prevalent. Each one has something significant to offer, and each one has costs associated with it before the first British thermal unit of power is delivered. Although they each rely on a "free" source of power—sun, wind, ocean, garbage, and so on—the system required to capture, convert, and deliver the free source is generally expensive, unattractive, larger than expected, and difficult to sell in a confused marketplace. For example, to retrofit a 3,000 square foot home with a solar power system in a Northeastern city might require eight years to pay for itself. Some people cannot see out eight years, or think they may move in the interim and elect to stick with gas or oil.

The energy trade-offs must be compelling to introduce an alternative energy system into the marketplace. To launch the strike plate company, which is only at the concept stage, the first and most immediate step is to see if the system can be built and to see if it works. At the same time its manufacturing costs can be ascertained, as well as its maintenance and service requirements.

Chester Carlson, the inventor of xerography and founder of Xerox Corporation, was in a similar spot in the early 1950s, trying to sell xerography against the highly popular mimeograph system. Mr. Carlson, a tall, cragged, slightly stooped man wearing a tan raincoat and a weathered hat, would go from corporation to corporation to find a sponsor and some capital. He went to Eastman Kodak, Bell and Howell, GAF, and to the large consulting firms such as Arthur D. Little to demonstrate in a rudimentary fashion the fundamentals of xerography.

With one hand he would reach into a raincoat pocket and pull out a small piece of stainless steel. From an inside jacket pocket he would remove a piece of typewritten paper. Then he would dive a hand into another pocket and pull out a rabbit's foot. He would take the rabbit's foot and vigorously polish the little bar of stainless steel. When polished, he would reach into another pocket and pull out a small container of powder. He would sprinkle the powder on a plain piece of paper and hold it, the stainless steel, and the typewritten paper up against a light. In a few minutes the typewritten paper would be transferred to the plain piece of paper.

"This method that Mr. Carlson is showing us will never replace the mimeograph machine," said the corporate planning officers of the major office equipment manufacturers. The venerable Arthur D. Little and Company was so bold as to put their strongly worded negative appraisal in writing.

After several years of show and tell, Chester Carlson met Joseph Wilson, a young man just returned from the Korean War, whose family had just recently turned over to him the Haloid Company to manage. Haloid, a manufacturer of copy papers, had annual sales of $6 million but it was not growing. Wilson was looking for new product ideas that did not require a lot of money to develop. When Carlson dropped by with the stainless steel bar and rabbit foot show, Wilson asked his close friend and the family's attorney, Sol Linowitz, to see the demonstration with him.

Jointly they decided that if an engineering firm could build a production model of the machine to carry out the patent design, and if the machine could then be manufactured for a reasonable cost, Haloid would acquire Carlson's rights for Haloid stock and finance the product launch. A small engineering and consulting firm in Columbus, Ohio, called Battelle, agreed to take on the engineering assignment. Happily, Haloid could not pay Battelle's fee, so the engineering firm took some of its payment in stock. The rest of the story is fairly well known. As Carlson received stock worth around $100 million, Battelle became a very well-known research organization and the University of Rochester, an early investor, built the third largest endowment of any university in the country. A few corporations purchased the first few Xerox machines, which became so popular that their personnel started reproducing books, menus, birth certificates ad nauseum to the point that the early Xerox machines needed operators. Haloid changed its name to Xerox, and one of the most profitable companies in the country was launched. But, it took Chester Carlson 12 years to get the first order for the Xerox machine.

The Xerox story is significant in any discussion of launching a capital-intensive productivity-improving or cost-saving product. There is an inertia that is more powerful than the force of the argument to convert to the newer, more efficient, cheaper product. Some of the alternative energy deals require building relatively large facilities, such as windmills and turbine housings, that are unattractive, or break up the landscape, or look peculiar or out of place. Windmills on top of houses look out of place in the early 1980s, but so did cars on roads in the 1910s. The strike plate deal requires small buildings situated on or underneath corners of city streets that occupy commercial space. Some town fathers may object to this.

Back to the reality of the product concept in search of a company, the required next step for the patent is to be engineered and costed. Two questions must be answered: (1) Will it do what it says it can? and (2) Can a device be built economically to do it?

There is an industry of consulting engineers such as Battelle and A. D. Little that answers these questions routinely for industry. Usually they work on an hourly charge basis, but it is not uncommon for them to take a portion of their fee in equity. It is possible for them to estimate in advance the probable cost of the assignment and whether or not they think the results of their study will be positive. They can also project the length of time the assignment will take. Given this information, the entrepreneur has the beginnings of a PERT chart.

There is at this point too little information to decide if the public offering is advisable. It may be too little money or too much dilution—or it may be a good deal. If the engineering job is priced at $150,000 over 120 days, it may be more prudent to raise that money from friends for 15% ownership, a $1,000,000 valuation, or to negotiate a consulting fee of $100,000 plus 5% of the company and raise the $100,000 privately. A third alternative would be to negotiate the engineering firm into a partial equity fee and use their endorsement to support a better public offering valuation.

But to merely go public with a product plan that is in an early concept stage and without a PERT chart or business plan will result in a loss of everyone's money. It violates Orson Welles' marvelous Paul Masson wine ad, "We will never sell a wine before its time," a line which should be used by brokerage firms more frequently. As more and more thoughtless new businesses are foisted on the public, the new issues market will dry up and blow away. New issues markets are not killed by the new issues houses doing their $2,000,000 deals with dice-rolling investors who enjoy that form of speculation and sport. Rather, the death knell comes when the major underwriters bring public slightly more mature companies to raise $25,000,000 or more. These companies are in the steep parts of their S-curves where it is necessary that the entrepreneurs either become managers or hand over day-to-day responsibilities to managers. Failing to do this usually results in business reversals and losses. As we are constantly reminded by our losses in the venture capital business, the risk is just as great at point B as it is at point A (see Exhibit 9):

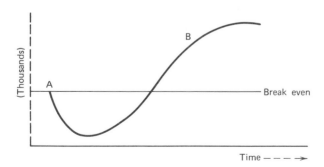

EXHIBIT 9.   The S-Curve

One final word on the alternative energy strike plate deal: entrepreneur inventors are occasionally guilty of confusing a product with a company. They are not the same. A company is formed by an entrepreneur to convey a product (solution) to a market (problem). The difference is pointed out more sharply by thinking of a company as a car and of a product as a package sitting in the back seat of the car, which is driven by a driver (entrepreneur) along a highway (business plan) to a destination (market). Some of the similes are as follows:

Car	Company
Driver	Entrepreneur
Gasoline	Capital
Tires	Salesmen
Motor	Factory
Dashboard	Accounting, finance
Package on seat	Product

Assume that the strike plate inventor is the entrepreneur and that he visits a venture capitalist for capital. Using the car example, it would be like taking the package from the back seat to a gas station and pouring gasoline on it. Now, let us assume that he incorporates and thus has a company (car). But, without a motor and tires, he has to push the car or have it towed into the gas station. The gas station attendant can then pour gasoline all over the package and all over the car. But, some of the gasoline must be used to buy a motor (production) or the car will never leave the station. The analogies can be drawn out infinitely.

I am fond of the comparison of cars with companies, because it is just simplistic enough to drive home the point that a *product* is not a company. Venture capitalists do not finance products, they finance companies.

The new issues market will finance products, disguised as companies, because it operates the same way as slot machines in Las Vegas. The new issue investor puts $1,000 into 20 different issues and *hopes* (we will come back to that word) that two or three investments will pay off in excess of 20 times. Operating on the principle of the bell-shaped curve, 10% should be winners, 10% should be losers, and 80% should break-even. See Exhibit 10.

Thus if the new issues investor risks $20,000 in 20 offerings, he anticipates $40,000 in gains from his two winners, $2,000 in losses from his two losers and break even on $16,000.

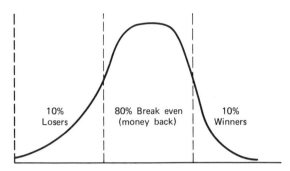

| 10% | 80% Break even | 10% |
| Losers | (money back) | Winners |

EXHIBIT 10.   Principle under which the New Issue Investor Operates

Professor James Lorie of the University of Chicago, in a project funded by Merrill Lynch, did a brilliant study of investment philosophy in 1963 which has come to be known as the "random walk" theory. The essence of the random walk theory is that an investor can do as well or better by picking stocks randomly than by receiving advice from securities analysts. In other words, if the investor throws a dart 20 times at the list of publicly traded stocks and buys the stocks in equal quantities that the darts hit, he will do as well or better than if he studied the companies before investing.

Mr. Lorie did not study the new issues market, but the random walk theory applies there as well, or perhaps better, because the alternative to throwing darts is not sufficiently available. That is, there is not much to study. Most new issues are start-ups and lack production capability, a reasonable business plan, and an experienced management team. A new issues investor can derive little satisfaction from reading the prospectuses, except to concentrate on the issues that deal with major social problems of the moment.

Whereas the new issues investor relies on emotion and psychological factors—he *hopes* that his investments will be in companies that capture other investors' fantasies—the professional venture capitalist does not rely on hope at all. Ask a hardened venture capitalist if he *hopes* he has just made a good investment in the strike plate deal and he will answer, "Hope is an emotion, and I don't deal in emotions."

A professional venture capitalist would do the strike plate deal only after going through the following steps:

1.   Have a patent attorney review the patent to determine the likelihood of defensibility.

2. Have an engineering firm review the patent to determine the feasibility of building the device.

3. Have a manufacturer of complicated capital equipment—Wheelabrator-Frye, Budd, Westinghouse, Allis-Chalmers, United Technologies, Boeing, and so on—determine the cost of manufacturing the device in quantity. Quantify energy trade-off.

4. Have city planners review the device to determine their interest in installing a device on a test basis.

5. Interview potential management team—senior level people from corporations that sell, install, and service capital items for municipalities.

6. Arrange financing through HUD (a UDAG grant) or other agency for the test and development order.

7. Divide the ownership between management, inventor, and investors.

8. Provide venture capital to pay the engineering firm, open a small office, pay salaries of managers, and build first two devices at Allis-Chalmers or on a contract basis.

9. Debug the first two installations and then generate accurate energy cost-saving figures.

10. Hire marketing personnel to begin demonstrating the device to other municipalities with the goal of obtaining enough orders to begin operations.

Naturally, a red light at any of the steps could kill the project or force the venture capitalist to take another route. One of the players could produce incorrect data along the way, which would be an expensive mistake. A deep recession could set the project back. But, by and large, the step-by-step approach to launching the strike plate deal is more likely to produce favorable results than is going straight to the new issues market for $1,500,000.

4. Q: I have started a medical instrumentation company. It has sales of $75,000 per month, and we are beginning to show profits. I need to raise about $600,000 of venture capital to expand sales, and I want to raise professional venture capital because I need a strong board and business planning advice. However, seven years ago I had to file personal bankruptcy and corporate bankruptcy in a previous venture. Will that kill my chances to raise the money?

4. A: The answer is "No," depending upon the circumstances of the bankruptcy and whether or not your debts were satisfied. Positive circumstances would include accidents such as fire, flood, or wind damage to your main plant that exceeded insurance coverage, a sudden change in a law, or extended delay in obtaining a ruling that delayed sales for many months, or perhaps the dumping of product in your market by a rapacious foreign competitor. Although a seasoned entrepreneur might have been able to circumnavigate these problems (and Monday morning quarterbacking is easy), they appear to be either surprises, accidents, or incredibly bad luck.

Negative circumstances would include the product did not work right when installed on the customer's floor, lack of competent sales personnel, inability to attract financing, or the bank got nervous and called the loan. These circumstances are in the category of bad management, and the entrepreneur would need to have shown some major achievements since the bankruptcy to overcome the bad odor of a management-caused bankruptcy.

The method of satisfying the bankruptcy has an important bearing on the worthiness of the entrepreneur to receive investors' trust once again. If all creditors were satisfied, the entrepreneur then fulfilled his obligation, and new sources of money can expect to receive fair treatment in the future. If, on the other hand, there are unsatisfied judgments, and if certain creditors are still looking to be paid seven years later, the entrepreneur may not expect better treatment from investors than he gave to his creditors. It would be pointless for the entrepreneur to attempt to raise professional venture capital once he had strewn that kind of mess all over his track.

Entrepreneurs in that predicament have a few doors shut in their faces, but not by any means are they at the bottom of a dry well. There is still the public in all of its forms: new issues investors, franchisees, or direct mail customers. Further, the SBA is slow to slam the door on an entrepeneur who has a record of failures if the new deal has great social benefits or creates many jobs.

What other things should be disclosed to an investor, and which of them are likely to kill a deal? Everything should be disclosed, because it will come out later and be more costly when it does. New issue prospectuses go back five years, so a lot of history can conceivably be quashed. But to a venture capitalist who digs and digs until he has a complete picture, it is best to assume that nothing can be hidden. Some venture capitalists use Bishops or Proudfoots, two detective agencies experienced in white collar crimes, to do a background check on an individual before investing.

This would have helped Creative Capital Corporation, the New York SBIC well known for financing a dress manufacturer run by an informer to the Justice Department who was being protected by the Federal Government with a new name, new Social Security number, and change in appearance. The entrepreneur had to be forcibly evicted when some of his decisions were leading to the company's ruin. Poor Creative had to take the write-off because the prospect of litigation was too costly and uncertain.

Another SBIC took a major write-off in 1981 after the entrepreneur it backed shot and killed another man who had insulted him in a yacht race. The SBIC officer had to spend three months running the company until a new chief executive officer could be found. The SBIC officer claims, partly in jest, that he will broaden his due diligence effort in the future to screen out potential murderers.

Husband and wife entrepreneurial teams should inform their investor beforehand as to whether their marriage is solid or shaky. If the latter, they should voluntarily develop a stock repurchase plan so that the spouse who leaves the company must sell his or her stock back to the spouse who stays at a predetermined value.

Entrepreneurs who have been convicted of felonies are pretty much frozen out of all sources of capital except franchising, friends, family, and direct mail. There are exceptions. If the entrepreneur-felon surrounds himself with a management team and board of directors composed of the proverbial "19 Bishops," he may be excused, subject to the circumstances of the crime.

An entrepreneur should in all cases reveal his true age. Ray Kroc was over 60 when he launched McDonald's, and Roy Little, the founder of Textron and dozens of other companies through Narragansett Capital Corporation, is going strong in his 80's. Youthfulness is no hindrance either. Steve Wozniak and Steve Jobs, the founders of Apple Computer Corporation were less than 26 years old when Arthur Rock invested in them. One of them is a fruitarian, hence the name "Apple."

5. Q: I think I have written a good business plan, the product sells fairly well without much marketing money—we will do $800,000 in our third year of operations—I have built a strong team, young but bright and eager. Yet every venture capitalist we go to turns us down. How can I raise venture capital?

5. A: You have to turn around the turn-downs. There is an expression in lending: "He wouldn't accept a turn-down." Some deals do not read very well and fail to impress investors and lenders, but the entrepreneur will not permit himself to be turned down. He keeps coming back with the "if-then-what" questions until he gets the money.

Avoiding the turn-down requires finding out from the least hostile and most helpful investor the precise reasons for his turn-down. Then the entrepreneur responds with, "Okay, if I jump through the hoop, what will you do?" The venture capitalist generally says, "Come back and we'll review it again."

So the entrepreneur returns and says, "I did the thing you asked me to do, now what can I do to get you to invest?" This give and take goes on and on for as many visits as necessary until the venture capitalist visits the entrepreneur's facility. At this point, he is on the entrepreneur's turf and off his own, thus less defensive and more open to the idea of investing. He can be closed, or at least give a conditional commitment.

A typical turn-down turn-around might go as follows:

Entrepreneur: Why?

Venture Capitalist: You haven't convinced me that you can sell the product, that there's a market for it. You have too much debt in the company senior to my position. You can have a deficit net worth. And I think I can make more money with other investments.

Entrepreneur: If I were to correct the things you object to to your satisfaction, would you then come out to visit the plant and meet the management team?

Venture Capitalist: Yes, but you're facing an uphill battle. I have many attractive opportunities. This is a busy time for me. And your deal is not what I'm looking for.

Entrepreneur: May I at least try to convince you? Will you take my calls as long as they are to inform you that I have corrected your objections?

Venture Capitalist: I will take your calls if that's what they're about.

Time passes, during which the entrepreneur calls his sales force and puts on a full court press to generate orders. Since the company cannot produce the orders thus generated, the entrepreneur must visit the key suppliers and ask them for more credit. If they refuse, or some of them refuse, the entrepreneur will have to go to his board or private investors and tell them that a venture capitalist has indicated a preliminary interest in investing—that is a long leap, but entrepreneurs, after all, are said to be people who record a receivable before they make a sales call—subject to certain conditions being met. The board or local investors agree to a "bridge financing," a short-term loan to accomplish a goal and to be repaid when the goal is achieved. Sometimes bridge financing becomes permanent capital, which demonstrates far greater faith in the company.

With $100,000 in bridge financing, the entrepreneur can comfortably reach out for more orders, run some advertising even, and move sales up to a higher plateau. After a few months of higher sales one or two suppliers may agree to extend more credit, which has the effect of allowing sales to grow to a still higher level. It is time to call the venture capitalist.

Entrepreneur: We have taken sales from $200,000 per month when I was in your office to $450,000 per month. I can maintain this level, but I cannot go higher.

Venture Capitalist: How did you increase sales?

Entrepreneur: My board plus two outside investors bought $100,000 of subordinated notes which the company can call at 150% of face value after one year. They have the right to put at the same price. Or they can convert the $100,000 into 5% of the company's stock. We then got two suppliers to raise their credit limits from $100,000 to $150,000. Several other suppliers have agreed to go out to 75 days from 60 days, which allows us to work with their money. We put new people into our receivables department who have brought average receivables days down from 52 to 36, so we're turning our cash faster. I cannot improve on receivables or supplier terms more than this. I can get sales up another 7.5% when we raise prices next month, but without long-term capital, we're stopped at this point.

Venture Capitalist: Sounds like you're on the right track. Where did the sales growth come from?

Entrepreneur: We opened several new markets with reps: the Northeast, Northern Middle West, and Pacific Northwest. We hired regional sales managers for these territories and trained the reps. The sales managers were given low bases and 10% overrides on the first $500,000 of new sales and 5% thereafter. The reps have standard commissions plus premiums for meeting goals, such as a trip to Hawaii. In our traditional markets, we have offered regular customers sharper discounts for volume orders and set up a series of premiums for the salesmen and reps there as well, with the top prizes of two Super Bowl tickets and a week in Mexico City. We began running national ads in five monthly trade magazines, and we took a larger booth at one of the regional trade shows.

Venture Capitalist: It seems to be working. Send me a list of customers with telephone numbers. I want to find out why they're buying.

Entrepreneur: Okay, and I'll send along about 20 product endorsements that we've gotten recently, as well as a comparison study done by one of the trade magazines that shows how we compare with the competition.

Venture Capitalist: How are you doing with the debt problem and the deficit net worth?

Let us assume that the company had cumulative losses of $1,000,000 and a $1,200,000 FmHA guaranteed term loan secured by plant and equipment as well as a line of credit from a commercial finance company secured by accounts receivable and inventory. Its balance sheet looks something like Exhibit 11.

The balance sheet portrays a company at the bottom but near the vertical portion of its S-curve, starved for expansion capital. To convince the venture capitalist to climb aboard, the entrepreneur has to eliminate the deficit and retire some senior debt. We assume that the company has been delinquent on its interest and principal payments to the FmHA. That is the logical place to discuss a refinancing.

The entrepreneur visits the FmHA and the bank and explains that the likelihood of the company becoming current on interest and principal is slim unless it can take in venture capital. In fact, a venture capitalist made that clear to the company after 30 others had turned down the deal out of hand.

The entrepreneur proposes that the FmHA and bank release the collateral to enable the company to do a sale and leaseback to an affiliated company. The company will then give the FmHA $600,000, or 50%, of its loan in cash and the remainder on a 15-year 2% sales royalty. The balance sheet effect, if the plant and equipment are sold for $900,000, is a $600,000 forgiveness of debt and a $300,000 injection of capital by the stockholders, seen in Exhibit 12.

EXHIBIT 11.   Balance Sheet Before Workout Financing

Assets			Liabilities and net worth		
Cash	$ 27,500		Accounts payable, accruals		$ 238,000
Accounts receivable	175,000		Notes payable		240,000
Inventories	342,000		Current portion long-term debt		200,000
Prepaid deposits	40,500				
Total current assets	585,000		Total current liabilities		678,000
Net plant, equipment	350,500		20-year term loan guaranteed by FMHA		1,000,000
Other assets	7,000				
			Investors subordinated debt		100,000
			Total liabilities		1,778,000
			Capital stock		175,000
			Accumulated deficit		(1,010,500)
			Stockholder's equity		(835,500)
			Total liabilities and		
Total assets	$ 942,500		stockholders' equity		$ 942,500

EXHIBIT 12. Balance Sheet After Workout Financing

Assets		Liabilities and Net Worth	
Cash	$ 327,500	Accounts payable, accruals	$ 238,000
Accounts receivable	175,000	Notes payable	240,000
Inventories	342,000		
Prepaid deposits	40,500		
Total current assets	885,000	Total current liabilities	478,000
Other assets	7,000	Investors subordinated debt	100,000
		Total liabilities	578,000
		Capital stock	475,000
		Accumulated deficit	(410,500)
		Stockholder's equity	315,000
Total Assets	$ 892,000	Total liabilities and stockholders' equity	$ 892,000

The entrepreneur must be extremely persuasive to the Government and the lead bank. They are not in the business of taking write-offs gratuitously. However, they respect the numbers, and in this case the numbers show that the company cannot pay off their loan without venture capital, which will not come into the company unless they agree to get off the balance sheet in a manner that adds to net worth. The entrepreneur returns to the venture capitalist and shows what he has done.

Venture Capitalist: I'll invest $600,000 if the bridge money converts.

Entrepreneur: We've gotten this far. I'm sure they'll agree to do it.

6. Q: My company was formed three years ago when I left the telephone company where I was a staff engineer for 10 years. My department had ordered a microcomputer and I got excited about it because it was as powerful as some of our mainframes. I felt that I could build a company using microcomputers.

Two friends in the retail business each invested $15,000 and so did I. We opened a personal computer store and began selling product and servicing our customers, as well as performing contract service work for a variety of manufacturers not carried in the store. I began taking on some data communications consulting work because of my telecommunications experience. A third division was formed to develop applications software for the ABC microcomputer, and this has led to our developing product for plumbing supply houses and building contractors. We also have a medical package.

We opened two more stores this year, but they did not come on stream fast enough, so we ran out of cash. The bank has gone to $75,000 secured by all of our assets and our personal signatures, but it will not advance any more.

Our operating statement for the fiscal year just ending in December 1981 is as follows:

	Percentage	Dollars (Thousands)
Revenues		
Retail stores—product	35.9	$ 575
—service	5.3	85
Telecomm. consulting	18.2	290
Systems integration	38.6	618
Other	2.0	32

	Percentage	Dollars (Thousands)
Total Revenues	100.0	1,600
Cost of goods sold	60.0	960
Gross profit	40.0	640
Selling expenses	7.5	120
Research engineering	5.8	92
General administrative	21.9	350
Net operating income	4.9	78
Interest expense	0.8	14
Net profit before taxes	4.1	$ 64

Our sales grew from $950,000 in our second year to $1,600,000 (nearly double), but our growth is stopped without more capital. I prepared a business plan and showed it to a few venture capitalists, but they all turned me down. If companies with huge losses in dull industries can raise capital, why can't I? What is wrong with our story?

6. A: The primary reason that you cannot attract venture capital is your lack of focus. The divisions do not relate to one another synergistically, although they make sense to you because you know a bit about each area. You have created a business that reflects your skills and interests, but that is as far as it goes.

So what if you raise $500,000? In another two years you will have grown to 10 stores and still be consulting and selling into a variety of vertical markets. You will have grown a small hodgepodge into a bigger hodgepodge. It will still lack focus.

Venture capitalists do not invest unless they can see their way out in five years. How would they get out of your company? The public does not like small conglomerates. A large corporation would be unlikely to acquire a company with three small divisions that have little relationship to one another. The revenue breakdown alone will scare off most investors because it shows a company running loose in three areas without a focus.

The solution is simple: sell the divisions with the lowest return on capital investment, reduce the costs of administering this octopus, and put all your energies and capital in the remaining division. Vertical market software has attracted high multiples in the public market because of the proprietary nature of the product. Many venture capitalists would prefer to see you exclusively in that business. The consulting activity may suit you personally and give you satisfaction, but it does very little for investors. "The assets go home at 5:00 p.m. in the consulting business," is the old saw. They may not come back in the morning.

The computer retail chain business is getting crowded, and that means that profits will begin to get thin. If you could grow it to 30–50 stores very quickly and make a serious dent in that market, it would be worth the shot. But having a few stores has got to be more trouble than its worth, and, moreover, eats up a lot of management time. You would probably be better off selling the stores.

You might sell the stores for inventory value plus 20% plus some administrative savings. The consulting business probably cannot be sold because the contracts are fairly personal, but it can be stopped and the contracts not renewed.

Then you can focus all of your energies in one direction, select one or two exciting vertical markets that need solutions for inventory control or list management and design a line of exceptional products for them. Within six months, you will have the investors knocking on your door.

7. Q: I have developed a practical and effective method of stress avoidance, and, rather than write a book about it, I would like to start a business to reach a lot of people with the method. Although I see it as a potentially exciting business, how do I finance it?

7. A: You have described a perfect example of the "service start-up," a generic kind of business that practically nobody wants to finance. The reasons are several: the product is intangible; the principal asset is in your brain; the other assets are people, and they can leave you without notice; and the product is nonproprietary, others can copy you with a better or less expensive product. These are the principal reasons, and then there are the normal areas of concern: Does it work? Can it be sold? Can it be sold profitably?

But service companies do get launched and some of them do amazingly well. Arthur Murray Dance Studios, Weight Watchers International, Century 21, Smoke-Enders, EST, Evelyn Woods Reading Dynamics, and a host of others. In each case the demand for the service had to be educated, and that requires large sums of advertising dollars. Note one of the newer service start-ups, the legal clinic, and the vast number of dollars spent on television advertising by the clinics. Relative to many manufacturing businesses, it generally takes more money to launch a service start-up. The entrepreneur must believe fervently in the value of his service because it takes more time and more capital to start a service company than any other kind of business. The entrepreneur can expect to own less of the company as a result.

There are some shortcuts, but not many. One is to obtain the endorsement of a famous person and market the service with the person's imprimatur. The Arthur Murray Dance Studio is an excellent example. There have been a number of failures where entertainers lent their names to businesses, but there is no causal relationship. Jerry Lewis Theaters did not succeed, neither did the Roger Williams piano schools. The Eddie Arnold fried chicken chain was a bust, as was Minnie Pearl's, Leroy Keyes', and Muhammad Ali's burger chains. Finding the correct endorsement can be difficult and time-consuming. It is necessary for the entrepreneur and the celebrity to develop a formula or system in concert so that the celebrity's ideas are involved and the entrepreneur can move ahead confidently knowing that the celebrity is behind him fully and completely.

For stress avoidance, it would be necessary to obtain the endorsement or the right to use the name of a well-known medical doctor or health and nutrition enthusiast with a high rate of national identification. A perusal of the health and nutrition books at any bookstore will produce numerous ideas. The entrepreneur should then explore the several candidates' philosophies, ideas, and formulas for better health, fewer anxieties, and less stress. There are a number of stress "gurus," but their names are simply not household words.

The entrepreneur must then arrange to meet with the celebrity and to negotiate a contract. This is usually in the form of a license to use the person's name in association with a certain system or package of services in a specified geographical territory for a certain number of years. A long time period, a broad territory, and unlimited services and products are in the entrepreneur's best interests. The celebrity may not be willing to go along with the blanket use of his name in an unlimited manner for an indefinite time. A relationship such as this requires a good deal of faith and trust. One of the more successful such arrangements has been the marketing of Charles Goren's name throughout the world by a bridge instruction and publishing company. The most successful business that bears the Goren endorsement is the cruise business. People who take cruises enjoy playing bridge and receiving instruction to improve their games. One of the nice features of the cruise business is that the customers pay in advance, thus providing most of the financing. The capital can be invested in bridge books and bridge table paraphernalia.

With or without the celebrity in tow, the most important factor in launching a service company is to determine the method of delivering the service. This will determine the source of financing. One of the fascinating aspects of Weight Watchers, EST, Smoke-Enders, and Arthur Murray Dance Studios is that the customer is asked to make the capital investment. He or she has to go to a place where the service is performed, pay an admission charge, and then participate in the service. Getting there requires transportation (capital) and fuel (energy). Payment for the service (labor) is essentially an advance payment prior to observing the efficiency of the service.

One of the more obvious examples of getting the customer to finance substantially all of the costs of a business is Lion Country Safari. Rather than keeping the animals in cages, as is done in zoos, which by the way are free, Lion Country Safari lets its animals roam free. The customer is in the cage (car), hence absorbs the capital cost of the plant and equipment. The car requires fuel (the utilities), which further reduces fixed overhead. Lion Country had to buy the land and the animals, but the locations selected are normally undesirable for commercial use, and the animals reproduce. Lion Country and its copiers provide an excellent example of customer financing to launch a service business.

For a service such as stress avoidance, where the principal market is corporate executives, the sell is probably to the corporation, who then offers the program to their executives. It is probably advisable, as well, to provide the service off the corporation's premises, since the corporation is the protagonist. Thus a neutral space such as a motel conference room is a more suitable location, or, alternatively, a conference center set in a rural area. The nicer the setting, the more capital is required.

The Pritikin Better Health Program, a fitness and diet advisory service priced at approximately $200 per seminar, is offered in hotel conference rooms and church social halls. Break even occurs at a relatively low revenue level, and the profits are reinvested in more advertising to increase the number of seminars. Usually some attendees are professionals who seek to purchase territorial licenses in their markets. This leads to the second source of financing for service start-ups: licensing. Selling marketing licenses to a service in a region that the entrepreneur had not considered moving into for awhile is an excellent source of financing. It requires careful documentation of the program to make certain that the service in one market will reflect that in another market. Licensing requires field supervision and training as well, but the entrepreneur can provide that the licensee must pay an ongoing service fee after he purchases the license. The selection and training of the people providing the service is the key. Advertising must be of a consistently high standard. Materials given or sold to customers must be consistent and of a high quality, as well. With these labor and capital costs, the first license sold may pay for the establishment of standards and the hiring of supervisors and trainers. Future licensees will produce profits.

To stabilize revenues from seminars, the parent organization should think of ancillary markets. The first thought is to offer take-home products for the seminar attendees. But there is a limit, perhaps $20, to what an attendee might buy at a seminar. The ancillary markets, then, should be nonattendees and might include products for corporations, such as training tapes, or documentaries of live seminars sold to network and cable television. Then there are the tried and true standby markets: books, newsletters, and cassettes.

The point of this elaborate discussion of service start-ups is to avoid conventional venture capitalists when launching a service company. It is less expensive and time-consuming to raise money from customers and licensees. Once the service company operates smoothly, it can seek conventional financing if additional capital is required.

8. Q: How many venture capital companies should I approach with my business plan, and am I required to tell them, if they ask, the names of the others funds that I am talking to?

8. A: It is best to approach at least 12 venture capital funds with the business plan and to meet with as many of them as possible. Unless your company has extremely unusual features, it is unlikely that any of the 12 funds will visit you at your plant after reading the business plan. If some of them do have the first meeting at your plant, then you can assume that your deal is a high priority situation.

More than likely, however, you will have to arrange the first meeting at their office. Venture capitalists are extremely busy but occasionally are in their offices with an hour or two free to hear a presentation. It is essential to have a meeting within 30 days after sending out the business plan, or the deal will get further down in the stack and be quietly forgotten.

It is unlikely that all 12 venture capital funds will be interested in the same deal. Thus, the 12 venture capital funds you select should be chosen as the most likely candidates to invest, based on the following criteria:

1. No competitive companies in their portfolios.
2. Ample capital to invest.
3. Sufficient manpower and time to consider the investment and to work on it.

There are several ways to determine the most likely venture capital funds to contact. The simplest is to ask them on the telephone when calling, prior to submitting the business plan. This is an extremely important step. An investor *must* be qualified before delivering a business plan. To do otherwise is to waste your time, because business plans mailed in blind are usually not read. Most venture capitalists feel that if an entrepreneur treats the issue of raising money that casually, he is likely to treat other business matters, such as marketing or hiring, equally as casually. It reflects poorly on the maturity and seriousness of the entrepreneur.

The second method of qualifying the interest and affinity of investors is to use the services of an investment banker or finder. The cost of this service is generally a consulting fee plus a closing fee, the total equalling perhaps 4 or 5% of the funds to be raised. The savings is in time, or more properly called "the cost of search."

The third method is to ask another entrepreneur how he raised venture capital and from whom. His introduction to his source of capital might result in one-stop-shopping; or if you get a turn-down, you can ask for their recommendations of likely investors.

Finally, there are directories of venture capitalists which are fairly up-to-date for a year or so. But new funds are formed with some frequency, and venture capitalists move around, so the directories tend to become obsolete fairly quickly. A one-year-old directory is at least 20% obsolete and inaccurate.

Assuming that you can find 12 interested venture capital funds and that they have been qualified and sent a business plan, you should then arrange to meet with as many of them as possible. It is important at these meetings to amplify and explain the strong points of the business plan. It is equally important to listen carefully to the questions you are asked. If the same questions come up again and again, then the business plan has probably failed to be explicit in that area, or the business plan is flawed and needs reworking. Thus, by going only to 12 candidates with the first plan, you have not burned all of your bridges. A revised and improved business plan can be sent around to 12 new candidates, and the process repeated perhaps this time with greater success.

If the venture capitalists ask you to name other funds that you have been to, there is no requirement to provide this information. The venture capitalist could be thinking in terms of putting together a syndicate or merely of sharing information with another venture capitalist. He may be thinking about following the lead of another venture capitalist. The professional venture capital industry operates in syndicate fashion. Rare is the fund that invests alone all of the time. Competent venture capitalists like to have other investment managers share in the analysis and investigation to minimize the risk that they may have overlooked something. They also like to share the investment to have someone they trust share the monitoring responsibility.

A proper answer is to say that you are speaking with several other funds and then to ask if there is anyone in particular whom they might suggest seeing. You should name one or two other funds, if pressed, to see if they register as suitable syndicate partners. There is less to be gained by being obtuse or defensive at this stage of seeking venture capital.

9. Q: Professional venture capitalists herald the fact that they provide a company with more than money. They claim that they provide management assistance, advice, and other services. Is this true, and, if true, is it consistently true from one venture capitalist to another?

9. A: Yes it is true, but it is not true for all venture capital firms. In fact, one of the primary reasons to obtain professional venture capital, rather than an SBA-guaranteed loan, a public offering, or a tax shelter, is to get help in managing the company. For an entrepreneur who thinks he does not need help, ask him to list the corporate success stories whose first round of capital came from the public. They are very few and far between.

Perhaps it is merely a trend, soon to vanish, but the entrepreneurial team is very much *de rigueur* in the early 1980s. Whereas in earlier decades investors were content to put garlands of dollars around the shoulders of a bright entrepreneur or innovative scientist and visit with him monthly or quarterly to monitor his performance, this method of operating is now considered hopelessly obsolete. Today's entrepreneur is more inclined to tell his investors: "Look chaps, I'm the most important resource that the company has and the last thing I need is for you to preoccupy me with questions about the company. If you want to visit the company occasionally, then you should plan to interface with members of middle management who can benefit from your advice and suggestions."

It is not the case that all venture capital funds provide constructive assistance to entrepreneurs. Many SBICs have been guilty of doing just the opposite: saddling the entrepreneur with numerous directors' meetings, directors' fees and expenses, and frequent telephone calls to the president to ask about various items on the financial statement. There is less of this going on than before because entrepreneurs are refusing to put up with it. But the fact still remains that SBICs pay a high rate of interest for the money they invest, and they loan it at higher rates of interest and occasionally tack on other charges to make a profit. They demand information from the company president because their board demands information from them. These SBICs do not perform as well over the long run as do the venture capital funds that provide constructive monitoring. However, close attention and frequent visits are very helpful in preserving capital.

The venture capital funds that are known for constructive monitoring have made a science of the company-launching business in an arena where only art once persisted. They surround the entrepreneur with a blanket of assistance drawing on resources that would be the envy of a large corporation.

For the entrepreneur-scientist whom they agree to back, they provide a chief executive officer (CEO) with company-launching experience in a similar or related industry. The entrepreneur is normally presented with several candidates from which to choose and selects the most compatible. They develop a business plan in concert that usually expands on the entrepreneur's product, broadens the line, vertically integrates it into more of a system, and usually includes the development of related products. The entrepreneur is usually delighted with the opportunity to be in charge of the product and future products and free of marketing, finance, personnel, and administrative duties.

The start-up experienced venture capitalists attempt to reduce the "management risk" by removing the entrepreneur from management. The Silicon Valley venture capital funds have become particularly adept at this. Usually, in cases where they are the investor, if the entrepreneur lacks company-launching experience they provide someone with that experience. There are a flock of company-launch entrepreneurs, particularly in the West, who some venture capitalists call on to manage a start-up for one year until someone else is found for the intermediate growth stage. The first person might be strong on planning, and the second might be strong on marketing. There may be another CEO after that whose long suit is finance and organization. This may sound like overweaning and the use of velvet handcuffs on the wrists of the entrepreneur. But in those instances where the product is outstanding and the market is enormous but the entrepreneur cannot be left in charge, this kind of overprotection seems to work.

The success story of Apple Computer Corporation owes quite a bit to this kind of careful selection of business managers to support the two entrepreneur-engineers, Steve Wosniak and Steve Jobs.

A variation on this theme is to incubate the entrepreneur for a year by giving him a desk at the venture capital firm and allowing him to review dozens of business plans. At the end of the entrepreneur training period, he is ready to write his business plan and begin selecting people, product lines, facilities, and the other necessary components, all with the input, advice, and assistance of the venture capital firm. This method is occasionally used when the entrepreneur-engineer shows management capabilities and instincts and would like to take a crack at being the company's CEO. Jim Treybig, the founder of Tandem Computer, was trained at the venture capital firm of Kleiner, Perkins prior to their investing. Bob Swanson, the CEO of Genentech, a successful biotechnology firm, was also trained at Kleiner, Perkins.

The classical entrepreneurial team is made up of two people: both are bright, but one is full of ideas and creative, innovative thoughts which he wants to implement and the other is more of a plodder, a more thorough person, an "i" dotter and a "t" crosser. The bright-innovative and the bright-thorough work hand-in-glove because the innovative one needs the thorough one to complete the things he begins and the thorough one needs the innovative one to initiate things for him to complete. This can be shown in the following example.

Two friends decide they will take a photographic safari to Africa. One of them buys a beautiful safari suit, scarf, expensive boots, and boards the plane to Kenya. The other shows up with a tent on his back, three cameras around his neck, shovel, ax, hammer, and first aid kit around his waist, two suitcases, and a duffle bag. They arrive in Africa and drive to the bush country and pick a site to pitch the tent. The well-dressed fellow hops out and says, "Why don't you put up the tent while I check out the area."

So he walks into the jungle and before long, he bumps into a ferocious lion. The lion chases him around a few trees, and the fellow heads straight back to the campsite with the lion in hot pursuit. The tent is up, and he bursts into the tent where his friend is working, swings around the pole with the lion on his tail, and shoots back out the front door. He looks over his shoulder and yells at his friend, "This one's for you. I'll go get one for me."

These two, if they survive the lion, will make a perfect entrepreneurial team. They enjoy the different launch challenges and support each other well. For the sole entrepreneur who begins a company without a bright-thorough partner, it has become increasingly the duty of the venture capitalist to find him that partner. It has taken the venture capital community several decades of learning how to launch companies to realize that pouring capital on a scientist or engineer does not mean you will grow a Henry Singleton or Bob Noyce.

Like other venture capitalists, I had to learn this the hard way also. I assembled $325,000 about nine years ago to back an entrepreneur who wanted to start a distribution company. A chief administrative officer was located within 90 days after the investment, so I felt that the financial records and production would be properly handled. The entrepreneur was marketing and sales oriented, particularly good at motivating people, from customers to salespeople to investors. His personality dominated that of the chief financial officer.

I would call the entrepreneur once a month for backlog information, sales results, expenses, and so forth. That was mistake one and mistake two. I would believe the numbers that I received—mistake three. I would relax and be pleased that things were going so smoothly—mistake four.

In the first place I should not have been calling the president for financial information. He was the company's most valuable resource, and I was occupying his time. Second, I should have been calling the chief financial officer to make sure he was keeping records, to get more accurate records, and to increase his importance in the company relative to the spotlight-stealing president.

The sales and backlog figures that the president would give me were a joke. He would book as a receivable the amount of goods he thought he might sell at a meeting he thought he might get. He was not lying;

rather, his self-confidence knew no limits. Whereas sales should have been the amount of shipments, his number for sales was always a projection. Thus, whereas I thought the company was doing well, it was really floundering. Fortunately, the entrepreneur's wife came up with an alternative business plan that was easy to implement without money, and it saved our skins. The company has grown to become one of the largest party-plan sales companies in the country.

It would have started differently this year from a decade ago. Assuming the entrepreneur sought professional venture capital and the venture capitalist liked the business concept, the business plan and the entrepreneur would be examined by another member of the firm and then by a marketing consultant. Questions would have been asked over and over. Similar companies such as Mary Kay, Shaklee, and Tupperware would have been studied. The estimates in the new company's business plan would be compared to the actual results at the existing companies. Cash flows and key operating ratios would be compared. The business plan would probably be adjusted to take into consideration lower gross profit margins, higher selling expenses, and a lower sales ramp.

Then the venture capitalist would present a plan to the entrepreneur involving funding the company with more money and attracting a chief operating officer from the industry to support the entrepreneur—a "bright-thorough." He would be given incentives with some founder's stock plus a stock option. The entrepreneur would keep 40% of the stock, the venture capitalists would receive 40% for their investment, and 20% would be divided between the chief operating officer (about 10%) and a reserve for future key employees (10%). The entrepreneur would receive two board seats, the chief operating officer one, the venture capitalists one, and the fifth board seat would go to a successful business executive from a related industry who would be approved by the venture capitalist and the entrepreneur. He might take a portion of the venture capitalist's investment to give him an equity incentive in proportion to everyone else.

The systematically launched company might not do as well as the haphazardly launched company, but most of the start-up risks would have been addressed intelligently. Sales projections, at least, would not be booked as receivables.

There are quite a few entrepreneurs who would resist this kind of structuring of their lives. After all, they are leaving the tightly structured corporate world behind when they start a new company.

10. Q: Can you describe the characteristics of an entrepreneur who would be the most likely to receive professional venture capital, other things being equal?

10. A: The universe of entrepreneurs seeking venture capital forms a pyramid. Sixty percent of the entrepreneurs who seek venture capital are blatantly incompetent and need to learn about managing a small business. They form the largest group. They are creative, energetic, bright, and driven, but they lack a sense of priority and the judgment that is so essential to launching a business. These entrepreneurs form the base of the pyramid. Some of them will learn by attending seminars, reading books, obtaining a mentor, actually raising money, and getting knocked around or, perhaps, going to work for a small company and having a variety of responsibilities.

The second largest group of entrepreneurs, say 20% of the universe, have a management background or a partner with management experience, but they have never been involved in launching a business. They have not demonstrated judgment in hiring people, getting a product to market, implementing a marketing plan, or any of the steps essential to grow a small business.

The next group, perhaps 15% of the universe of entrepreneurs, have gained management experience or have a partner with those tools. This entrepreneur has been employed at a small or rapidly growing company, has seen some of the steps necessary to get a product into the market, but has been one step removed from making the judgement calls. Perhaps he has knowledge in two of the four key areas—marketing, production, engineering, and finance—administration—but not in all four. He will need strong team players or a venture capital firm willing to help him find partners or members. He has earned a salary all of his working life, had no equity in the company he worked for, and his principal asset is his house. To develop his prototype he has either raised some family or friendly money or borrowed against the house. In any event, very little of his own money is in the company, yet he has begun advertising the product and has an excellent response—but no dollars to fill orders with. He is up against a time clock because his marketing plan is too far out in front of his ability to produce. Thus, although he has demonstrated drive, ambition, and a popular product, he has shown management weaknesses in not being able to deliver product. If given venture capital, the key decisions will probably have to be taken away from him until he learns how to disengage his sales effort until his production effort gets into gear.

The smallest group of entrepreneurs in the universe, representing 5% or so, are the most popular with venture capitalists. They have been deeply involved in a previous launch, either entrepreneurially or as the first or second employee hired. They know (the judgment issue) to fill the key positions of marketing, production, engineering, and finance/administration with proven managers who have also been involved with other start-ups. They understand that there will be several rounds of financing and that after incentives to all the key people, the venture capitalists take their bite, and the second round is completed they will be fortunate to still own 20% of the company. This group of entrepreneurs made a capital gain on the stock of the first company they helped launch and are willing to invest a substantial portion of that money in the new company. They have tied down all the loose ends, from having their financial statements audited to preparing a "Welcome to Our Company" brochure for new employees. Their business plan could not be written better if they hired McKinsey and Company to do it, and all of the key managers have positive track records, two dozen outstanding references from superiors, peers, and subordinates as well as some of their money in the deal. Venture capitalists froth for entrepreneurs like this.

The pyramid of the universe of entrepreneurs is shown in Exhibit 13.

Over time, some of the D entrepreneurs move up to C, and C to B, and so forth. But at a point in time, there are too few A entrepreneurs to go around. Or, other things are *not* equal, and an A entrepreneur has selected a weak product or market and must be turned down. Or a B entrepreneur has selected an excellent product or market, but needs the kind of time-consuming monitoring that we discussed above. Thus only some A entrepreneurs are selected, and a few B's, and a small number of C entrepreneurs—with lots of support and monitoring.

My own hypothesis of why new issue markets collapse is that quality underwriters become so eager to get into the excitement of launching new Intels and Xeroxes that they take public companies run by C and D entrepreneurs. Nothing turns off stock market investors more quickly than quality investment bankers putting their names on companies that are not ready to receive capital. Morgan Stanley, a blue chip underwriter, once took public a small software company called Computer Usage Corporation, which promptly went "South." If a small, inexperi-

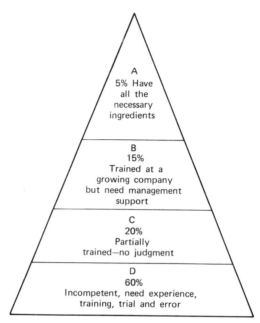

EXHIBIT 13.   The Universe of Entrepreneurs

enced underwriter had taken this company public, the market would not have been aghast. But firms like Morgan Stanley are supposed to have judgment and experience and sufficient profits from steel, oil, and airline clients not to require the fees from a small new issue.

The experienced, professional and well-funded venture capital firms attract the A entrepreneurs. These entrepreneurs know who the top venture capitalists are and vice versa. As the venture capital industry matures, the uncertainty that used to exist in raising capital becomes less and less, and A and B entrepreneurs have an easier time finding the kind and amount of venture capital that they seek. It is greed and mistakes in judgment that lead some venture capitalists, investment bankers, and new issue investors into the C and D areas of the pyramid to find investment opportunities.

11. Q: I have been in several negotiations to make leveraged buy-outs, but in the middle of the deal, it seems that the seller usually gets a better offer from another buyer and I lose out. Are there any tried and true formulas to help me complete these acquisitions?

11. A: There are several dangers in doing leveraged buy-outs, including taking a lot of personal financial risk to own a zero net worth business that someone else has discarded. But, assuming that your nerve endings can live with the risk of leverage, the principal danger in doing a leveraged buy-out is losing the deal to a more qualified buyer. The solution to this particular problem is to move quickly and professionally.

It is important to remember that in an entrepreneurial leveraged buy-out, the sellers are quite nervous about the ability of the entrepreneur to meet obligations. After all, they ran the business and they know all the trouble it can be. To offset this concern, which can be substantial enough to break a deal, the entrepreneur should have a professional team at all meetings with the seller, dispatching them to do their part of the deal as required. The team members should include an attorney, accountant, investment banker, and marketing consultant. By delegating critical functions to these team members, the entrepreneur can move more quickly and the seller is more confident about the stability and management depth of the buyer. For smaller deals, the entrepreneur needs fewer team members. But for divisional spinoffs of large corporations, all of the team members must be very strong. In a leveraged buy-out of a $26 million division of a $15 billion (sales) manufacturer for which I acted as investment banker in 1980, even the venture capital fund that put up $6 million was thoroughly investigated by the seller. Never take too casually the importance that a seller places on maintaining a quality image for the division that is being spun off.

Let us review the sequence of events and then consider how to compress the events to complete the acquisition in the shortest possible time.

1. Examination of financial statements to determine if the assets exist to use leverage and if the income is sufficient to support leverage.

2. Examination of the company's product and market to determine if the company's prospects are attractive.

3. Offer to seller.

4. Offer negotiated and/or accepted and a date set for closing. Permission granted by seller for in-depth investigations and audits.
5. In-depth investigations and audits.
6. Closing date.

The first step can be done in a few minutes on the legendary back of an envelope. The second step, examining the company's products and markets, requires one to two weeks. Investigation of future prospects for the market requires reading industry studies and brokerage house research reports as well as speaking with analysts who follow the industry. Investigation of the company's products requires talking with customers, former customers, noncustomers, and people with industry relationships and experience such as leasing companies (if the product is a leased item) and officers or former officers of competitive companies. The information gathered during the first two steps provides the purchaser with an idea of how much the company is worth and the assets and liabilities that he may choose to include or exclude in making the offer.

The third step—the offer—is usually the most critical step in the buy-out process. The offer, or Letter of Intent as it is frequently called, must include a sufficiently attractive package of price and terms of payment to interest the seller and convince him to take the company off the market, while providing the purchaser with enough "outs" should some "horribles" appear during the audit phase of the buy-out (Step 5).

Let us go through a sample letter of intent on the next few pages that provides the seller a "firm deal," that is, the purchaser cannot claim lack of financing or uncover some "horribles" and try to weasel out while permitting the purchaser to drop the price (primarily the cash portion of the price) if a significant portion of the inventory is found to be obsolete during the audit phase (Step 5). As you can well imagine, there are certain instances in which the seller thinks his inventory is "Southern Fried Chicken" while the purchaser thinks it is chicken feed. A compromise in this type of situation is for the seller to keep it and have the purchaser sell it on consignment for the seller. If it does not turn over within a year or so, the purchaser can buy it for a few cents on the dollar price. If it turns over, the purchaser presumably has received his costs plus a profit.

A Letter of Intent appears as follows in its entirety, with analysis and commentary following:

LETTER OF INTENT
TO CORPORATE SELLER
FROM ENTREPRENEURIAL PURCHASER

DATE

Mr. President
Seller Corporation
Street Road
City, State

Dear Mr. President:

The purpose of this letter is to summarize and evidence our discussions relative to the proposed transaction whereby Purchaser Corporation, a State corporation ("Purchaser") shall acquire from Seller Corporation ("Seller") substantially all of the assets of Seller Subsidiary, Inc. ("SSI"). The objective of our discussions has been the expeditious execution and consummation of a definitive Purchase Agreement (the "Agreement") which, among other things, would provide for the various matters set forth below. This letter does not constitute a binding agreement on any of the parties. The respective rights and obligations of the parties remain to be defined in the Agreement which will entirely supersede this Letter; provided, however, that the respective obligations of the Seller and SSI under paragraph 11 shall be binding upon them when signed and delivered by them to Purchaser. If the Agreement is not executed on or before PA Signing Date, then the parties hereto will be deemed, unless otherwise agreed, to have abandoned any intent to complete the Agreement.

1. Purchaser will purchase from Seller substantially all of the assets, subject to current liabilities, franchises and business of SSI as a going concern as of Latest Financial Statement Date such assets ("Transferred Assets") to include but not be limited to the following: accounts receivable, inventory, customer lists, research data, contracts, prepaid expenses, patents, formulas, trademarks and tradename(s), copyrights and goodwill associated therewith, equipment, leasehold improvements, furniture, and fixtures. Excluded from the Transferred Assets being purchased are all capitalized corporate allocations of the Seller that are not applicable to the ongoing business of SSI.

2. At Closing, Purchaser will pay to Seller a price of Three Million Five Hundred Thousand and no/100 ($3,500,000.00) Dollars of which One Million Five Hundred Thousand and no/100 ($1,500,000.00) Dollars will be in cash, One Million Two Hundred-Fifty Thousand and no/100 ($1,250, 000.00) Dollars will be in the form of a five percent (5%) royalty on sales for a term of five years payable annually, no later than 90 days following Purchaser's fiscal year end and Seven Hundred Fifty Thousand and no/100 ($750,000.00) Dollars will be in the form of

a five year unsecured subordinated note bearing interest at the rate of ten percent (10%) per annum and repayable in three equal annual installments beginning three years after Closing Date.

The accounts receivable, inventory, and equipment shall be certified by Seller's independent public accountants as of 30 days prior to Closing Date. In the event that the sum of the audited net book value of the accounts receivable, inventories, and equipment of SSI as of the Closing Date is less than the sum of the net book value of those assets as of Latest Financial Statement Date, as set forth below, the price will be reduced proportionately. As of the Latest Financial Statement Date, Transferred Assets and related liabilities have been represented to be approximately as follows: accounts receivable of $870,000.00, prepaid expenses of $20,000.00, inventories of $3,738,000.00, net fixed assets of $160,000.00, accounts payable of $235,000.00, accrued payables of $66,000.00, employee withholdings of $11,000.00, accrued payroll and taxes of $119,000.00, other accrued expenses of $23,000.00. In addition, Purchaser may decline to purchase certain items of inventory which it determines have no immediate commercial value to it, in which event the net book value of those items will be deducted from the purchase price. Such deductions to be applied first to the cash portion of the purchase price up to Five Hundred Thousand and no/100 ($500,000.00) Dollars and then to the royalty portion of the purchase price up to Two Hundred Fifty Thousand and no/100 ($250,000.00) Dollars.

The balance sheet shall be prepared in accordance with generally accepted accounting principles, consistently applied following those practices of the Seller used in preparing year-end statements heretofore.

Purchaser will assume the existing lease on the SSI facility at Street Road, City, State.

Purchaser will assume no liabilities for payments to the employees pension plan.

3. Purchaser will assume and pay as the same shall be due the following disclosed liabilities of SSI.

A. All current liabilities incurred in the normal course of business, with the exception of accrued payroll taxes and payroll taxes withheld, the aggregate not to exceed the sum of $400,000.00.

B. All liabilities to SSI's customers for undelivered merchandise on order with SSI.

C. All purchase orders or commitments of SSI with SSI's vendors at Closing Date.

D. All leases of personal property used by or in SSI.

4. From PA Signing Date until Closing Date (the "Interim Period"), Seller will perform for Purchaser the following services or functions for SSI to wit:

A. Seller shall agree to permit inspection of all financial and operating data and other information relating to the business and property of SSI by Purchaser or its lenders or appraisers and to permit Purchaser to meet with and discuss the nature of operations with SSI's key distributors, sales representatives, customers, vendors and key employees.

5. *Accounts Receivable.* Seller will guarantee the collection of all of the accounts receivable shown on the Balance Sheet as of Closing Date. Seller may, at its expense, have an employee located within Purchaser's premises for a period of six months to observe the collection of the accounts receivable. Purchaser agrees to furnish, at its expense, office space, and telephone (exclusive of long distance calls) for said employee of Seller. Seller's employee will have the right to view the opening of the mail of Purchaser containing checks, cash, or other instruments of payment of SSI customers. All accounts or notes receivable guaranteed by Seller but uncollected by 6 months after Closing Date will be sold to Seller at one hundred (100%) percent of the then outstanding amount.

6. *Sales Applicable to Royalty.* The royalty shall be applied to the unit selling price exclusive of taxes, tariffs and duties, of SSI's full product line exclusive of service charges, maintenance fees, and miscellaneous charges.

7. *Conditions Precedent*

A. The obligations of Purchaser to consummate this transaction shall be subject to the following:

i. Receipt by Purchaser of certified resolutions of its Board of Directors authorizing and approving the execution of and consummation of the Agreement.

ii. Receipt by Purchaser of customary assurances of Seller, or its certified public accountants if required by Purchaser's lender, that as to the Interim Period no material adverse change in the operation of SSI has occurred or to its knowledge is threatened.

iii. Receipt of opinion of counsel satisfactory to Purchaser.

iv. Execution of employment agreements satisfactory to Purchaser by Key Employees of SSI as identified by Purchaser during the Interim Period.

v. Seller shall agree to subordinate to all other lenders its note and lease of real property to Purchaser.

vi. Favorable review of Purchaser's counsel of the corporate status and proceedings of Seller and SSI and title of Seller to the Transferred Assets.

B. The obligations of Seller to consummate this transaction provided for in the Agreement will be subject to the following:

i. Receipt of opinion of counsel satisfactory to Seller.

ii. All cash, notes, royalty agreements, leases, and Closing documents that are required to be furnished by Purchaser at Closing are ready for delivery.

iii. Representations and warranties of Purchaser, as set forth in the Agreement, at the time of Closing are correct.

iv. That Seller has received certified copies of resolutions of Purchaser's Board of Directors and stockholders (if necessary) authorizing the execution of this Agreement.

8. *Closing.* The Closing will take place in City, State on or before twenty (20) days after receipt by Purchaser of the audited balance sheet of SSI, but no later than 60 days after the Audit Date.

9. The Agreement shall contain the customary representations and warranties by Seller and Purchaser regarding the corporate existence and authority to enter the Agreement; the assets, liabilities, contracts, claims, commitments, financial statements, and financial business conditions of SSI, Seller, and Purchaser. Representations and Warranties shall survive the Closing of the tansaction, but not past two years after the Closing Date.

10. The Agreement shall provide that Seller will not compete with Purchaser in certain selected business activities as mutually agreed upon for the period ending Five Years After Closing Date, and a portion of the purchase price will be allocated to this covenant.

A. For a period of two (2) years from Closing, Seller agrees not to employ key employees of SSI to be cited by Purchaser during the Interim Period.

B. Seller shall not prepay any SSI debt or obligation (except as set forth in the Agreement) or, without prior permission of Purchaser, incur any significant indebtedness for borrowed money or make any significant capital improvements or commitments or sell or dispose of any of SSI's assets or properties except in the ordinary or regular course of business, or increase the compensation payable to any of SSI's key employees.

11. In consideration for the substantial expenditures of time, effort, and expense to be undertaken by Purchaser in connection with preparation and execution of the Agreement and the investigation referred to in this Letter, Seller and SSI undertake and agree (a) that they shall not, between execution of the Letter and PA Signing Date or the Closing date if the Agreement is executed on or prior to PA Signing Date, enter into or conduct any discussions with any other prospective purchaser of the Transferred Assets or SSI stock; (b) that they shall use their best efforts to preserve intact SSI's business organization and goodwill.

12. Please indicate your assent to the foregoing by signing in the space provided below on the enclosed copy of this letter and returning it to the undersigned. Upon delivery, counsel for Purchaser and Seller shall prepare, and the parties shall execute, the Agreement containing provisions in accordance with the foregoing together with such further appropriate terms and conditions as such counsel may mutually determine, subject to approval of the parties.

Sincerely,

PURCHASER CORPORATION

BY _____

Title President and Chief Executive Officer

Date Signed _____

The foregoing is hereby assented to subject to the terms and conditions stated herein.

SELLER CORPORATION

By _____

Title _____

Date _____

Notice the reference to four separate and important dates:

1. Purchase Agreement or PA Signing Date.
2. Latest Financial Statement Date.
3. Closing Date.
4. Six Months After Closing Date.

Certain other dates are frequently used as well, such as the date some years after the purchase is completed at which time the Purchaser must cease using the seller's logo or trade name in product sales literature. Another occasionally important date, also in the future, specifies the termination of the purchaser's agreement to service products located on customers' premises that were sold and installed by the seller. But the critical dates in all letters of intent reference the date of the balance sheet that the purchaser is buying, the interim period between the signing of a definitive purchase agreement and the closing date during which the assets and the company are audited and a date six months in the future usually, but sometimes longer or shorter, in which adjustments to the purchase price are made. These adjustments can arise due to an inability to collect all of the accounts receivable that were purchased, to sell all of the inventory that was purchased, or to reflect balance sheet changes that arose when the definitive audit was completed after the closing date. For example, auditors send letters to a company's customers and suppliers asking them to verify the company's records. Frequently the responses to these queries take 45 to 60 days to be returned and reviewed. If the closing must occur before the return of these letters, both the purchaser and the seller would be interested in adjusting the purchase price to reflect the changes.

Thus the first critical date in a letter of intent is the Latest Financial Statement Date, which is normally a few weeks earlier than the date of the Letter of Intent. The balance sheet reviewed at this date will be rendered obsolete by the balance sheet reviewed by the purchaser's auditors, which is usually completed near the closing date and reflects the changes in the primary assets. Note also in the Letter of Intent that the seller is specifically asked not to use its cash to repay indebtedness or to make capital improvements, and it is asked not to incur any significant indebtedness in the interim period prior to closing. One can immediately see from these and other items in the Letter of Intent the mutual trust and good faith required on both sides.

The first numbered paragraph of the Letter of Intent lists the assets that are to be transferred to the purchaser. Leveraged buy-outs are always asset purchases as opposed to stock purchases, in order for the purchaser to permit immediate and direct transfer of title to or permit the encumbrance of liens on the assets by secured lenders.

The second numbered paragraph outlines the terms of the purchase. In this example, the purchaser is dubious about the salability of the inventory and desires to reduce the purchase price if "it determines [that they] have no commercial value." This determination would be made unilaterally by the purchaser. It would hire auditors and industry-experienced consultants to investigate the commercial value of certain items in the product line, including finished goods, work in process, and raw material. The second key ingredient of the terms of payment is the audit, which changes the purchase price if the numbers change from those on the Latest Financial Statement Date. In buy-outs of closely held corporations, the seller frequently desires to hold back certain personal assets, such as cars, memorabilia, and club memberships.

The third numbered paragraph enumerates the liabilities that the purchaser is willing to accept and those it does not want to accept. Usually "normal course of business" liabilities are included and others, such as advances from the parent, are excluded. Payroll taxes and payroll withholding taxes are normally not included, because they should be paid by the seller in order that the purchaser begin with a clean slate in its obligations to the IRS.

The fourth numbered paragraph addresses the topic of the events that will occur during the Interim Period. The seller must be willing to "permit inspection" of the company, warts and all. During this period, the purchaser will audit financial statements, personnel, and contracts, sometimes referred to as the financial, management, and legal audits. The purpose of the financial audit has been discussed; the reason for the management audit is to identify the most important personnel, to find out the mistakes the seller has been making in the management of the company, to find areas of waste and unnecessary expenditures, and to ascertain the problems of the company and set priorities for solving them. The internal management is usually eager for an entrepreneurial buyer to take over the company and they may try to hide some of the problems. Conversely, internal management might prefer a competitive purchaser, or may want to purchase it for themselves, in which case all of the warts and some other horribles might be cited and indeed exaggerated. However, by interviewing several different members of management as well as knowledgeable middle-level personnel, the facts can be compared and weighed and some semblance of reality extracted.

The legal audit can produce interesting surprises. Occasionally the contracts on which the company has been relying for its exclusive sources of supply of vital products or components may not be in the company's favor. Worse, they may be near expiration. At the other end, the company's dealer, distributor, and product maintenance contracts might be written to the company's detriment. Or they too may be expiring. There could be a plethora of litigation against the company for faulty products or nonpayment of liabilities. One or two members of management, perhaps weak managers, may have long-term employment contracts. I can remember the purchase of an insect trap manufacturer a few years ago where every product was shipped with a card entitling the customer to return the product within 90 days if unsatisfied. You guessed it, sales were peaking in May and June and products were being returned in August and September full of bugs. The legal audit pointed up to the purchaser the need to amend this procedure.

The Interim Period is a busy time for the purchaser. It must not be forgotten that the Interim Period is a busy time for the lender as well. The credit approval process at an asset-based lending organization is one that involves the new business officer collecting and presenting the data to the credit officers to obtain the necessary approvals to make the loan. This usually involves sending in appraisers to assess the value of the inventory on a quick-sale basis and the value of the fixed assets under the auctioneer's hammer. If the lender in the case at hand cannot approve a $1.5 million loan secured by the assets listed above, this will create an additional problem for the purchaser during the Interim Period. Another lender must be found quickly.

The fifth numbered paragraph sets forth the purchaser's requirement for having the collectibility of the accounts receivable guaranteed. This is a fairly standard request and the paragraph goes on to explain the mechanism for assuring the seller that as the receivables are collected, the ones it has guaranteed will be credited first. Any sums not received within 6 months must be then paid to the purchaser by the seller. The seller's employee who opens the mail will be able to verify the amount due.

Paragraph 6 describes the royalty on sales and enumerates those assets for which royalty will be paid and those for which it is not applicable. Clearly income on service calls and maintenance calls does not warrant a royalty.

The Conditions Precedent section, paragraph 7, lists the "outs." In this particular Letter of Intent, in which the purchaser has not offered a binder forefeitable if the buy-out does not occur, it is difficult to have a set of outs favorable to the purchaser. Thus the outs available to the purchaser include material adverse changes during the Interim Period and an unsatisfactory opinion of counsel. The outs available to seller are minimal as well, however, since this Letter of Intent was prepared by the purchaser and does not include negotiating points that are in favor of the seller. The revised Letter of Intent may include some strong terms from the seller. For example, the seller might like to see that the purchaser has $500,000 in liquid net worth to invest in the company or to demonstrate that there exists more than hope and prayer of making the note and the royalty have value. In fact, if the seller were to accept the above Letter of Intent without having the purchaser put some strength behind the note (personal guarantee, side collateral, cross-default provisions, and so forth) or improve the payment terms of the royalty (perhaps a "hell-or-high-water" clause customary in leases which would make the royalties payable come hell or high water, whether or not sales were made), then the purchaser could be sure that the company is failing and the seller is delighted to have its problems assumed by someone else. This particular Letter of Intent very plainly says, "Dear Seller, I am paying you with cash generated from your balance sheet, with royalties generated from selling some of your inventory and with a note for the balance, if there is anything left after interest, expenses, and royalties. If your management is fairly competent and if there is no major downturn in business, you will probably get paid. Wish me luck." This set of conditions is usually asking too much of a seller, thus the sellers revisions to the Letter of Intent will usually seek to tighten up the terms of payment.

The eighth numbered paragraph sets forth the Closing Date, which occurs at the end of the Interim Period and usually after the audit is completed. Paragraph 9 defines the representations and warranties that are to be included in the Purchase Agreement. Paragraph 10 informs the purchaser that it may not go back into the company's business for five years. This will permit the purchaser to assign a hefty portion of the purchase price, if it chooses to do so, to this "noncompete agreement." The agreement can be amortized over five years, thus reducing taxes. This paragraph also warns the seller against trying to hire key personnel from the company for a period of two years.

The eleventh numbered paragraph asks the seller to refrain from soliciting other candidates. Normally, the seller requests a forfeitable binder in consideration for removing the company from the market. The amount of the binder and the conditions under which it is forfeitable are both subjects for negotiation.

The Letter of Intent is a road map that points the way for both sides to proceed quickly to a closing. By preparing a carefully written Letter of Intent, the seller is put on notice that the purchaser is serious—he has begun spending money on legal advice—and he intends to proceed methodically to a closing. It can help make an entrepreneurial purchaser appear more substantial, thus obviating one of the reasons that sellers hold out for corporate purchasers.

12.Q: I understand that a well-written business plan is the key factor in raising capital and borrowing money. But you hear stories of entre-

preneurs who go into a venture capital fund or a bank and come out
with a check. Surely this is an exaggeration. Or perhaps it is true that
there is an art to communicating with lenders and investors.

12.A: It is true that some entrepreneurs are able to raise capital with
greater facility than others because they are better talkers and make a
better impression than others. Although the oral presentation is very
important in raising capital, it cannot take the place of a well-written
business plan. After all, the business plan inaugurates the meeting.

When lenders discuss financing opportunities, they refer to the better situations as "credits." A credit is a loan proposal that makes the
lender feel reasonably confident he will get his money back. He feels
good about the situation and wants to make the loan.

When lenders discuss entrepreneurs, they refer to the more competent ones as people who can "sell a credit." To sell a credit is to convince your lender of the merits of the loan and your company's ability
to repay it when it comes due. To say that an entrepreneur knows how
to "sell a credit" is the highest compliment a lender can pay.

The greatest art form in the money-raising field is to be able to sell a
credit for a financing opportunity that is not a credit. That is, to raise
money for a situation where the return of that money is uncertain. This
is one of the primary challenges of entrepreneurship. But a great deal of
entrepreneurial success depends on how well the entrepreneur talks.
The ability to raise money frequently may determine a new company's
success or failure, regardless of the merits of the situation. Rarely is the
failure to raise money the fault of the financial community. There are
thousands of sources of money and hundreds of sources for any particular situation. The failure to raise money is usually the entrepreneur's
inability to sell a credit.

Oral communication skills are necessary for entrepreneurs to convince the customers and suppliers to bend their policies as well. Frequently you will hear that large corporations have shipped raw materials to zero net worth companies and given them 90 days to pay. In these
instances, the suppliers usually believe that the entrepreneur has the
ability to sell the product, pay them, place larger orders in the future
and become a loyal customer. If the inventory is not paid for in a timely
manner, future shipments may be C.O.D., but the supplier has evi-
denced its good faith and willingness to be helpful. I once asked the
Treasurer of U.S. Steel why that company was not an investor in a venture capital fund. He told me, "Son, we have over 200 venture capital
investments. We ship product to young companies some of which we

know may never be able to pay us. But we need to keep building new customers."

Talking to Lenders

There are three types of lenders: no risk, calculated risk, and risk. No risk lenders are banks; calculated risk lenders are commercial finance companies; risk lenders are venture capitalists. Many new companies raise money from all three sources either at various times in their growth or at the same time as a packaged financing (sometimes called a "blended rate") deal. It is imprudent and a waste of everyone's time to seek risk capital from a bank without offering the bank collateral, cash flow, and secondary collateral or, as it is sometimes referred to, belt, suspenders, and safety pins. No matter how well you talk, the obstacles to your success are overpowering. Even with a government loan guarantee, the odds of succeeding are slim, no matter how skilled your oral communications.

The entrepreneur must understand his company and its assets, both hidden and visible, to know from which of the three sources to raise capital and at what magnitude. For example, a manufacturer seeking to purchase machinery and equipment might be able to borrow on an unsecured basis from a bank if the present cash flow exceeds the pro forma loan repayment schedule. The situation might require a commercial finance loan secured by the machinery and equipment if the ability to repay is questionable—for example, if the company has experienced a loss year or had too brief a track record of positive cash flow. Venture capital would be the solution if there are doubts about the ultimate productivity of the machinery and equipment. There are, of course, variations and exceptions to all of these rules, but exceptions are usually the result of extraordinary circumstances.

The fourth type of lender is the guarantor, usually government guarantor, generally Federal but occasionally state, and generally in the person of a local civil servant manning an area office and trying just as hard as you to understand the guidelines under which he can approve a loan guarantee for your company. Clearly no equity is given up to the government. In speaking with civil servants an entirely different orientation is required. You must realize that your listener has been depersonalized somewhat by his monolithic client and that no matter what you say at the first meeting, he will feel compelled to find a reason to turn down your application. It is his job, he feels, to find a reason to criticize your submittal, and no matter how perfectly the application has been filled out, the civil servant feels that if he does not turn it down at least once, he has not executed his duties properly.

Therefore, the entrepreneur should make his conversation especially pleasant and attempt to personalize the civil servant. He should find like experiences to share and strive to discover common interests. The entrepreneur should be self-effacing. The entrepreneur should make the government guarantor feel that his turn down of the application is actually (1) a search for information from him, and (2) an opportunity to visit with each other again. The civil servant has the opportunity to assist the entrepreneur in achieving wealth, which is a commodity the civil servant may never have or may be envious of. Thus it is important to make the civil servant feel an important part of the process. The same applies to unsecured and secured lenders as well.

The rules of selling a credit are the same whether the entrepreneur is raising money from a no risk, calculated risk, or risk lender. The rules apply, however, only if the entrepreneur is selling to the appropriate lender. No matter how outstanding the verbal presentation, a credit cannot be sold to a lender if granting the loan violates his policies and objectives. In summary, these policies are as follows.

Commercial Bank.   The ability to repay the loan must be absolutely certain and protected in three ways: cash flow, asset coverage and side collateral. These are made up, for example, of historical cash flow that exceeds the pro forma repayment schedule, accounts receivable substantially in excess of the value of the loan, and a guarantor willing to pledge liquid collateral in support of the loan.

Commercial Finance Company.   The ability to repay the loan must be highly probable and supported by assets—accounts receivable, inventories, or plant and equipment—which in liquidation would aggregate more than the value of the loan. In addition, the commercial finance company must be familiar with the kinds of assets used to secure the loan so that it will know to whom they might be sold in the event of liquidation. Personal guarantees usually are required to show good faith and to keep the entrepreneurs from running off to some other company.

SBIC or MESBIC.   The loan must have a high probability of repayment, but it is not supported by assets pledged to secure the loan. Rather, the venture capitalist generally takes a full risk on the principal amount of the loan, in consideration for which he purchases a significant minority equity position in the borrowing company. The venture capital company will sell its equity position at a profit to the public, a larger company, or back to the entrepreneur at some future date, when and if it has increased in value.

Government Guarantor.   The loan must have a high probability of repayment, which the government believes is more likely to occur if the entrepreneurs invest approximately 10–20% of the total proceeds in the form of equity, or if the borrower's net worth is equal to a similar percentage of the loan. The government, whenever possible, seeks to collateralize its loans with "negative incentive" assets, such as a lien on the entrepreneur's house or other hard assets. When this is not possible, the borrower must present overriding social benefits as a reason for granting the guarantee.

Using the foregoing guidelines, an entrepreneur in many cases will be able to determine which type of lender to attempt to sell. It is pointless to seek risk money from a bank or commercial finance company, and it is costly to seek no-risk money from a venture capitalist.

Before meeting the lender or investor the entrepreneur should bear in mind the plight of the first person to have ever eaten a crab. Although he may have enjoyed the taste, communicating his pleasure to others must have been a difficult assignment. I can hear the people saying to him, "But it crawls on the bottom of the sea," and "It is so terrible looking," and, perhaps, "How did you prevent it from grabbing your nose with its pinchers?"

There are parts of a business plan which need quite a bit of explaining as well. Although the entrepreneur may understand the nuances of market and product, a lender or investor may not understand them all. Consider the small business computer industry. Few are the lenders who understand words and phrases such as "Mbyte," "floppy disk," and "vertical market software." The entrepreneur who expects to accomplish anything at the meeting should be prepared to begin at the beginning.

Getting the Meeting

Many entrepreneurs use intermediaries to submit their business plans and arrange meetings. Sponsorship is the best means of getting the meeting. Naturally, there is a fee, but it is usually worthwhile to pay 5% if the chance of raising capital depends on it. Without the services of a financial intermediary, then, it is advised that the entrepreneur deliver the business plan in person and attempt to sell the credit at the first meeting while the lender skims the material. In order to get the appointment, the entrepreneur should ask the lender or investor if he may "Come by and drop off the material." At that point, the lender or investor will probably reply with: "Why don't you just mail it and I'll give you a call after I have read it." Persistence and tenacity are appreciated by lenders and investors, and the entrepreneur should rebut with: "I have to be near your office tomorrow anyway, and it would not be out of my way to drop it off." This proposal might fit neatly into the lender's or investor's schedule, but assuming it does not, the entrepreneur can choose one of several other options:

1. "If the afternoon is not good for you, I can change my other appointment and see you in the morning."
2. "If tomorrow is not acceptable, I need to be back your way in one or two days." (Leaving options open.)
3. "I have lunch open on my schedule if that would be a convenient time."
4. "If your schedule is tight right now, why don't we get together for breakfast?"
5. "Perhaps you could squeeze me in after work one day this week."

I firmly believe that lenders and investors are more interested in tenacious entrepreneurs than in relaxed or casual entrepreneurs. Intimidation mixed with charm is an excellent initial impression to make on an investor or lender. For example, if the person absolutely will not see you, you might laughingly say something like, "Gee, you guys must have a lot of good deals in there now."

In attempting to arrange the meeting, the entrepreneur must be careful to balance his persistence, so that he does not appear "pushy" but creates a busy, important image—running off to meetings with other lenders, customers, suppliers, lawyers, and advertising agencies. If nothing seems to be working, but the lender or investor still has not hung up the telephone, the entrepreneur might take a few minutes to explain the key ingredients, entrepreneurial team, market size, and product niche. If these are indeed interesting, then the lender or investor will try to find time for a meeting.

Selling the credit begins the moment you enter the room. I suggest entering quickly and confidently with a glowing smile, an extended hand, and an unexpected remark such as "Thank you for seeing me. Sorry to be late— we've just completed our biggest month in history . . .," or "a major order from____," or "a session with our patent counsel. . . ." Thus the first impression is that you are a "doer."

One entrepreneur I know always says "It's done" as he enters the lender's or investor's office for the first time. "It's done" is a surprising remark. My entrepreneur friend claims that it is the single best opener beause it is completely unexpected, it makes you look like a doer—an accomplisher—and it subjectively encourages the lender to do something with you also. If yours is an entrepreneurial team, the two of you could enter the room, one saying to the other, "It's done!" and then gleefully introducing yourselves to the lender. Chances are the lender will ask "What's done?" Then you can lead into the verbal presentation with a positive tone of accomplishment. The "What's done?" question could elicit a response from the lender to write something in the margin of a page (more on writing during the meeting and its significance further on).

Dress is a topic that is important in selling a credit. When a lender decides to grant a loan, in the back of his mind there is a nagging concern that the entrepreneur may lack the judgment to spend the money wisely.This concern is definitely not major once a positive decision has been reached, but the entrepreneur's appearance could affect the positive decision just enough to skew it from slightly bullish to slightly bearish. Hence the entrepreneur's clothing should suggest conservatism more than liberalism, risk aversion more than risk taking, caution rather than devil-may-care optimism. They dress for their superiors (to whom they sell their brains, hearts, and souls daily) who expect them to be judicious with the institution's money. Roe Stamps, a partner in the venture capital fund of TA Associates, says that successful entrepreneurs usually speak Yiddish and dress British. This is a reference to the incorporation of colorful Yiddish terms of commerce, of which there are many, while dressing like a Saville Row banker.

Colors of clothing may reflect conservatism in one part of the country and liberalism in another. The following dress code was given to me by a colorful, spicy entrepreneur who kept pulling out different attire as we traveled from city to city raising venture capital.

1. *New England.*   Dark blue suit, blue shirt, semiwide paisley tie, lace-up shoes.

2. *New York.*   Grey, pin-stripe suit, blue shirt, red and blue striped tie, lace-up shoes or conservative loafers.

3. *Chicago and Industrial Midwest.*   Grey or dark brown suit, dark tie, lace-up shoes. Give appearance of being ready to slap a hard hat on your head and tramp through a foundry right after the meeting.

4. *South and Southwest.*   Light grey or light brown suit, any color shirt except white, bright tie, lace-up shoes or conservative loafers.

5. *Los Angeles.*   Similar to the South and Southwest, except colors should be coordinated and loafers may be tassled.

6. *San Francisco.*   Dark blue suit, white shirt, bright tie, lace-up shoes or conservative loafers.

Women should follow the color guidelines stated above, translating suits and ties to simply tailored suits and scarves worn with conservative shoes. Jewelry should be plain and understated. Since there are relatively few women involved in finance and entrepreneurial ventures at the time of this writing, it is hard to make generalizations about women's dress, and in turn, there are no set formulas expected by lenders.

Lenders derive some of their personality characteristics from the entrepreneurs to whom they lend money and whose plans, dreams, and aspirations become their own plans, dreams, and aspirations. It is inevitable that the lender will ask himself, "Do I see a part of myself in that entrepreneur? Could I possibly share common goals with him? Are we at all alike?" It is in this area that dress plays a role, albeit secondary to the substance of the conversation, but important in that the entrepreneur should provide an appearance more appropriate to handling money wisely than to going to a ball game.

Select the most comfortable seat nearest the lender and at all times sit forward but straight. Never lean back or become relaxed. If the lender sits behind his desk, you should sit in front of his desk and place your material on the desk in a folder in front of you. The entrepreneur should never appear at ease. The subject is money and that is not a casual topic. One entrepreneur with whom I have worked believes that the entrepreneur should be very ill at ease and uncomfortable.

One of the best credit selling meetings I attended involved a commerical bank officer and an entrepreneur whose company, in bankruptcy proceedings at the time, had just completed its second year of operations with revenues of $75,000. The entrepreneur was a skilled salesman, and he pulled out all the stops in the empathy game. He pretended he was too hot, and asked if he might remove his jacket. It was the South, so jacket removal was acceptable. He put the jacket over the arm of his chair and then tugged at his collar, still looking like a fully dressed man in a steam room. All the while, he was describing his business and its prospects once it obtained financing. In the meantime, he coordinated collar tugs with knocking his jacket down to the floor, picking it up, pushing it down, picking it up, shifting around, folding and unfolding it, and finally letting it fall to the floor and stepping on it. At that point, the lender literally left his seat and came over to the entrepreneur, obstensibly to see his material more closely.

Another style that is fascinating to watch is the entrepreneur who becomes so excited about the prospects for his company that he has to stand up and walk around. The excitement, if you will, causes him to leave his seat. While standing, he has two basic moves to employ: the grip and the stroll. The grip involves holding tightly to the back of a chair for support and reassurance and the stroll is simply an animated walk around the office of the lender, one hand in a jacket pocket, the other moving furiously to stress various points. An apology then follows, on the order of "I'm sorry but I get so excited sometimes I can't keep my seat." Sound corny? It would be if everyone did it. But many entrepreneurs are frightened in meetings with lenders and sit in a fetal position in a womblike corner of the office, praying silently that the lending community is like "Monopoly" and this particular office is "Free Parking."

Hands are fascinating to watch. The best entrepreneurs use their hands in syncopation with their voice. Billy Graham slices the air up and down and side to side. Oral Roberts, while saying "Let me help you," "Let me give you," rolls his hands outward to his audience. Reverend Ike shoots his bejeweled hands skyward. Johnny Carson, who sells shyness, leaves his hands in his pockets, and brings them out Jack Benny-style to underscore surprise. The list of "handtalkers" is endless, and much can be learned from watching them. For entrepreneurs who are poor speakers, I recommend hiring a speech tutor or coach.

There are dozens of body language signs to watch for in a meeting with a lender. If his arms and legs are folded or crossed, you're not reaching him. His mind is closed to your proposal. If his arms and legs unfold, he is beginning to show interest. If he leans back with his hands behind his head and his legs spread apart, he is saying, "Sell me, I'm yours."

It is possible to effect a positive change in body language in the listener by a number of actions on your part. For example, you can push things toward his hands that he has to reach for in order to receive and examine. If the product you manufacture is small enough to bring with you, you can place that in easy reach of the lender. You can push the product off the desk to get his feet untangled—he'll have to get up in order to retrieve it.

If you are an entrepreneurial team, one of you should take out a pencil and write during the meeting. This encourages the listener to take notes also, hence opening up his hands and arms. Excessive body movement on your part will tend to open up the lender in the same way that people watching a high jumper will raise their legs as he kicks up to the bar. It is instinctive to want to get in motion with someone in motion.

Never, but never, use the word "problem" in a meeting with a lender. Avoid a sentence like "Here's our problem," "Our problem is this," or "We have a cash flow problem." The lender has problems in his portfolio and he doesn't want more of them. If he thinks you will become a problem to him, he will turn you down. Always bring a lender solutions, not problems.

Avoid street language such as "con," as in "We were conned by a supplier." Avoid inferences to crime, fraud, felony, dishonesty, and, if possible, avoid discussing litigation or government action regarding your business. These words raise the specter of uncertainty and business interruption or the possible loss of the lender's money and embarrassment to him.

I have vivid memories of a lender's face turning from smiles to frowns when an entrepreneur, who was just about to get financed, launched into a crime story replete with an impersonation of a thug. The story was about a meeting the entrepreneur had, accidentally, with a "street lender," and although it was humorous, it placed the lender in the same category by association and also indicated that the entrepreneur was stupid enough or hard-pressed enough to have had that kind of meeting in the first place. The lender wants to deal with Rockefellers, Watsons, and Phippses, but since they do not need money, he wants to deal with people who act like them: proud, self-reliant, honest, competent, and absolutely right.

Finally, the lender or investor wants answers to at least five questions at the meeting:

1. How much can I make?
2. How much can I lose?
3. How do I get my money out?
4. Who else is in the deal?
5. Who says you are any good?

These questions refer to other points we have covered, including upside potential, areas of risk, future public offering potential, names of suppliers, customers, investors, and lenders who are involved, and the track record of the entrepreneurial team. While being aware of speech, dress, posture, and body language, these questions must be dealt with clearly and carefully.

13.Q: Why do some small businesses succeed and others fail? Why do some small businesses raise money easily and others have difficulty? Is there a common denominator among successful small businesses?

13.A: This is not a simple question to answer. Ask it of any two venture capitalists and you will receive three different answers. My answer to the question is based on my personal experiences; other venture capitalists will have other experiences that produce different answers.

The definition of entrepreneurship is the process of conceiving and launching a new company to market a product or service which has "demonstrable enconomic justification."

There are eight characteristics of demonstrable economic justification which I call the eight "DEJ" factors. The more DEJ factors an entrepreneur has in his new company, the more likely is the new company to succeed.

Demonstrable economic justification, or DEJ, is a condition of a marketplace wherein a qualified buyer, when solicited by a seller, will purchase the product or service from the seller the majority of the time. A new company markets a product that has demonstrable economic justification if in more than 5 sales calls out of 10 a sale is made or if in 10 sales there are 5 or more reorders. Venture capitalists always look for a company's reorder rate. The more DEJ factors an entrepreneur has in his new company the greater its chance for success, because (1) the greater will be its volume of sales, (2) the faster growing will be its earnings, (3) the less its need for capital, (4) the greater the return on that capital, and (5) the larger the entrepreneur's eventual wealth.

As an example, pretend a book entitled *Entrepreneurship: The Road to Riches* is a new company's product. Ten aspiring entrepreneurs go into a bookstore and see this book and thumb through it, and if more than five purchase it, then the book probably has all eight DEJ factors because the majority of the potential customers purchased it. The title of the book may have been less important than the advertising, location in the store, the persistence of sales clerks, and so forth. The 50% who did not buy the book may have been unqualified buyers; that is, they did not have a problem for which the book offered a solution. The other buyers may have been influenced by one of the following eight DEJ factors:

1. Existence of qualified buyers.
2. Existence of competent management.
3. Homogeneity of buyers.
4. Large number of buyers.
5. Lack of institutional barriers to selling.
6. "Hey, it really works!" phenomenon.
7. Optimum price–cost relationship.
8. Invisibility of the new company.

Each of these factors should be a component of the new company's business plan. The existence of all eight DEJ factors in many instances is predictive of a major entrepreneurial success.

Electronic Data Systems Corporation, H. Ross Perot's company, grew to sales of $36 million in less than 5 years and had a market value of more than $1 billion by the sixth year. This record of entrepreneurial success has been approached but not exceeded by any other new company since 1960. Electronic Data Systems (or "EDS") possessed all eight DEJ factors. The company was formed in 1964 to solve data processing problems for large corporations and institutions. EDS offered facilities management contracts to its customers. It hired the customer's data processing personnel and purchased the customer's data processing equipment. It ran the customer's work at the customer's budget (EDS's revenues). If it brought in the job for less than the budget, the difference was EDS's profit. Additional customers meant fewer personnel and less equipment per job, hence more profit.

Existence of Qualified Buyers.   Corporate data processing inefficiency was a very real problem. Buyers did not have to be educated—that is, told they had a problem. Buyers knew they had a problem and knew they had to pay for a solution. A minimal amount of buyer education was required.

Existence of Competent Managers.   H. Ross Perot, the EDS entrepreneur, hired managers who were skilled in providing solutions to the problems of the EDS customers. Perot, a former IBM salesman, was an able salesman and he hired personnel in his image. He was competitive and competent and so were the managers he hired.

Homogeneity of Buyers.   The problem that EDS solved was essentially the same for all buyers with minor differences in degree or severity. The solution did not have to be tailor-made or customized for each buyer. Selling off the racks is cheaper and provides more rapid cash flow than selling custom made.

Large Number of Buyers.   The number of potential buyers sharing essentially the same problem was in excess of 3000 corporations and institutions. Assuming each one had an annual data processing budget of $1 million, the market size for EDS's solution was $3 billion and no other competitor was within two years of sharing a piece of the pie. More than any other single factor, this explains why EDS's initial public offering was at a common stock price in excess of the then unheard of 115.0 times earnings. Facilities management, five years after EDS began operations, was to become the fastest growing segment of the data processing industry.

Lack of Institutional Barriers to Selling.   The buyers were not organized. They belonged to no association. There was no regulatory body to which they were responsible for their activities such as the American Medical Association or Civil Aeronautics Board. The buyers were new to computers and new to their problem. Their purpose in seeking a solution was to save money, and for no other purpose for which they would have to seek permission or clarification from an outside or collective institution.

"Hey, It Really Works!" Phenomenon.   EDS's solution was passed along from buyer to buyer by word-of-mouth advertising. Not only is word-of-mouth the cheapest form of advertising, it is also the most effective.

Optimum Cost–Price Relationship.   The price of the solution was equal to the cost of the problem, that is, the buyer's data processing budget. EDS's price could not be questioned as being excessively high or unwarranted, because the buyer was paying the same price for his problem that he was to pay to have it solved. If the same $100 that brought him problems would now bring him solutions, he was $100 ahead. As they say in *The Godfather*, EDS made them an offer they couldn't refuse.

Invisibility of the New Company.   EDS operated quietly and without fanfare. It did not advertise or promote heavily. It did not gain attention so that it could be copied by competitors. In 1973, 10 years after the formation of EDS, General Electric was the first company larger than EDS to enter the facilities management business. By that time, Perot had banked nearly $1 billion in capital gains.

Now that we've seen how the DEJ factors worked in a specific case, let's consider them more generally.

Existence of Qualified Buyers

This is the education factor. It means that if buyers do not know they have a problem, there will be no demand for the solution. They will have to be educated to realize (a) they have a problem, and (b) there exists a solution.

Automatic Data Processing, Inc. (ADP), founded around 1960 by Henry Taub, Joseph Taub, and Frank Lautenberg, began by operating data processing service bureaus. These service bureaus, located in over 30 cities in the United States, prepare payroll checks and provide bookkeeping services for many large and small companies. ADP began in the payroll processing business with a solution to a problem that many company managers did not know they had; that is, the preparation and processing of payroll checks is expensive, time-consuming, subject to errors, and allows certain employees to know everyone else's salary.

When ADP was formed, no payroll processing problem existed. Henry Taub had to educate the market. Today, ADP's market value is greater than $700 million. By comparison with EDS, however, ADP grew to a market value 50% less than that of EDS in more than twice EDS's time period because, among other things, ADP had to educate its market. Whereas EDS began with $25,000 and never required venture capital, ADP raised over $6 million in venture capital in order to generate sales equal to EDS's at the time of the latter's initial public offering.

Telling buyers that they have a problem is a very difficult task. People who are successful at this task are called, among other things, marketing geniuses.

For example, most of us are aware of bad breath and underarm odors, because we have been told that these are problems and we accept them as such. We spend over $3 billion each year on mouthwash and deodorant. Getting into Heaven is also a problem and the evangelical market is inestimably large and buoyant and possesses some of the greatest marketing geniuses in our country.

One approach such geniuses have developed over the years is to "sell the sizzle, not the steak." Selling the sizzle means presenting a picture in the buyer's mind of a satisfied buyer who has purchased the solution. For example, "finger lickin' good" tells us how we will feel after eating Kentucky Fried Chicken. McDonald's tells us "we deserve a break today," and, of course, we all feel we deserve a break today. The successful evangelist Reverend Ike brings successful small businessmen to surround him on the stage, to show the power of faith and hard work.

Many entrepreneurs know little about marketing and sell the problem rather than the solution. Entrepreneurs are happy to tell a buyer that he has problems, but the buyer knows how stupid he is for not having found the solutions himself. Thus sell solutions, not problems.

Entrepreneurs most frequently eliminated by the marketplace are wiped out by the education factor for the simple reason that they have developed a solution for a nonexistent problem. These are generally referred to in the venture capital industry as "black-box companies." The black box performs a service faster, better, and cheaper than the present mechanism. Unfortunately, the people using the present mechanism do not regard their malediction as a problem. They have not commissioned anyone to find a solution. They are pleased with their slower, more costly method. Hence this market is difficult to sell.

The "black box" entrepreneur might call on the purchasing vice president of a major United States airline, for example, with a black box which, when installed in every seat of the airplane at a cost of $0.05 per seat per flight, will enable each passenger to serve himself a meal. This could be a solution to the rising costs of cabin attendants. But maybe the passengers do not want self-service; maybe they like to have cabin attendants around for assistance, ambience, and to comfort frightened children. This black box probably cannot be sold, because the rising cost of cabin attendants is not uniformly regarded as a problem. If a solution cannot be sold, it has very little economic justification.

The airline industry has some very serious problems. The airlines have relatively low aggregate market values and p/e ratios. The companies that solve identifiable airline problems, however, have high market values and p/e ratios: Inflight Services (movies), Sperry (computers), Ingersoll–Rand (compressors), Marriott (food), and so forth. This points out that if a company solves a problem well for a beleaguered industry, its earnings will grow rapidly. An improved system of baggage handling at a cost of no more than a penny per bag would be of interest to airlines. A system for defogging runways would find ready customers. And should you find a way to put a paying passenger in every seat on every flight, you will have hit the jackpot.

Fried chicken dinners prepared by some of the fast food fried chicken franchisors have a random taste, sometimes greasy, sometimes dry. An entrepreneur came to see me one day with an invention for a new chicken fryer that would be self-cleaning and eliminate grease from the bottom of the pot, thus providing a consistent taste. We called on a few of the fried chicken franchisors to see if they knew they had a taste variance problem. It turns out they did not know and did not care. The entrepreneur went back to designing computer systems for satellites and missiles, and fast-food fried chicken still varies in taste. Were the fried chicken franchisors to begin losing sales because of random product taste, they would appreciate a solution.Should you develop a solution ahead of the problem that it solves, you would be well-advised to put yourself in the hands of a marketing consultant. He should be able to develop a strategy for marketing the solution in such a way that customers either will never have to be advised of their problem or will be advised in such a way that they become eager buyers. Most venture capitalists are not interested in companies that sell solutions for which no problem exists. These types of companies are not socially useful. Companies that offer dune buggy rentals, ingenue-type magazines, and so forth, are marketing "rip-offs" and problem creators. They are rotten apples that take advantage of large numbers of young and unknowing buyers and lead to more anticompetitive government intervention.

The education factor—the existence of qualified buyers—is the premier DEJ factor. If there is no problem to solve, the solution to be conveyed by the new company is not economically justifiable. The additional marketing costs to create a demand for the solution means (a) greater amounts of venture capital, (b) a relatively longer development period, and (c) a lower rate of return on invested capital.

Existence of Competent Managers

Entrepreneurs are characteristically problem solvers, or sellers. Corporate personnel are characteristically problem finders, or buyers. Problem finders do not have to be competent, because the marketplace preserves them, competent or not. Problem solvers are competent, or the marketplace soon eliminates them. Consequently, entrepreneurs have the very difficult assignment of finding and hiring competent managers to manage the selling of the new product.

How important is good management to a new company? General Georges Doriot, founder of American Research and Development Company, Inc., and the grandfather of the venture capital industry, said, "There are three all-important facts to a new company: people, people, and people." Arthur Rock is a successful venture capitalist who launched Personal Software Inc. and Apple Computer Corp. and, in conjunction with Tommy Davis, is credited with having provided the venture capital for Teledyne Corp. and Scientific Data Systems Corp. Rock said that he generally will invest in a new company, no matter how speculative, if it has strong management.

Occasionally a new company will be fortunate in having an entrepreneurial team skilled in covering the four functions of a new company: marketing, production, engineering, and Finance. Very simply stated, one person designs the product, one makes the product, another sells it, and a fourth makes sure it is all done at a profit.

It is rare to find a perfectly balanced foursome of entrepreneur/managers in a new company. It existed at Automatic Data Processing, where one man designed the product, another sold it, and the third made sure it was done at a profit. Sometimes if the team members get along too well with one another there will be an insufficient amount of debate, dissension, and testing of new ideas. They might be subject to the same blind-sidedness. Therefore, one member should be the front end of the gun—the visionary and the catalyst. A second should be the firing mechanism—product responsibility. The third should keep the gun clean and be sure it fires live ammunition each time. The fourth should make sure that the exercise is a profitable one and that there is enough capital to keep the team going.

You will notice that many times an entrepreneurial team is successful at launching a new company but incompetent at managing its growth. They have to be replaced by the investors to avoid a failure. Entrepreneurial management requires an ability to control an entire situation while thinking three moves ahead. The quarterback has the hirable skill; the team owner builds the team into a profitable franchise. It is the unwise entrepreneur who fails to hire good managers to carry out his or her dreams and plans which have been put on paper. The days of the solo entrepreneur who can do it all are over.

Some venture capitalists demand a three-man team before they will invest. The team members are nicknamed People, Pencil, and Paper.

People is the entrepreneur, the Mr. Outside, the front end of the gun. He is the driving force, planner, and sometime dreamer. He is a concept man. His eventual responsibilities will be marketing because he is good with people.

Pencil is the thorough executor of People's plans. He is Mr. Inside, a good administrator of an idea. He cannot sell. He can produce a product. He can describe a product or service, and put a pencil in his hand and he will give you a nuts and bolts description of the production process.

Paper is the clean-up man, the financial man, the numbers man. He is likened to a green eyeshade. His world is green columnar paper with budgets, projections, cash flow statements, purchase orders, and bank statements. Paper is responsible for bank relationships, controls, payrolls, and cash management.

If a new company can be an attractive investment without all three men, the least dispensable is People, because there is no business to run unless there are sales.

Homogeneity of Buyers

It is important to the new company's ability to make a profit that it addresses one identical problem shared by all of its customers. For example, if the problem is clothing, the solution can come in different shapes, sizes, colors, and fabrics, but it should remain a standard solution to a standard problem.

Frequently an entrepreneur will have conceived an excellent solution which could be used to solve a number of problems, that is, address several markets simultaneously. Holography is such a product. Do you point it at the cancer in bone marrow problems or stresses in steel problems or others? Part of the answer is to point it at the problem with the most homogeneous buyers.

Henry Ford said that he would make the Model T in any color you wanted so long as it was black. His entrepreneurial brilliance cannot be taken lightly. Founders of new companies who bid on a variety of different contracts, each calling for a variation of their basic product, will end up with manufacturing losses and no marketing program with which to grow.

If you want to measure the great entrepreneurial fortunes in this country, think of the most universally demanded standardized, off-the-shelf products and you will see the largest fortunes: computers, cars, oil, electronics, foods, and department stores; but there will be few lawyers, doctors, or teachers and no advertising executives, book publishers, accountants, architects, designers, or other customizers.

The homogeneity factor is also known as the "multiplier" or "cookie cutter." If it costs $100,000 to develop a standardized product that will sell over and over again at a significant markup, the investors will achieve a greater return on $100,000 than if each sale has to be customized or tailor-made to fit the customer's needs. If a new product or service is knocked out like your grandmother cut cookies from a big piece of dough, the profits will be greater and more rapidly achieved.

The basic problem caused by nonhomogeneous buyers is a need for a greater amount of start-up capital. In 1970 approximately 150 computer time-sharing companies were launched. Time-sharing is the ability of a customer to lease time and storage space on a computer, along with 100 or so other customers, and without interfering with the access to the computer of any other customer. Time-sharing has a crisp logic to it: why should small companies own or lease entire computers when they need to store and retrieve data only a small portion of the time?

At the time, this new business idea was the hottest new area for venture capitalists. Approximately 150 venture capitalists, as well as the public market, invested approximately $500 million in the new time-sharing companies. Today, about five of these companies still exist. Many were deficient in several of the DEJ factors, but the principal reasons generally cited for their failure was that they ran out of capital. Since they had no earnings to attract second-stage investors, many were unable to raise additional capital and quitely folded their tents.

Time-sharing customers are nonhomogeneous. Their problems differ. They must be sold individually. They must be serviced individually. Different programs must be written for each to keep them hooked up to the computer. But the critical mass of capital necessary to launch a time-sharing company and support a marketing program is about 10 times greater than many investors ever imagined.

The requirement for greater amounts of start-up venture capital does not by any means obviate the interest of venture capitalists. If the projected rate of return on the $5 million is greater than the projected rate of return on the $500,000, the larger investment will be the more attractive one, because one company rather than ten companies, will be added to the overworked venture capitalist's portfolio. Venture capitalists, on average, like to see a five times rate of return after capital gains taxes in three years. If a new company cannot get into the black in 24 months, it probably has one or two missing DEJ factors. However, if it is profitable in its second year, the investors will look for a public offering after the completion of the third or fourth year's audit.

Assume that two companies simultaneously visit a venture capitalist. Christopher Columbus Explorations, Inc., requires $500,000 to sail three ships to India in search of precious metals. Americus Vespucci needs $100,000 to purchase a printing press to produce and sell maps of India after he returns on the voyage with Columbus. Both entrepreneurs, Columbus and Vespucci, are willing to give up one-half of the ownership of their companies in exchange for $500,000 and $100,000, respectively.

Vespucci's three-year profit projections from the sale of maps are $25,000 in 1493, $50,000 in 1494, and $100,000 in 1495. Vespucci thinks that the market will capitalize that growth rate at a p/e ratio of 30 times, but in his business plan he uses a 10 times p/e. He shows the venture capitalist that 50% of 10 times $100,000 is equal to $500,000 or five times the investment in three years.

What kind of potential rate of return must Columbus show to attract venture capital? Assuming a 10 times p/e ratio, Columbus must necessarily project third-year earnings of $500,000 to have a rate of return comparable to Vespucci's. A larger projected dollar amount of earnings usually means that a larger problem is to be solved. And the greater the problem, the greater the p/e ratio. Thus the venture capitalist, in this case Queen Isabella, selects Columbus over Vespucci, because the eventual p/e will be larger.

Large Number of Buyers

Ideally, the market for the new product should contain an infinite number of buyers. This is usually attainable if the problem reflects a fairly ubiquitous incompetency among the buyers—like managing money, managing leisure time, transportation, beauty aids, and if the product becomes obsolete or replaces itself—razor blades, stamps, cosmetics.

For example, the market created by our inability to stop tooth decay has been an exciting area for new products. The electric toothbrush achieved an 8% market share of the United States toothbrush market. The Water Pic oral hygiene device manufactured by a Teledyne Corp. subsidiary is a popular gift, graduation, and wedding shower item. Sugarless chewing gum has grown in popularity and ultrasonic denture cleaners are showing an increased market share. The tooth decay market is a marvelous area for entrepreneurs. It involves hundreds of millions of customers making billions of purchases each year. A solution for cavities could be an entrepreneurial challenge.

On the other hand, if the number of potential buyers of a solution is relatively small—less than 1 million—the unit price of the product must be fairly large and there must be either repetitive sales or sales of ancillary products and services. For example, biomass plant manufacturers sell entire production operations that cost over $3 million each, plus expensive service and maintenance contracts. Some products require the purchase of replacement or spare parts.

Many venture capitalists consider the "success" level of a new company to be sales or market value of approximately $50 million five years after start-up. Sales and market value are not always identical, but rules of thumb are easy to adopt and use. In the world of venture capitalists it is assumed that companies normally will not earn more than 10% of their sales volume after taxes, or have p/e ratios greater than 10 times. Hence with sales of $50 million, 10% = $5,000,000 × 10 = $50,000,000 market value—an easy rule of thumb.

Therefore, if a company has a product selling for 25 cents—bubble gum cards, sugarless gum, breath fresheners—it needs 200,000,000 unit sales per year. Obviously, there must be repetitive sales as well as quantity purchases to achieve 200,000,000 individual sales each year.

At a unit price of $1.00, the company needs 20,000,000 sales per year. *Playboy* at $2.50 per copy is extraordinarily successful with nearly 15,000,000 sales per month, at least three-fourths of them on a prepaid, subscription basis.

At a risk of overgeneralizing, the scale of market sizes needed to achieve annual sales of $50,000,000 is as follows:

Unit Price($)	Number of Sales
0.10	500,000,000
1.00	50,000,000
10.00	5,000,000
100.00	500,000
1,000.00	50,000
10,000.00	5,000
100,000.00	500
1,000,000.00	50

Growth companies are growth companies regardless of the unit prices of their products. Xerox charges 5 cents per copy, Automatic Data Processing charges less than 30 cents per payroll check. McDonald's collects around $1.95 per customer order. Polaroid charges approximately $8 for a package of 10 pictures. Avon's cosmetics are less that $10 per unit. Holiday Inns collect $30–40 per room. Hospital Corporation of America charges $100 per room. And so forth, up to IBM's $3 million computers.

Inventors frequently make the error of inventing a line of ten or so products, each having a $1–2 million annual market, the sum of which, with a little pushing, might reach $20 million. Unfortunately, in many cases the products bear no relation to one another and require different production techniques and multiple sales forces and financing programs. Inventors frequently are not comfortable as members of entrepreneurial teams, which is another reason why they frequently do not build successful companies.

Submarkets, or favorable product niches, are more difficult to find and to convince venture capitalists about, but they are frequently explosive. Niches are problem areas restricted to a fewer number of buyers. *New York* magazine broke into the black more quickly than any magazine since *Sports Illustrated* by shooting with a rifle at relatively well-educated upwardly mobile middle-income New Yorkers who were finding it increasingly difficult to survive economically and emotionally in New York. Health foods, such as "Crunchy Granola" are popular with both organic and health food enthusiasts, and there have been several growth companies in the health food area. Note the explosive growth of the silicon chip companies such as Intel Corp., National Semiconductor Corp., Fairchild Semiconductor Corp., and Advanced Microsystems Corp., which, by reducing the cost of computer power for single-purpose solutions to less than $10, led the way for the creation of hobbyist computers to expand into the $1 billion personal computer market.

Lack of Institutional Barriers to Selling

Companies in the same industry and people sharing the same problem form associations to prevent the introduction of solutions to their problems.

The thickest book in my office library is *The Encyclopedia of Associations,* and in it are the names of all of the associations in the United States, their addresses, telephone numbers, and the names of their executive directors. If an entrepreneur develops a new tractor attachment that will ostensibly eliminate a present tractor attachment, I am able to call the Association of Farm Equipment Manufacturers and, after probing a while, learn that there is no problem in that area, thank you very much. Associations are don't-rock-the-boat oriented. They are not peopled with forward-thinking, progressive, entrepreneurial executives.

How important are industrial barriers to entrepreneurs? Ask the entrepreneurs, venture capitalists, and commercial bankers who lost more than $200 million in modular housing. State and local zoning codes began coming out of the woodwork to prevent the on-site erection in residential areas of homes built in factories. The housing industry, too, has its incompetence to protect.

Entrepreneurs with ideas for safe vehicles might just as well forget it. The establishment isn't buying. Detroit didn't offer energy-efficient cars until it had to. There are certain television sets that emit more radiation than an X-ray machine, but were you to invent a cheap consumer device to measure radiation from home television sets, who would you get to run your ads? Not television. And not the newspapers who are affiliated with television stations through common ownership. There are hundreds of formal and informal associations aimed at keeping out the problem solvers.

Associations are created by their members to prevent the solution for one member without the solution for all. For example, say New Farm Implements Corporation has developed an apple picker so revolutionary that it picks, peels, and cores apples in the field and bottles applesauce and applejuice on the ride back to the factory at a total cost of one-tenth of what it presently costs to pick apples, much less make applesauce.

The entrepreneur at New Farm Implements could elect to (1) manufacture and sell direct to apple processors, (2) license a farm implements manufacturer to produce and sell the new product, (3) build the equipment and lease it to apple processors, or (4) enter into contracts with apple processors to manage their picking/canning process at a fee equal to one-half their present budget. The first two methods of marketing probably will not work, whereas the third and fourth choices do not end run the manufacturers. If you charge into the offices of the large manufacturers of farm equipment or machinery, you may find that you get absolutely nowhere. They can do very well without you, so it is up to you to end run them. Charging directly into an old industry with a revolutionary new product is dangerous, foolhardy, and expensive. Nobody ever made money carrying coals to Newcastle.

Problems do not cost anything if nobody admits they exist. Solutions cost something. Associations, confederations, bureaucracies, and unions are formed by the members to lock the problems in and keep the solutions out. For an auto maker to license an air pollution device maker in 1960 would have been an admission of a problem. Therefore, to sell an auto maker a new air pollution product before the problem is made public, you must either end run the industry or create a demand among auto users around the country.

Informal institutional barriers—traditions, habits, buying patterns, inertia, insecurities, lack of confidence, and so forth—are frequently dealt with in the industry's trade journal. Hardware stores were being "sold" minicomputers and software packages in the late 1960s for inventory control. The hardware store trade magazine listed the pros and cons of computerization. In general, it was negative on computerization, feeling that good judgment required a wait-and-see attitude. Buyers read their trade journals, and as a rule of thumb, trade journals don't rock the boat. Ten years later the attitudes had changed. But for the entrepreneur who introduced small business computers to hardware stores before 1980, the cost of making a sale was very high.

Informal barriers, like trade journals, are almost as stiff as formal institutional barriers. Both are walls that stand in the way of the entrepreneur, and make the unknowing entrepreneur end up like Humpty Dumpty.

"Hey, It Really Works!" Phenomenon

In the context of entrepreneurship, advertising means "building solution awareness." It is not the creation of the demand for the product, which is the education factor but, rather, the identification of a specific source of supply:

Education factor   Identifies the problem
                           Creates the demand
Advertising factor   Identifies the problem solver
                           Identifies a specific source of supply

Sometimes the problem is sold along with the solution, as in "halitosis—try Listerine," or "tired blood—try Geritol." Where mass consumer markets are involved, it is possible to detect a problem, establish a demand curve, and move in with a specific solution before the competition is aware of what you have done.

However, for the most part, it is terribly expensive to create awareness for a problem. People just do not want to hear that they are in trouble. Entrepreneurs who have successfully convinced people of their problems and then provided them with a solution are marketing geniuses of the first order.

Most entrepreneurs are not geniuses. It is therefore more expedient for us to begin companies in areas where a definite problem exists: energy costs, cancer, crime, venereal disease, drug addiction, fear among old people, educational inadequacies, diabetes, deafness, and so forth. Assuming this is the case, and we must then spend a substantial portion of our budget on advertising, the solution may not be appropriate, timely, or suited to the problem.

If a new company must spend a substantial amount of capital on advertising, then investors regard the product as a "tough sale." One possible reason for its being a tough sale is that it is difficult to measure the success of the product's solution. In other words, heavily advertised products frequently lack the "Hey, it really works" factor.

For example, assume there is a new company that offers training for assembly-line personnel in encounter groups to increase personnel productivity. How do you measure productivity? This could be a valuable and necessary service for many corporations, but it will be a hard service to sell if the purchaser has no means of measuring success. On the other hand, a drug addiction treatment program for line personnel would be an easier sell because if the men on the assembly line stay awake during an eight-hour day, the program probably has been successful. The buyer will tell his friend, "Hey, it really works!" And that's free advertising.

If an entrepreneur must spend a substantial percentage of his budget to build awareness for his solution, then it is conceivable that his solution is not the best one for the problem. This condition usually exists in easy to enter, highly competitive markets. Breakfast cereal is a good illustration, because huge amounts of advertising are needed to generate solution awareness.

Venture capitalists, in general, tend to back away from advertising-intensive companies. Economic justification implies that in the marginal case, a qualified buyer will purchase a solution conveyed to him most of the time. Advertising should be employed merely to keep him qualified and aware of the solution. A projection of more than 5% of revenues as an advertising expenditure makes many venture capitalists nervous.

Optimum Price–Cost Relationship

There are principally two aspects to a price: the dollar amount and the form of payment. Companies that sell established products are more concerned with the amount, because it is a function of the cost of producing the product and competitive factors. Entrepreneurs do not need to concern themselves with the dollar amount. If an entrepreneurial solution has either serious competition or a narrow spread between price and cost, it is not a solution with high rate of return possibilities.

On the other hand, the form that the price will take is of grave concern to the entrepreneur. The several forms that a price can take are the following:

1. Direct sale
2. Installment sale
3. Lease
4. Rental

5. Meter or usage charge
6. Giveaway
7. Any of the above, plus:
    a. Service contract
    b. Related product purchases
    c. Replacement parts

For example, the Xerox copier is priced on a usage charge plus service contract basis. Cement plants are leased with service contracts. The Polaroid camera is sold with related products. A bank sells small loans on an installment basis. Hertz, Avis, National, and Budget rent cars, then charge for the number of miles driven.

Malcolm McLean was the entrepreneur primarily responsible for the development of the container shipping industry in the United States. The problem he identified was the increasing cost of shipping freight on steamships plus the shrinkage of product, such as Scotch whiskey at the unloading dock. The costs were particularly high at the loading and unloading points. McLean believed that if the van or container parts of the tractor were used to hold the freight on board, they could be lifted on and off trucks at dockside with cranes rather than dock workers. His idea resulted in the creation of a billion dollar market and the sale of his container shipping company, McLean Industries, Inc., to the R. J. Reynolds Corp. for more than $100 million.

McLean bought more than a dozen fully depreciated, mothballed ships under a sale-leaseback arrangement with private investors. He gutted the insides and welded in steel honeycombed walls in order to stack the containers. McLean then sought shipping business from international shippers. How did he price this revolutionary new container shipping service? The amount of the price was sufficient to cover McLean's ship-lease costs and operating expenses and provide a substantial gross profit margin, while substantially cheaper than traditional cargo shipping prices. The form of the price was the traditional space-occupied-times-distance-traveled fee used in the cargo-and-people shipping business for centuries.

With millions of dollars of monthly lease obligations, and competitors the like of Moore & McCormack and U.S. Lines, the new challenger in the cargo shipping industry stuck with traditional pricing methods. McLean was in a position to revise the form of payment drastically since he made shipping less expensive and quicker and virtually eliminated dockside shrinkage. He elected the wiser, more moderate course of action.

Many new products and services solve a specific problem sufficiently well to the extent that they produce greater profit margins than traditional products and services. For example, privately owned hospitals which provide profit-sharing incentives to doctors whose patients use the hospitals have greater profit margins than not-for-profit hospitals who care less about how many patients occupy beds. With greater profit margins, a company can afford to wait longer for payment. Hence these new proprietary hospital companies are able to offer credit or instaliment payments to their customers.

If you make it easier for people to pay, there will be less resistance to buying. Politicians are bad entrepreneurs. They sell themselves exhaustively to a mass audience every two, four, or six years, using millions of dollars of other people's money. Yet they make voting difficult and time consuming. Voting is like buying. A politician as competent as H. Ross Perot would legislate for a change in the method of voting to a much simpler way. For example, on election day each year, all registered voters could dial a computer from their homes and register their votes by touching appropriate buttons. Perhaps this will come about someday if enough successful entrepreneurs enter politics.

Once you have settled on a dollar price or form of payment for your new product or service, the price must be related to the cost of producing and marketing the product over time. This exercise is twofold: the first part is PERT chart analysis and the second part is Cash Flow analysis.

PERT chart analysis is a time study flow of events through your company that creates receipts and disbursements. For example, lets start a company that recycles and resells scrap paper. Assume that we occupy the proper plant. The time study of events will include:

1.   Contract with large paper users to provide scrap paper (1st–90th day).

2.   Hire unemployed people to pick up scrap paper (7th–21st day).

3.   Contract with sources to purchase recycled paper (21st–120th day).

4.   Close on all contracts (180th day).

Thus the new company has all costs and no receipts for its first 180 days. In its cash flow analysis, it must then account for a substantial initial cash deficit.

Cash flow analysis is a time study of receipts and disbursements which is done to determine how much capital a new company requires in order to match its proposed deficit. If the cash flow deficit is too great, such as $5 million in 12 months, the plan to launch the new company should probably be reevaluated. If the cash flow deficit is very small, like $20,000, then you should finance it yourself, like H. Ross Perot financed EDS.

The cash flow projection should begin by listing all the receipt and disbursement items, then varying each about three times, then taking the arithmetic mean of all the cash flow deficits thus generated. It is possible to purchase computer programs for this data problem to reduce the time requirement,

The greater the gross profit margin, the greater the available cash flow to build a management team and market the product and the smaller the reliance on venture capital.

Invisibility of the New Company

It is axiomatic in the company-launching business that anything worth doing is worth duplicating. You could have a patent on a cure for depression, but if it is selling well, dozens of competitors will emulate you and some of them will say to hell with patent infringement litigation. Their potential profits will cover legal fees and litigation.

For every successful new company, there will be many followers. Time-sharing had over 150 entrants. Modular housing had over 400 entrants. Even disposable thermometers had a dozen new company formations. To head off potential competition, an entrepreneurial company should keep a low profile. Invisibility is the entrepreneur's friend. To reverse Zero Mostel's famous quotation: "When you got it, *don't* flaunt it."

Do not advertise until you can deliver. Someone may beat you to the delivery date. Avoid all product publicity until the product can be produced in quantity.

Entrepreneurs are new to the company-launching business and full of optimism and enthusiasm. But what if you trip and fall on your face? Bear in mind the Entrepreneurial Laws of Gravity:

First Law. When things fall, they fall into the most difficult to reach places or break into the greatest number of pieces and all at the same time.

Second Law. When things fall, they do so in such a way as to cause the most damage to the greatest number of objects.

It is better to have a low profile in case things fall.

FINAL THOUGHTS

The 1980s will be remembered as the beginning of the Age of Entrepreneurship, a period in which social, medical, and industrial problems will be solved in many cases by small companies formed specifically to perform specific tasks such as increase the world's food supply at affordable prices, reduce the cost of energy through alternative sources, find inexpensive cures for serious diseases, and so forth. The process of raising capital to develop and market innovative solutions to difficult problems is becoming more systematic. In a decade or so, when entrepreneurial teams become more competent and when there are more experienced venture capitalists, the financing process will become routinized, in fact, probably as simple as getting a job. Then there will be more successful entrepreneurs who will look for other mountains to climb. It would not surprise me to see more and more entrepreneurs begin to enter government, create charitable foundations, become teachers, and begin to use their organizational and leadership gifts, their courage and tenacity, and indeed their wealth to try to make the world a truly better place for everyone.

APPENDIX 1

SAMPLE OPTION AND PROXY USED TO GAIN CONTROL IN LEVERAGED BUY-OUTS

General Proxy
(Shares of XYZ Corporation)
Expiration Date: _____, 1982

KNOW ALL MEN BY THESE PRESENTS, that

The undersigned shareholders(s) ("Grantor") of capital stock of XYZ Corporation, a (State) corporation ("Company"), do hereby constitute and appoint (your name) ("Grantee"), as true and lawful attorney for Grantor and in Grantor's name, place, and stead, for a period ending on the expiration date set forth above, to vote as Grantor's proxy all shares of the Grantor in said Company, at any and all meetings, regular and special, of the shareholders of the Company, or any adjournments thereof which may be held during said period, giving and granting to my said attorney all the powers the undersigned Grantor would possess if personally present (subject to the limitations contained in the next sentence), and Grantor hereby revokes all proxies heretofore made by me. Notwithstanding the foregoing the proxy granted herein, so far as it applies to the election of Directors of the Company, shall be limited to the election of not more than four (4) Directors out of a total Board of seven (7) Directors.

This proxy is coupled with an interest in that it is granted in express reliance upon similar proxy grants by other shareholders of the Company, and it is also granted in reliance upon Grantee's immediate undertaking to direct the affairs of the Company and to perform as herein provided. In the event (*a*) of the death, incapacity, or unwillingness of the Grantee to perform the undertakings hereinafter set out and actively direct the affairs of the Company as Chairman of the Board of Directors, or (*b*) of the failure of the Company to obtain a certified audit by a national accounting firm issued not later than (90 days) 1982 containing at least a signed qualified opinion (as contrasted to a more adverse audit report, "the certified audit"), then this option shall, in any such event, be deemed to be revoked and shall be of no further force and effect.

Subject to the terms of the preceding paragraph and prior to the exercise or expiration of this proxy grant, this proxy shall be *irrevocable* during the period and binding upon the heirs, personal representatives, and assigns of the Grantor *except and unless* the Grantee shall fail to perform in a timely manner any one of the following conditions within the time specified therein (and such failure shall not be expressly waived in writing by the Grantor), in which event this proxy shall be deemed to be revoked and shall be of no further force and effect:

1. Not later than sixty (60) days following completion of the certified audit of the Company, Grantee shall cause to be provided to Company such advances, loans, or contributions of cash and/or delivery or pledge of assets and/or negotiated net reduction of Company debt so that working capital of the Company is thereby increased by not less than $____, such financial arrangements to be made on such terms and conditions that the working capital additions thereby provided shall not be repaid within a period of one (1) year and one (1) day from infusion into the Company.

2. Not later than one hundred fifty (150) days following completion of the certified audit of the Company, Grantee shall cause to be provided to Company such additional advances, loans, or contributions of cash and/or delivery or pledge of assets and/or negotiated net reduction of Company debt so that working capital of the Company is thereby increased by $____ (making a total of $____), such financial arrangements to be made on such terms

and conditions that the working capital additions thereby provided shall not be repaid within a period of one (1) year and one (1) day from infusion into the Company.

During the period that Grantee is entitled to exercise the proxy rights granted herein, he expressly agrees:

1. To permit (inside person), on behalf of the Grantor and the Company at the expense of the Company, or such other financial advisor as a majority in interest of the shareholders (including Grantor) granting similar proxies to Grantee shall determine, to examine the financial and operational status of the Company and, in particular, compliance with the several conditions hereinabove provided, and to report back to Grantor. At all reasonable times during normal working hours, the said (inside person) or other financial advisor shall be provided timely and reasonable access to all books and records of the Company, operating reports and plans, capital and financing commitments and appropriations, and operating personnel, in order to carry out his assigned duties. In addition, Grantee shall routinely provide said advisor or other financial advisor, at least once a month, with information of a nature that would show significant changes in financial, operating and personnel matters, and conditions of the Company.

2. To refrain from causing the Company to issue or otherwise transfer to Grantee, to any person related by blood or marriage to Grantee, or to any corporation, trust, partnership or other entity in which Grantee has an interest, shares of stock of any class (or other security convertible into shares of stock of any class) of the Company, except as may be approved by Judge (in bankruptcy, trustee), or his successor in Chapter XI proceedings now pending with respect to the Company.

3. To operate the affairs of the Company in a sound and business-like manner with due regard for the best interests of Grantor and other shareholders similarly situated and so long as the Company is involved in Chapter XI proceedings in compliance with the orders and directions of Judge (bankruptcy, trustee), or his successor.

4. During the pendency of this proxy grant, Grantee agrees to cause the day-to-day affairs of the Company to be monitored by

an Advisory Committee of the Board of Directors consisting of four (4) members and (key manager) and (other key manager) shall serve as two (2) such members.

_____   _____   _____
Shares Owned   Shares
                                           Subject to Option

             _____
                   Granted

Dated: (closing) ____, 1982

Agreed:

_____
(Your name)

APPENDIX 2

SAMPLE
BUSINESS PLANS

Sample: *Operating statement projections for a start-up manufacturer of an exact measuring device used by helicopter operators in marking sites for oil-drilling, mining, land development, and so forth*

LIST OF ASSUMPTIONS

1. *Fiscal Year End:* May 31.
2. *Closing Date of This Private Placement:* 7/31/82.
3. *System Sales Price:* Assume all product sales are at a retail price of $150,000, less sales commission or dealer discount of 15% on that portion of the system exclusive of the carbon clocks. The carbon clocks cost the Company approximately $18,950 each, and there are three carbon clocks in each system for a total clock cost of $56,850; the discount of 15%, or $14,000, applies to the non-clock part of the system, for an assumed net sales price of $136,000 per system.

Assume all system sales to helicopter operators are in the Gulf Coast and follow an initial sale of four base stations at $50,000 each. Then the helicopter sales would involve mobile units requiring one diamond clock system each at a gross sales price of $15,000, less a 15% discount of $1,397, for an assumed net sales price of $12,750 per mobile unit.

4. *Sales or Rentals:* Assume the Company management discourages rentals until its third year of operations, and that all of the systems are sold through dealers until the third full year of the projections. Assume that the rental charge for the systems, when implemented, will be equal to 1/11 of the gross sales price per month, or:

	Carbon Clock Systems	Diamond Clock Systems
Gross sales price	$ 150,000	$ 120,000
Net sales price	136,000	102,000
Monthly rental (1/11)	13,636	10,908
Net monthly rental	12,363	9,272

Assume further, that each rental is for a period of 6 months, that a system comes off rental for 6 months, and that it is rerented for 6 months, and so forth.

5. *System Deliveries:* The following assumptions* have been made by Company management for the twelve months ended 5/31:

	1982	1983	1984
Oceanographic commercial (C)[c]	8-S[a]	20-S	15-S
Navy (C)	2-S	8-S	12-S
Helicopter (D)[b]	—	2-S	10-S

6. *Terms of Payment:* Assume that the Company receives a down payment on sales of 10% of the gross sales price upon receipt of order, 20% two months thereafter, and the balance of the net sales price upon delivery, as follows:

	Carbon	Diamond
Down payment	$ 15,000	$ 12,000
Installment	30,000	24,000
Final payment	90,600	66,000
Total	$135,600	$102,000

C = carbon; D = diamond; S = sales; R = rental.

*Rounded up to nearest $500.00.

Assume that all rentals require a security deposit equal to one month's rental upon receipt of order; that is, $13,636 for carbon and $10,908 for diamond.

7. *Replacement Parts Sales:* Assume they begin in year two at a rate equal to 25% of year 1 sales.

8. *Production Cycle:* Assume that the first five orders of both systems require 5 months to complete and deliver and that all subsequent orders require 3 months to complete and deliver.

9. *Production Costs:* Assume that the direct labor cost component of each system is $5,000 and that the cost of goods sold excluding direct labor are $70,500 for carbon clock systems and $42,600 for diamond clock systems, the difference arising from the fact that the former requires three carbon clocks at a cost of $18,950 (per unit) each and the latter requires one carbon clock and two diamond clocks at a cost of approximately $5,000 each.

The components of the system, and their costs to the Company (as recently quoted by vendors) are as follows:

MAJOR COMPONENTS

Mobile Station

2	Receiver	$ 1,602.96	Each
2	Crystal assembly	110.00	Each
1	Instrumentation	3,400.00	
1	Frequency standard	18,950.00	
1	Strip chart recorder, dual channel	840.00	
1	Antenna (2)	976.00	

Base Stations, *Each* (minimum of two stations required)

1	Exciter	1,086.50
1	Linear amplifier	
1	Frequency standard	18,950.00
1	Antenna (3)	488.00

Plug-In Modules

Receiver

1	R.F. module	235.30
1	I.F. module	66.77
1	Sideband multiplier	67.38
1	Sideband VCXO	41.16
1	Sideband VCXO	41.16
1	R.F.I. filter assembly	7.00

Receiver

1	Local oscillator	54.73
1	Mother board	37.50
1	Voltage regulator	98.33
2	Sideboard 0 lock loop	78.40
1	AGC and APC assembly	55.47
1	Carrier lane gen. and sync.	50.69
1	Output interface	39.47
1	Synthesizer	49.70
1	Potted crystal plug. assembly (4)	100.00

Instrumentation

2	Unambiguous phase meter	300.00	Each
1	Lane accumulators	195.00	
1	Master divider	140.00	
1	Frequency selector	115.00	
1	Histogram analyzer	220.00	
1	Tone generator	100.00	
2	Carrier synthesizer	110.00	Each
1	Balanced modulator	70.00	
1	Antenna splitter matcher	140.00	
1	Lane display	240.00	
1	Output bus control	70.00	
1	Front panel	620.00	
1	Power supply	130.00	

Exciter

1	Exciter balanced modulator	75.00
1	Tone generator	100.00
1	Carrier synthesizer	100.00
1	Exciter freq. scl.	120.00
1	Exciter master divider	100.00
1	Pre amplifier	100.00
1	Power supply	110.00
	Total component costs	$70,500.00*

10. *Selling Expenses:* Assume one full-time salesman employed beginning June, 1982 at a salary of $30,000 per year plus a 5% sales commission based on net sales price. Assume that he is responsible for one-half of total sales, but that consultants are responsible for the balance of the sales, and receive a commission of 5% of net sales price. Assume sales support expenses of $5,000 in Year 1, $10,000 in Year 2, and $15,000 in Year 3. These expenses will include the salesman's travel and entertainment budget, catalogs, advertisements in trade journals, and booths at trade shows.

11. *General and Administrative Expenses:*   Assume G&A expenses of $154,000 per year (plus 10% annual escalator) which includes the following:

Officer's salary	$ 25,000
Engineering salaries (3)	48,000
Clerical salary	8,000
Rent (6,000 ft^2 × 150)	9,000
Telephone ($1,000/mo.)	12,000
Taxes, franchise fees	6,000
Audit	6,000
Legal	6,000
Patent counsel	12,000
Employee benefits (20%)	16,000
Insurance and misc.	6,000
Total annual G&A	$154,000

Assume in Year 2 the addition of a full-time president and/or chief marketing and administrative officer at a salary of $30,000 per year plus benefits and an increase of 10% in all salaries.

Assume in Year 3 the addition of a full-time vice-president finance at a salary of $20,000 per year and increase of 10% in all salaries. Assume also an increase of 50% in rent and telephone expenses.

12. *Engineering Expenses:*   Assume that the Company spends $25,000 per annum for applied engineering expenses in Year 1 and $100,000 per annum thereafter.

13. *Royalties:*   The Company is contractually obligated to pay ABC Company royalties on the sales or rental income on the Precise Radio System as follows:

Sales or Rental Income	Royalty (%)
Up to $1.0 million	0
$1.0 million–$6.0 million	3%
$6.0 million–$11.0 million	2%
$11.0 million–$16.0 million	1%
Over $16.0 million	0

14. *Interest Expenses:* Assume all present indebtedness either repaid if owed to banks or converted to equity if owed to stockholders.

15. *Depreciation:* Assume $30,000 of production equipment purchased after the closing of this financing and depreciated over 10 years at a cost of $250.00 per month. Present depreciation of production equipment is at the rate of $333.00 per month. Hence, total depreciation is projected at the rate of approximately $600.00 per month through the projection period.

THREE-YEAR OPERATING
STATEMENT PROJECTIONS*

EXACT MEASURING DEVICE CORPORATION

First Year

	Quarter 1	Quarter 2	Quarter 3	Quarter 4	Total 5/31/83
Systems Orders					
Oceanographic	—	2	2	4	8
Navy	—	—	—	2	2
Helicopters	—	—	—	—	—
Revenues					
Oceanographic	—	$ 30	$ 90	$ 301	$ 421
Navy	—	—	—	$ 30	$ 30
Helicopters	—	—	—	—	—
Total revenues	—	$ 30	$ 90	$ 331	$ 451
Cost of goods sold					
Oceanographic	—	76	76	227	379
Navy	—	—	—	76	76
Total cost of goods sold	—	76	76	303	455
Gross profit (loss)	—	(46)	26	28	(4)
Selling expenses	—	—	—	5	5
General and admin. exps.	38	38	38	40	154
Engineering expenses	—	5	10	10	25
Total SG&A and eng. exps.	38	43	48	55	184

	Quarter 1	Quarter 2	Quarter 3	Quarter 4	Total 5/31/83
Net operating income	$ (38)	(89)	(22)	(27)	(188)
Interest expense	—	—	—	—	—
Royalty expense	—	—	—	—	—
Net profit (loss) before taxes	$ (38)	$ (89)	$ (22)	$ (27)	$(188)

*Dollar amounts are given in thousands.

Second Year

	Quarter 5	Quarter 6	Quarter 7	Quarter 8	Total 5/31/84
Systems Orders					
Oceanographic	4	5	5	6	20
Navy	2	2	2	2	8
Helicopters	—	—	—	2	2
Revenues					
Oceanographic	$ 361	$ 542	$ 557	$ 693	$2,153
Navy	90	271	271	271	903
Helicopters	—	—	—	102	102
Total revenues	$ 451	$ 813	$ 828	$1,066	$3,158
Cost of Goods Sold					
Oceanographic	302	339	377	414	1,432
Navy	152	152	152	152	608
Helicopters	—	—	—	48	48
Total cost of goods sold	454	491	529	614	2,098
Gross profit	(3)	322	299	452	1,060
Selling expenses	40	60	70	70	240
General and admin. exps.	40	50	50	60	200
Engineering exps.	15	20	20	20	75
Total SG&A and eng. exps.	95	130	140	150	515
Net operating income	(98)	192	159	302	545
Interest expense	—	—	—	—	—
Royalty expense	—	—	—	95	95
Net profit before taxes	$(98)	$ 192	$ 159	$ 207	$ 450

Third Year

	Quarter 9	Quarter 10	Quarter 11	Quarter 12	Total 5/31/85
Systems Orders					
Oceanographic—S	3	3	4	5	15
R	3	3	4	5	15
Navy	3	3	3	3	12
Helicopters	2	2	3	3	10
Revenues					
Oceanographic—S	$ 678	$ 679	$ 322	$ 467	$2,146
R	—	114	280	345	739
Navy	286	316	407	407	1,416
Helicopters	129	27	27	27	210
Replacement parts	—	30	40	50	120
Total revenues	$1,093	$1,166	$1,076	$1,296	$4,631
Cost of Goods Sold					
Oceanographic	452	452	528	678	2,110
Navy	190	228	266	342	1,026
Helicopters	64	17	17	17	115
Total cost of goods sold	706	697	811	1,037	3,251
Gross profit	387	469	265	259	1,380
Selling expenses	60	60	70	70	260
General and admin. exps.	60	60	60	60	240
Engineering expenses	15	20	20	20	75
Total SG&A and eng. exps.	135	140	150	150	575
Net operating income	252	329	115	109	805
Interest expense	—	—	—	—	—
Royalty expense	—	—	—	135	135
Net profit before Taxes	$ 232	$ 329	$ 115	$ (26)	$ 670

Sample: *Operating statement for a first-stage retail chain operator (restaurant, clothing, and the like)*

LIST OF ASSUMPTIONS

Projected Store Operating Income and Expenses for First Three Years of Operation of Typical Store (2,300 Square Feet)

1. Net sales for the first year of operation of new stores are projected to equal the sales of the two existing stores, adjusted for square footage, for their first year of operation. Net sales for the second year of operation are projected to exceed first year sales by 30%, and net sales for the third year of operation are projected to exceed second year sales by 15%.

2. Cost of goods sold is projected at 50% of net sales, after allowing for freight, cleaning, alterations, markdowns, and discounts, based on present margins and previous experience.

3. Sales salaries are projected at 12% of net sales in accordance with the Corporation's incentive pay system of commissions and bonuses.

4. Rent is projected at 6% of net sales as provided in the Corporation's existing and proposed lease agreements.

5. Store utilities are projected at $6 per square foot per year for an average store size of 2,300 square feet, or approximately $14,0000 per year. Telephone expense is estimated at $1,000 per year.

6. Advertising and promotion are projected at 1% of net sales with planned expenditures limited to the months of October, November, and December. Cooperative advertising agreements between the Corporation and several of its key suppliers have been entered into in order to provide additional nonbudgeted funds for advertising.

7. Store office supplies expense is projected at 1/2% of net sales based on previous experience.

8. Packaging supplies expense is projected at 1/2% of net sales based on previous experience.

9. Credit card discounts are projected at 1% of net sales based on previous experience.

10. Customer bad debts expense is projected at 1/2% of net sales based on previous experience.

Projected Administrative Expenses
for Operating Levels
of 5, 11, and 20 Stores

1. Executive salaries are projected as follows: president, $36,000 per year plus 5% of the Corporation's net income per year in excess of $150,000, executive vice-president, $24,000 per year.

2. Other administrative salaries are projected to allow the Corporation to hire and retain qualified personnel in the areas of finance, purchasing, and administration, as needed.

3. Interest expense is projected to allow for accrued interest on subordinated debentures as well as short-term working capital loans for expansion.

4. Travel and entertainment is projected to allow monthly visits to all store locations by general office personnel.

5. The cost of equipment leases is projected to allow the Corporation to completely computerize its accounting, inventory control, and sales management systems.

Actual and Projected (P) Income
and Expenses for the Fiscal Years
Ending September 30, 1982 through 1985

1. The actual income statement and expenses for the fiscal year ending September 30, 1981 are taken from the Corporation's unaudited financial statement as of that date.

2. The projected income and expenses for the fiscal year ending Septemer 30, 1982 are an extension of the Corporation's actual income and expenses from the corporation's unaudited financial statement for the 9-months ending June 30, 1982.

3. The projected income and expenses for the fiscal years ending September 30, 1983, 1984, and 1985 are the result of multiplying the projected number of stores in operation and levels of maturity for the fiscal years ending September 30, 1983 through 1989 by the projected store operating income and expenses for the first three years of operation of a typical store (2,300 square feet) and subtracting the projected administrative expenses for operating levels of 5, 11, and 20 stores and allowing for estimated corporate federal and state income taxes.

Actual and Projected (P) Assets
and Liabilities as of the Close of Three
Fiscal Years Ending September 30, 1983 through 1985

1. The actual assets and liabilities as of the close of the fiscal year ending September 30, 1981 are taken from the Corporation's unaudited financial statement as of that date.

2. The projected assets and liabilities as of the close of the fiscal year ending September 30, 1982 are an extension of the Corporation's actual assets and liabilities from the corporation's unaudited financial statement for the 9 months ending June 30, 1982.

3. The projected assets and liabilities as of the close of fiscal years ending September 30, 1983, 1984, and 1985 are the result of giving effect to the projected income and expenses for the fiscal years in question as well as significant nonincome or—expense transaction, including the following:

    a. Increases in trade accounts receivable projected at $8,000 per new store.

    b. Increases in merchandise inventory projected at $40,000 per store.

    c. Collection of notes receivable of $20,000 in the fiscal year ending September 30, 1983.

    d. Increases in prepaid and deferred expenses as projected.

    e. Increases in store fixtures and equipment projected at $10,000 per store.

    f. Increases in store leasehold improvements projected at $57,000 per store.

    g. Increases in office furniture and equipment and automobile equipment as projected.

PROJECTED NEW STORE OPENINGS
FOR THE FISCAL YEARS ENDING
SEPTEMBER 30, 1982 THROUGH 1984

Geographic Region	Metropolitan Market Area	Openings FYE 9/30/82	Openings FYE 9/30/83	Openings FYE 9/30/84
West	San Francisco	Palo Alto	Stanford	Marin
				Berkeley
	Los Angeles		West Covina	Montclair
	San Diego		Fashion Sq.	La Jolla Acres
Midwest	Chicago	Northbrook		Heightstown
		Tall Oaks		Elm Hill
	Detroit		Bayfair	Lake Shore
	Cleveland			Millville Park
South	Atlanta		Northpark	
	Houston		The Galleria	
	Dallas			Westbrook

The foregoing new store openings represent the Corporation's tentative plans for expansion within its present market and into new markets during the next three years.

Final lease negotiations have been entered into with respect to locations scheduled for opening in the fiscal year ending September 30, 1982, and preliminary lease negotiations have been entered into with respect to locations scheduled for opening in the fiscal year ending September 30, 1983. The new store openings scheduled for the fiscal year ending September 30, 1984 are only tentative.

It is the goal of the Corporation that stores scheduled for opening in a given fiscal year will be open by the first day of that fiscal year. All financial data and projections included herein assume new store openings in accordance with that schedule.

PROJECTED NEW STORE OPENING
COSTS FOR THE FISCAL YEAR ENDING
SEPTEMBER 30, 1982 THROUGH 1984

	Projected New Store Opening Costs per Store	FYE 9/30/82 3 New Stores to Be Opened (8,500 ft²)	FYE 9/30/83 6 New Stores to Be Opened (13,800 ft²)	FYE 9/30/84 9 New Stores to Be Opened (20,700 ft²)
Leasehold improvements	$ 57,500	$172,500	$345,000	$517,500
Merchandise inventory	40,000	120,000	240,000	360,000
Fixtures and equipment	10,000	30,000	60,000	90,000
Total	$107,500	$322,500	$645,000	$967,500

The per store cost of leasehold improvements is calculated by multi-plying estimated average square footage per store (2,300 square feet) by the dollar cost per square foot ($25) for construction of the Corpora-tion's present two stores. No reduction is made for cash construction al-lowances from landlords although such allowances are a standard re-quirement in the Corporation's lease negotiations.

PROJECTED NUMBER OF STORES IN OPERATION
AND LEVELS OF MATURITY FOR THE FISCAL YEARS
ENDING SEPTEMBER 30, 1982 THROUGH 1984

	FYE 9/30/82	FYE 9/30/83	FYE 9/30/84
Number of stores in first year	3	6	9
Number of stores in second year	1	3	6
Number of stores in third year	1	2	5
Total	5	11	20

PROJECTED STORE OPERATING INCOME AND EXPENSES
FOR FIRST THREE YEARS OF OPERATION
OF TYPICAL STORE (2,300 SQUARE FEET)

	First Year		Second Year		Third Year	
	Amount	Percent of Sales	Amount	Percent of Sales	Amount	Percent of Sales
Net Sales	$500,000	100.0	$650,000	100.0	$750,000	100.0
Cost of Goods Sold						
Merchandise	237,000	47.3	307,000	47.3	355,000	47.3
Freight, cleaning, and alterations	6,000	1.2	8,000	1.2	9,000	1.2
Markdowns and discounts	7,000	1.5	10,000	1.5	11,000	1.5
Total	$250,000	50.0	$325,000	50.0	$375,000	50.0
Gross Profit on Sales	$250,000	50.0	$325,000	50.0	$375,000	50.0

Store Operating Expenses

	Amount	%	Amount	%	Amount	%
Sales salaries	60,000	12.0	78,000	12.0	90,000	12.0
Payroll taxes and benefits	9,000	1.5	10,000	1.5	11,000	1.5
Rent	30,000	6.0	39,000	6.0	45,000	6.0
Utilities and telephone	15,000	3.0	15,000	2.3	15,000	2.0
Maintenance and upkeep	1,000	0.2	1,000	0.1	1,000	0.1
Taxes and insurance	2,000	0.4	2,000	0.3	2,000	0.3
Advertising and promotion	5,000	1.0	6,000	1.0	7,000	1.0
Display and decoration	1,000	0.2	1,000	0.1	1,000	0.1
Office supplies	2,000	0.5	3,000	0.5	4,000	0.5
Packaging supplies	2,000	0.5	3,000	0.5	4,000	0.5
Credit card discounts	5,000	1.0	6,000	1.0	7,000	1.0
Customer bad debts	2,000	0.5	3,000	0.5	4,000	0.5
Equipment leases	1,000	0.2	1,000	0.1	1,000	0.1
Depreciation and amortization	8,000	1.6	8,000	1.2	8,000	1.1
Other store expenses	1,000	0.2	1,000	0.1	1,000	0.1
Total	$144,000	28.8	$177,000	27.2	$201,000	26.8
Store Operating Profit	$106,000	21.2	$148,000	22.8	$174,000	23.2

PROJECTED ADMINISTRATIVE EXPENSES
FOR OPERATING LEVELS OF 5, 11, AND 20 STORES

	5-Store Operation		11-Store Operation		20-Store Operation	
	Amount	Percent of Total	Amount	Percent of Total	Amount	Percent of Total
Administrative Expenses						
Executive salaries	$ 60,000	22.2	$ 70,000	18.4	$ 80,000	16.0
Other administrative salaries	75,000	27.8	100,000	26.3	125,000	25.0
Payroll taxes and benefits	10,000	3.7	11,000	2.9	14,000	2.8
Rent	12,000	4.4	18,000	4.8	24,000	4.8
Utilities and telephone	10,000	3.7	15,000	3.9	20,000	4.0
Maintenance and upkeep	1,000	0.3	2,000	0.5	4,000	0.8
Taxes and insurance	3,000	1.1	6,000	1.6	12,000	2.4
Office supplies	3,000	1.1	6,000	1.6	12,000	2.4
Legal and accounting	5,000	1.9	10,000	2.6	15,000	3.0
Interest	30,000	11.1	40,000	10.5	50,000	10.0
Automobile operation	5,000	1.9	10,000	2.6	15,000	3.0
Travel and entertainment	25,000	9.3	50,000	13.2	75,000	15.0
Equipment leases	15,000	5.6	20,000	5.3	25,000	5.0
Depreciation and amortization	15,000	5.6	20,000	5.3	25,000	5.0
Other adm. expenses	1,000	0.3	2,000	0.5	4,000	0.8
Total	$270,000	100.0	$380,000	100.0	$500,000	100.0

INDEX

Accountants, requirement for, 21, 58,
    151, 181, 188
Accounts payable as source of cash,
    20–21, 161–162, 192
Accounts receivable financing, 9, 17,
    95–102, 190
ACS America, Inc., 78
Advanced Microsystems Corp., 213
Advance ratios on secured loans,
    97–102, 108
Alaska Renewable Resources Fund, 57
Allen & Co., 82
Allied Corporation, 34
Allis-Chalmers Corp., 158
Allstate Insurance Co., 23, 146
Alternative energy sources, 35, 111, 152,
    154, 211, 220
American Cyanamid Corp., 36
American Electronic Association, 39
American Express Corp., 110, 112
American Hospital Supply Corp., 117
American Motors Corp., 117
American Research and Development
    Corp., 40, 207
American Standard Corp., 118
Amoco Venture Capital Company, 43
Apollo Computer Corp., 122, 125
Apple Computer Corporation, 4, 160,
    175, 207
Arcoa Corporation, 4
Arthur Murray Dance Studios, 105,
    168–170
Associated Southwest Investors, 44
Atari Inc., 122
Audited financial statements,
    requirement for, 50
Automatic Data Processing Corp., 108,
    204, 212

Baca, Ben, 44
Bankrupt companies, purchase of,
    13–20, 97
Bankruptcy in entrepreneur's back-
    ground, 158–159
Battelle Memorial Institute, 153
Bell & Howell, 153
Biogen, 36
Biotechnology, 35, 71, 83, 111
Bird in the hand, value of, 53
Bishops report, 159
Body language, 198–200
Boise Cascade Corporation, 34
Bradford Computer Systems Corp., 108
Bridge financing, 162
Bushnell, Nolan, 122
Business Development Corporations,
    55–60, 91
Business plan, 28, 65, 85, 93, 121–145,
    152, 156, 167, 172
Business Week, 144

Capital, amount to raise, 132
Carlson, Chester, 4, 153
Carnegie, Andrew, 77
Carson, Johnny, 199
Central Data Corporation, 127
Century 21 Corporation, 168
Cetus Corporation, 4, 36
Chicken Delight legal battle, 106
Chrysler Corporation, 126
Cisneros, Ignacio, 43
Citicorp Venture Capital Ltd., 23, 122,
    146
Codenol, Inc., 82
Commercial banks:
    as lenders under SBA program,
    91–92, 95

Commercial banks (*Continued*)
  as no risk lenders, 95, 193–194
Commercial finance companies, 11, 17,
  96–97, 190, 193–194
Commitment fees, 97, 190, 191
Computer Usage Corp., 179
Connecticut, grant program, 78
Consulting business, form of customer
  financing, 111
Consumer Electronics, 144
Container shipping, 133
Control Data Corp., 36
Control of company by investors, 50,
  83, 131, 134
Convertible subordinated debentures,
  48, 134, 162
Corporate planning departments,
  117–118, 153
Corporate venture capital investing,
  33–37
  objectives other than capital gains,
  34
Co-sale agreements, 52
Crane Corp., 118
Creative Capital Corporation, 160
Cross default covenant, 49, 191
Cummins Engine Corporation, 122
Customer financing, 5, 103–113, 169

Davis, Tommy, 207
Decision-making process at SBICs and
  venture capital funds, 47–48
Delorean, John Z., 126
Demonstrable economic justification
  (DEJ) factors, 201–219
Diablo Corp., 122
Diamond Shamrock Corporation, 34
Digital Equipment Corporation, 30, 34,
  41, 122
Dilution of entrepreneurs' ownership,
  85
Direct mail, customer financing,
  110–113, 128, 159
Divisional spin-offs, 7
Doriot, General Georges, 40, 207
Dow Chemical Company, 34
Dress code for entrepreneurs, 197–
  198
Dun & Bradstreet reports, 89
Durham, Walter, 43

Eastman Kodak Corp., 148, 153
Eaton Corporation, 34
Economic Development Administra-
  tion (EDA), 91
Electronic Data Systems Corp., 104,
  202, 219
Electronic funds transfer systems,
  typical new industry growth pat-
  tern, 110–111
Employment, creation of, 39, 45, 55, 58,
  79, 159
Encyclopedia of Associations, 213
Endorsements of entrepreneurs, 138,
  146, 169, 195
Entrepreneurial team, importance of,
  173, 200, 207–208
Entrepreneurs, rankings of, 178–180
Equipment financing, 9, 11, 13, 17,
  95–102
Equitable Life Assurance, minority in-
  vesting, 42
EST, 105, 168, 170
Evelyn Wood Reading Dynamics, 168,
  170
Expansion:
  first stage, 29, 123
  mezzanine stage, 31, 163
Expenses of various financings, 68, 85
Exxon Enterprises Inc., 34–35

Facilities management, as customer
  financing, 104, 108–110, 202–203, 204
Fairchild Semiconductor Corp., 213
Family money, 26, 148–151
Family owned companies, 7, 11
Farley, Peter, 4
Farmers Home Administration
  (FmHA), 91, 163
Federal Express Corporation, 4, 30, 109,
  125, 127, 146
First National Bank of Chicago, 146
First stage of expansion, 29, 123
Food supply, 220
Forbes, 138
Ford Motor Company, 42, 82
Foreign governments as venture capi-
  talists, 37–38
Franchising, 73–74, 105, 106–108, 151,159
Freedom and Capitalism, 109
Friedman, Dr. Milton, 79, 109

Frost and Sullivan, 127
Full disclosure to investors, 158–159

GAF Corp., 153
Genentech Corporation, 28, 83, 136, 175
General Electric Co., 204
General Foods Corp., minority invest-
    ing, 41
Gerstenberger, Richard, 34
Goldman, Sachs & Co., 82
Government-guaranteed loans, 5, 13,
    53, 56, 78, 91–94, 98, 126, 193
Graham, Dr. Billy, 199
Granitelli, Andy, 118
GTE Corp., 34
Gulf Oil Corporation, 34
Gulf + Western, 20
Guren, Charles, 169

Haloid Company, 153
Hay, Timothy, 130
Heinze, Walter, 118
"Hell-or-high-water" clause, 191
Hewlett-Packard, 3, 28, 29, 136
Hockey stick valuation method, 124–125
Holiday Inns Corporation, 104, 212
Home computers, 111, 143–144, 166
Home satellite antennas, 103, 141–143
Home video, 111
Hospital Corporation of America, 212
Hughes Aircraft Company, 142
Hybritech Inc., 82, 136

Iaccoca, Lee, 126
IBM Corp., 104, 212
Industrial Development Authority, 27,
    58, 76
Industrial Revenue Bonds, 127
Inflation, positive factor in tax shelter
    financings, 76
Information processing, 35, 139–140,
    204, 214
Insurance, requirement for, 50
Intel Corporation, 4, 30, 213
Interferon, 83, 220
Internal Revenue Service, 15, 58, 69–71,
    74, 189
International Harvestor Corp., 51
International Water Saving Systems,
    Inc., 118

Inventory financing, 9, 95–102
Investment banker, 25, 62, 64, 75, 85,
    119, 121, 138, 146, 172, 181
Invisibility, requirement for, 85, 204, 219
Israel, high technology in, 37
Itek Corp., 148

Jobs, Steve, 160, 175
Johnson, Wallace, 104
Johnson & Johnson, 34
Joint ventures and licensing, 115–120,
    170
JS&A, 112
Judgment of entrepreneurs, 4, 179

Kentucky Fried Chicken, 105, 205
Kleiner, Perkins and Co., 29, 136, 175
Kroc, Ray, 160

Lautenberg, Frank, 204
Lawyers, requirement for, 21, 64, 68, 75,
    107, 151, 157, 181, 188
Leasing, 128, 191, 213
Lee, David, 122
Letter of Intent, 184–187
Leveraged buy-out, 7–21, 31, 180–191
    diagrams, 8, 12, 18, 19
    method, 180–191
    ways to get hurt, 21, 181
Licensee/dealership tax shelter
    financing, 72–76
Ling, Jimmy, 82
Linowitz, Sol, 154
Lion Country Safari, 170
Liquidifying investments, 131, 137–138,
    167
Little, Arthur D. Inc., 153
Little, Royal, 160
Lloyds of London, 102
Loan guarantee insurance, 101–102
Lorie, James, 157
LTV Corporation, 82

McDonalds Corp., 105, 106, 151–152,
    160, 205, 212
McLean, Malcolm, 133, 217
McMurtry, Burton, 138
McNeish, Peter F., 42
Magazine financings, 69–70
Mailing lists as collateral, 101, 105

Market, problem seeking a solution, 156, 205, 210, 214
Markulla, Michael, 4
Mary Kay Cosmetics, 105, 176
Massachusetts Technology Development Corp., 57
MCI Communications Corp., 125
Merrill Lynch, 157
MESBIC Financial Corporation, 43
Mezzanine stage of expansion, 31, 163
Minority Enterprise Small Business Investment Companies (MESBIC), 39, 41–43, 95, 194
Minority Equity Capital Company, 43
Monogram Industries, 30
Monsanto Corp., 36
Morgan Stanley & Co., 179
Motorola Corp., 34
Movie financing, 42
Ms. Magazine, 110

Narragansett Capital Corp., 160
National Science Foundation grants, 77
National Semiconductor Corp., 213
Negative planning, 129
Negotiating with investors, 52
Networking, 57–60
New Issues, 81
Newsletter publishing, 110, 111, 170
New York magazine, 212
Non-complete agreement, 191
Not-for-profit corporation, 78
Noyce, Robert, 176
Nutrition market, 111, 169

Oil and gas drilling programs, 64
Option and proxy, 17, 221–224

Party-plan selling, 105, 128
Payment Systems, Inc., 110
Penny stock market, 81, 89, 152, 156–157, 159, 173
Perot, H. Ross, 104, 202–203, 218–219
Personal Software, Inc., 207
PERT Chart, 26, 128–129, 131, 133–134, 136, 152, 155, 218
Pink sheets, 89, 180
Pizza Time Theaters Inc., 122
Plant visit by potential investor, 47
Playboy, 104, 212

Playtex, 118
Poduska, Bill, 122
Polaroid Corporation, 30, 118, 133, 212, 217
Preferred stock, venture capital funds use of, 49, 134
Prime computer Corp., 122
Pritikin Better Health Program, 170
Production model of new product, 152–153, 158
Professional launch, by venture capitalists, 67, 173–174, 178–180
Project financing, 35–36
Proudfoots, 159
Psychology Today, 4, 111
Public offerings, 53, 65, 68, 78, 81–86, 87, 126, 155
Public shells, 87–89
Put and call provisions in loans, 162

Qume Corp., 122

R & D tax shelter, 5, 53, 63–67, 70–71, 78, 126
Real estate financing, 17, 60, 76
Research and Development Grants, 77–80
Retail chains:
    projections for, 127, 151–152, 168, 233–240
    reliance on SBA loans, 93, 152
Reverend Ike, 199
Risk, major areas of, 135–136
R. J. Reynolds Corp., 217
Roberts, Oral, 199
Rock, Arthur, 23, 160, 207
Roloff, Jeffrey, 127
"ROI", target for venture capitalists, 32, 66, 123–126, 150, 207, 210–211

Satellite broadcasting, 37
Schoen, Dr. Leonard, 4
Schroeder, Robert, 122
Scientific Data Systems Corp., 207
S-curve, 132, 136, 155, 163
Sears, Roebuck and Company, 110, 112
Securities and Exchange Commission (SEC), 66, 68, 83
Security Pacific Capital Corp., 130

SEC, Form S-18, A Monitoring Report
(March, 1981), 84
Seminar businesses, customer
financing, 105, 111, 170
Service company start-up, 168–170, 216
Shaklee Corp., 176
Shell merchants, 89
Silicon Valley, 38, 96, 174
Singleton, Henry, 176
Small Business Administration (SBA),
39, 91–95, 96, 98, 100, 152, 173
Small Business Investment Companies
(SBIC), 39–53, 95, 151, 160, 174, 194
Smith, Fred, 4, 126, 145
Smoke-Enders, 168, 170
Software for small computers, 143–144, 166
Solar energy, 115, 152
Spector, Charles, 122
Sports Illustrated, 212
Spouse, importance to entrepreneur,
148, 177
Stages of financing, 25, 123
Stamps, E. Roe, IV, 197
Stanford Research Institute, 127
Start-up stage, 25–29, 123, 130, 148, 157,
168, 210, 225
Storage Technology Corp., 126
STP Corp., 118
Subchapter S, when to form, 26
Sugarman, Joe, 112
Sutter Hill Management, 122
Swanson, Robert, 175
Syntex Corp., 82

TA Associates, 197
Tandem Computer Corporation, 29,
136, 175
Taub, Henry and Joseph, 204
Tax shelters, 61–76, 107, 121, 126, 135,
151, 173
negatives of, 67–68
when to use, 68–69
Teleconferencing, 143
Teledyne Corp., 20, 207, 211
Terms and conditions of venture capi-
tal investments, 49, 134
Textron Corp., 160
Time Inc., 34
Time requirement of various
financings, 68, 83, 85

Transart Industries, Inc., 105
Treybig, James, 29, 136, 175
Tupperware Corp., 105, 176
Turn-downs, avoidance of, 160–166,
194
TV Guide, 141

U-Haul System, 4
Union Carbide Corporation, 34
University of Chicago, 157
Urban Development Action Grants
(UDAG), 79–80, 158
Use of Proceeds section in Business
Plan, 136–137
U.S. Steel Corp., 192

Valuation procedure, 30, 124–125,
148–151, 211
Venture capital, 4, 13, 73, 83, 89, 94, 111,
122, 124, 128, 130, 151, 152, 156, 161,
171, 181, 193, 216
Venture capital financings, time requirement, 125–126, 157, 161, 171
Venture capital funds, 23–32, 109, 126,
136, 174
Venture capital investments:
reasons for failures, 130–132
terms and conditions, 49, 134
Venture capitalists, reasons for forming syndicates, 130, 172
Verbal communications skills, 2,
192–201

Wall Street Journal, 15, 21, 85, 106
Weight Watchers International, 3, 105,
168, 170
Wholesale distributors, as buy-out can-
didates, 20, 99, 101
Wiks 'n Stiks, 106
Wilson, Joseph, 153
Wilson, Kemmons, 104
Windpower, 152
Women entrepreneurs, financing
available to, 42, 198
Women's liberation movement, typical
new industry growth pattern, 110
Workout financing, 163
Wozniak, Steve, 160, 175

Xerox Corp., 4, 30, 128, 133, 153, 217